Advanced Machine Le with Python

Solve challenging data science problems by mastering cutting-edge machine learning techniques in Python

John Hearty

[PACKT] open source
PUBLISHING
community experience distilled

BIRMINGHAM - MUMBAI

Advanced Machine Learning with Python

First published: July 2016

Production reference: 1220716

Published by Packt Publishing Ltd.
Livery Place
35 Livery Street
Birmingham B3 2PB, UK.

ISBN 978-1-78439-863-7

www.packtpub.com

Credits

Author

John Hearty

Reviewers

Jared Huffman

Ashwin Pajankar

Commissioning Editor

Akram Hussain

Acquisition Editor

Sonali Vernekar

Content Development Editor

Mayur Pawanikar

Technical Editor

Suwarna Patil

Copy Editor

Tasneem Fatehi

Project Coordinator

Nidhi Joshi

Proofreader

Safis Editing

Indexer

Mariammal Chettiyar

Graphics

Disha Haria

Production Coordinator

Arvindkumar Gupta

Cover Work

Arvindkumar Gupta

About the Author

John Hearty is a consultant in digital industries with substantial expertise in data science and infrastructure engineering. Having started out in mobile gaming, he was drawn to the challenge of AAA console analytics.

Keen to start putting advanced machine learning techniques into practice, he signed on with Microsoft to develop player modelling capabilities and big data infrastructure at an Xbox studio. His team made significant strides in engineering and data science that were replicated across Microsoft Studios. Some of the more rewarding initiatives he led included player skill modelling in asymmetrical games, and the creation of player segmentation models for individualized game experiences.

Eventually John struck out on his own as a consultant offering comprehensive infrastructure and analytics solutions for international client teams seeking new insights or data-driven capabilities. His favourite current engagement involves creating predictive models and quantifying the importance of user connections for a popular social network.

After years spent working with data, John is largely unable to stop asking questions. In his own time, he routinely builds ML solutions in Python to fulfil a broad set of personal interests. These include a novel variant on the StyleNet computational creativity algorithm and solutions for algo-trading and geolocation-based recommendation. He currently lives in the UK.

About the Reviewers

Jared Huffman is a lifelong gamer and extreme data geek. After completing his bachelor's degree in computer science, he started his career in his hometown of Melbourne, Florida. While there, he honed his software development skills, including work on a credit card-processing system and a variety of web tools. He finished it off with a fun contract working at NASA's Kennedy Space Center before migrating to his current home in the Seattle area.

Diving head first into the world of data, he took up a role working on Microsoft's internal finance tools and reporting systems. Feeling that he could no longer resist his love for video games, he joined the Xbox division to build their Business. To date, Jared has helped ship and support 12 games and presented at several events on various machine learning and other data topics. His latest endeavor has him applying both his software skills and analytics expertise in leading the data science efforts for Minecraft. There he gets to apply machine learning techniques, trying out fun and impactful projects, such as customer segmentation models, churn prediction, and recommendation systems.

Outside of work, Jared spends much of his free time playing board games and video games with his family and friends, as well as dabbling in occasional game development.

First I'd like to give a big thanks to John for giving me the honor of reviewing this book; it's been a great learning experience. Second, thanks to my amazing wife, Kalen, for allowing me to repeatedly skip chores to work on it. Last, and certainly not least, I'd like to thank God for providing me the opportunities to work on things I love and still make a living doing it. Being able to wake up every day and create games that bring joy to millions of players is truly a pleasure.

Ashwin Pajankar is a software professional and IoT enthusiast with more than 8 years of experience in software design, development, testing, and automation.

He graduated from IIIT Hyderabad, earning an M. Tech in computer science and engineering. He holds multiple professional certifications from Oracle, IBM, Teradata, and ISTQB in development, databases, and testing. He has won several awards in college through outreach initiatives, at work for technical achievements, and community service through corporate social responsibility programs.

He was introduced to Raspberry Pi while organizing a hackathon at his workplace, and has been hooked on Pi ever since. He writes plenty of code in C, Bash, Python, and Java on his cluster of Pis. He's already authored two books on Raspberry Pi and reviewed three other titles related to Python for Packt Publishing.

His LinkedIn Profile is https://in.linkedin.com/in/ashwinpajankar.

I would like to thank my wife, Kavitha, for the motivation.

www.PacktPub.com

eBooks, discount offers, and more

Did you know that Packt offers eBook versions of every book published, with PDF and ePub files available? You can upgrade to the eBook version at www.PacktPub.com and as a print book customer, you are entitled to a discount on the eBook copy. Get in touch with us at customercare@packtpub.com for more details.

At www.PacktPub.com, you can also read a collection of free technical articles, sign up for a range of free newsletters and receive exclusive discounts and offers on Packt books and eBooks.

https://www2.packtpub.com/books/subscription/packtlib

Do you need instant solutions to your IT questions? PacktLib is Packt's online digital book library. Here, you can search, access, and read Packt's entire library of books.

Why subscribe?

- Fully searchable across every book published by Packt
- Copy and paste, print, and bookmark content
- On demand and accessible via a web browser

Of the many people I feel gratitude towards, I particularly want to thank my parents … mostly for their patience. I'd like to extend thanks to Tyler Lowe for his invaluable friendship, to Mark Huntley for his bothersome emphasis on accuracy, and to the former team at Lionhead Studios. I also greatly value the excellent work done by Jared Huffman and the industrious editorial team at Packt Publishing, who were hugely positive and supportive throughout the creation of this book.

Finally, I'd like to dedicate the work and words herein to you, the reader. There has never been a better time to get to grips with the subjects of this book; the world is stuffed with new opportunities that can be seized using creativity and an appropriate model. I hope for your every success in the pursuit of those solutions.

Table of Contents

Preface

Hello! Welcome to this guide to advanced machine learning using Python. It's possible that you've picked this up with some initial interest, but aren't quite sure what to expect. In a nutshell, there has never been a more exciting time to learn and use machine learning techniques, and working in the field is only getting more rewarding. If you want to get up-to-speed with some of the more advanced data modeling techniques and gain experience using them to solve challenging problems, this is a good book for you!

What is advanced machine learning?

Ongoing advances in computational power (per Moore's Law) have begun to make machine learning, once mostly a research discipline, more viable in commercial contexts. This has caused an explosion of new applications and new or rediscovered techniques, catapulting the obscure concepts of data science, AI, and machine learning into the public consciousness and strategic planning of companies internationally.

The rapid development of machine learning applications is fueled by an ongoing struggle to continually innovate, playing out at an array of research labs. The techniques developed by these pioneers are seeding new application areas and experiencing growing public awareness. While some of the innovations sought in AI and applied machine learning are still elusively far from readiness, others are a reality. Self-driving cars, sophisticated image recognition and altering capability, ever-greater strides in genetics research, and perhaps most pervasively of all, increasingly tailored content in our digital stores, e-mail inboxes, and online lives.

With all of these possibilities and more at the fingertips of the committed data scientist, the profession is seeing a meteoric, if clumsy, growth. Not only are there far more data scientists and AI practitioners now than there were even two years ago (in early 2014), but the accessibility and openness around solutions at the high end of machine learning research has increased.

Research teams at Google and Facebook began to share more and more of their architecture, languages, models, and tools in the hope of seeing them applied and improved on by the growing data scientist population.

The machine learning community matured enough to begin seeing trends as popular algorithms were defined or rediscovered. To put this more accurately, pre-existing trends from a mainly research community began to receive great attention from industry, with one product being a group of machine learning experts straddling industry and academia. Another product, the subject of this section, is a growing awareness of advanced algorithms that can be used to crack the frontier problems of the current day. From month to month, we see new advances made, scores rise, and the frontier moves ever further out.

What all of this means is that there may never have been a better time to move into the field of data science and develop your machine learning skillset. The introductory algorithms (including clustering, regression models, and neural network architectures) and tools are widely covered in web courses and blog content. While the techniques at the cutting edge of data science (including deep learning, semi-supervised algorithms, and ensembles) remain less accessible, the techniques themselves are now available through software libraries in multiple languages. All that's needed is the combination of theoretical knowledge and practical guidance to implement models correctly. That is the requirement that this book was written to address.

What should you expect from this book?

You've begun to read a book that focuses on teaching some of the advanced modeling techniques that've emerged in recent years. This book is aimed at anyone who wants to learn about those algorithms, whether you're an experienced data scientist or developer looking to parlay existing skills into a new environment.

I aimed first and foremost at making sure that you understand the algorithms in question. Some of them are fairly tricky and tie into other concepts in statistics and machine learning.

For neophyte readers, I definitely recommend gathering an initial understanding of key concepts, including the following:

- Neural network architectures including the MLP architecture
- Learning method components including gradient descent and backpropagation
- Network performance measures, for example, root mean squared error
- K-means clustering

At times, this book won't be able to give a subject the attention that it deserves. We cover a lot of ground in this book and the pace is fairly brisk as a result! At the end of each chapter, I refer you to further reading, in a book or online article, so that you can build a broader base of relevant knowledge. I'd suggest that it's worth doing additional reading around any unfamiliar concept that comes up as you work through this book, as machine learning knowledge tends to tie together synergistically; the more you have, the more readily you'll understand new concepts as you expand your toolkit.

This concept of expanding a toolkit of skills is fundamental to what I've tried to achieve with this book. Each chapter introduces one or multiple algorithms and looks to achieve several goals:

- Explaining at a high level what the algorithm does, what problems it'll solve well, and how you should expect to apply it
- Walking through key components of the algorithm, including topology, learning method, and performance measurement
- Identifying how to improve performance by reviewing model output

Beyond the transfer of knowledge and practical skills, this book looks to achieve a more important goal; specifically, to discuss and convey some of the qualities that are common to skilled machine learning practitioners. These include creativity, demonstrated both in the definition of sophisticated architectures and problem-specific cleaning techniques. Rigor is another key quality, emphasized throughout this book by a focus on measuring performance against meaningful targets and critically assessing early efforts.

Finally, this book makes no effort to obscure the realities of working on solving data challenges: the mixed results of early trials, large iteration counts, and frequent impasses. Yet at the same time, using a mixture of toy examples, dissection of expert approaches and, toward the end of the book, more real-world challenges, we show how a creative, tenacious, and rigorous approach can break down these barriers and deliver meaningful results.

As we proceed, I wish you the best of luck and encourage you to enjoy yourself as you go, tackling the content prepared for you and applying what you've learned to new domains or data.

Let's get started!

What this book covers

Chapter 1, Unsupervised Machine Learning, shows you how to apply unsupervised learning techniques to identify patterns and structure within datasets.

Chapter 2, Deep Belief Networks, explains how the RBM and DBN algorithms work; you'll know how to use them and will feel confident in your ability to improve the quality of the results that you get out of them.

Chapter 3, Stacked Denoising Autoencoders, continues to build our skill with deep architectures by applying stacked denoising autoencoders to learn feature representations for high-dimensional input data.

Chapter 4, Convolutional Neural Networks, shows you how to apply the convolutional neural network (or Convnet).

Chapter 5, Semi-Supervised Learning, explains how to apply several semi-supervised learning techniques, including CPLE, self-learning, and S3VM.

Chapter 6, Text Feature Engineering, discusses data preparation skills that significantly increase the effectiveness of all the models that we've previously discussed.

Chapter 7, Feature Engineering Part II, shows you how to interrogate the data to weed out or mitigate quality issues, transform it into forms that are conducive to machine learning, and creatively enhance that data.

Chapter 8, Ensemble Methods, looks at building more sophisticated model ensembles and methods of building robustness into your model solutions.

Chapter 9, Additional Python Machine Learning Tools, reviews some of the best in recent tools available to data scientists, identifies the benefits that they offer, and discusses how to apply them alongside tools and techniques discussed earlier in this book, within a consistent working process.

Appendix A, Chapter Code Requirements, discusses tool requirements for the book, identifying required libraries for each chapter.

What you need for this book

The entirety of this book's content leverages openly available data and code, including open source Python libraries and frameworks. While each chapter's example code is accompanied by a README file documenting all the libraries required to run the code provided in that chapter's accompanying scripts, the content of these files is collated here for your convenience.

It is recommended that some libraries required for earlier chapters be available when working with code from any later chapter. These requirements are identified using bold text. Particularly, it is important to set up the first chapter's required libraries for any content later in the book.

Who this book is for

This title is for Python developers and analysts or data scientists who are looking to add to their existing skills by accessing some of the most powerful recent trends in data science. If you've ever considered building your own image or text-tagging solution or entering a Kaggle contest, for instance, this book is for you!

Prior experience of Python and grounding in some of the core concepts of machine learning would be helpful.

Conventions

In this book, you will find a number of text styles that distinguish between different kinds of information. Here are some examples of these styles and an explanation of their meaning.

Code words in text, database table names, folder names, filenames, file extensions, pathnames, dummy URLs, user input, and Twitter handles are shown as follows: "We will begin applying PCA to the handwritten `digits` dataset with the following code."

A block of code is set as follows:

```
import numpy as np
from sklearn.datasets import load_digits
import matplotlib.pyplot as plt
from sklearn.decomposition import PCA
from sklearn.preprocessing import scale
from sklearn.lda import LDA
import matplotlib.cm as cm

digits = load_digits()
data = digits.data

n_samples, n_features = data.shape
n_digits = len(np.unique(digits.target))
labels = digits.target
```

Any command-line input or output is written as follows:

```
[ 0.39276606  0.49571292  0.43933243  0.53573558  0.42459285
  0.55686854  0.4573401   0.49876358  0.50281585  0.4689295 ]
```

```
0.4772857426
```

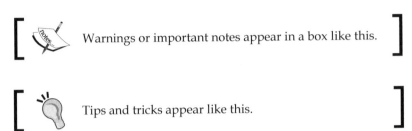

Warnings or important notes appear in a box like this.

Tips and tricks appear like this.

Reader feedback

Feedback from our readers is always welcome. Let us know what you think about this book—what you liked or disliked. Reader feedback is important for us as it helps us develop titles that you will really get the most out of.

To send us general feedback, simply e-mail feedback@packtpub.com, and mention the book's title in the subject of your message.

If there is a topic that you have expertise in and you are interested in either writing or contributing to a book, see our author guide at www.packtpub.com/authors.

Customer support

Now that you are the proud owner of a Packt book, we have a number of things to help you to get the most from your purchase.

Downloading the example code

You can download the example code files for this book from your account at http://www.packtpub.com. If you purchased this book elsewhere, you can visit http://www.packtpub.com/support and register to have the files e-mailed directly to you.

You can download the code files by following these steps:

1. Log in or register to our website using your e-mail address and password.
2. Hover the mouse pointer on the **SUPPORT** tab at the top.
3. Click on **Code Downloads & Errata**.
4. Enter the name of the book in the **Search** box.
5. Select the book for which you're looking to download the code files.
6. Choose from the drop-down menu where you purchased this book from.
7. Click on **Code Download**.

Once the file is downloaded, please make sure that you unzip or extract the folder using the latest version of:

- WinRAR / 7-Zip for Windows
- Zipeg / iZip / UnRarX for Mac
- 7-Zip / PeaZip for Linux

The code bundle for the book is also hosted on GitHub at `https://github.com/PacktPublishing/Advanced-Machine-Learning-with-Python`. We also have other code bundles from our rich catalog of books and videos available at. `https://github.com/PacktPublishing/` Check them out!

Downloading the color images of this book

We also provide you with a PDF file that has color images of the screenshots/diagrams used in this book. The color images will help you better understand the changes in the output. You can download this file from `https://www.packtpub.com/sites/default/files/downloads/AdvancedMachineLearningwithPython_ColorImages.pdf`.

Errata

Although we have taken every care to ensure the accuracy of our content, mistakes do happen. If you find a mistake in one of our books—maybe a mistake in the text or the code—we would be grateful if you could report this to us. By doing so, you can save other readers from frustration and help us improve subsequent versions of this book. If you find any errata, please report them by visiting `http://www.packtpub.com/submit-errata`, selecting your book, clicking on the **Errata Submission Form** link, and entering the details of your errata. Once your errata are verified, your submission will be accepted and the errata will be uploaded to our website or added to any list of existing errata under the Errata section of that title.

To view the previously submitted errata, go to `https://www.packtpub.com/books/content/support` and enter the name of the book in the search field. The required information will appear under the **Errata** section.

Piracy

Piracy of copyrighted material on the Internet is an ongoing problem across all media. At Packt, we take the protection of our copyright and licenses very seriously. If you come across any illegal copies of our works in any form on the Internet, please provide us with the location address or website name immediately so that we can pursue a remedy.

Please contact us at `copyright@packtpub.com` with a link to the suspected pirated material.

We appreciate your help in protecting our authors and our ability to bring you valuable content.

Questions

If you have a problem with any aspect of this book, you can contact us at `questions@packtpub.com`, and we will do our best to address the problem.

1
Unsupervised Machine Learning

In this chapter, you will learn how to apply unsupervised learning techniques to identify patterns and structure within datasets.

Unsupervised learning techniques are a valuable set of tools for exploratory analysis. They bring out patterns and structure within datasets, which yield information that may be informative in itself or serve as a guide to further analysis. It's critical to have a solid set of unsupervised learning tools that you can apply to help break up unfamiliar or complex datasets into actionable information.

We'll begin by reviewing **Principal Component Analysis (PCA)**, a fundamental data manipulation technique with a range of dimensionality reduction applications. Next, we will discuss **k-means clustering**, a widely-used and approachable unsupervised learning technique. Then, we will discuss Kohenen's **Self-Organizing Map (SOM)**, a method of topological clustering that enables the projection of complex datasets into two dimensions.

Throughout the chapter, we will spend some time discussing how to effectively apply these techniques to make high-dimensional datasets readily accessible. We will use the **UCI Handwritten Digits** dataset to demonstrate technical applications of each algorithm. In the course of discussing and applying each technique, we will review practical applications and methodological questions, particularly regarding how to calibrate and validate each technique as well as which performance measures are valid. To recap, then, we will be covering the following topics in order:

- Principal component analysis
- k-means clustering
- Self-organizing maps

Principal component analysis

In order to work effectively with high-dimensional datasets, it is important to have a set of techniques that can reduce this dimensionality down to manageable levels. The advantages of this dimensionality reduction include the ability to plot multivariate data in two dimensions, capture the majority of a dataset's informational content within a minimal number of features, and, in some contexts, identify collinear model components.

For those in need of a refresher, collinearity in a machine learning context refers to model features that share an approximately linear relationship. For reasons that will likely be obvious, these features tend to be unhelpful as the related features are unlikely to add information mutually that either one provides independently. Moreover, collinear features may emphasize local minima or other false leads.

Probably the most widely-used dimensionality reduction technique today is PCA. As we'll be applying PCA in multiple contexts throughout this book, it's appropriate for us to review the technique, understand the theory behind it, and write Python code to effectively apply it.

PCA – a primer

PCA is a powerful decomposition technique; it allows one to break down a highly multivariate dataset into a set of orthogonal components. When taken together in sufficient number, these components can explain almost all of the dataset's variance. In essence, these components deliver an abbreviated description of the dataset. PCA has a broad set of applications and its extensive utility makes it well worth our time to cover.

Note the slightly cautious phrasing here—a given set of components of length less than the number of variables in the original dataset will almost always lose some amount of the information content within the source dataset. This lossiness is typically minimal, given enough components, but in cases where small numbers of principal components are composed from very high-dimensional datasets, there may be substantial lossiness. As such, when performing PCA, it is always appropriate to consider how many components will be necessary to effectively model the dataset in question.

PCA works by successively identifying the axis of greatest variance in a dataset (the principal components). It does this as follows:

1. Identifying the center point of the dataset.
2. Calculating the covariance matrix of the data.
3. Calculating the eigenvectors of the covariance matrix.
4. Orthonormalizing the eigenvectors.
5. Calculating the proportion of variance represented by each eigenvector.

Let's unpack these concepts briefly:

- **Covariance** is effectively variance applied to multiple dimensions; it is the variance between two or more variables. While a single value can capture the variance in one dimension or variable, it is necessary to use a 2 x 2 matrix to capture the covariance between two variables, a 3 x 3 matrix to capture the covariance between three variables, and so on. So the first step in PCA is to calculate this covariance matrix.

- An **Eigenvector** is a vector that is specific to a dataset and linear transformation. Specifically, it is the vector that does not change in direction before and after the transformation is performed. To get a better feeling for how this works, imagine that you're holding a rubber band, straight, between both hands. Let's say you stretch the band out until it is taut between your hands. The eigenvector is the vector that did not change direction between before the stretch and during it; in this case, it's the vector running directly through the center of the band from one hand to the other.

- **Orthogonalization** is the process of finding two vectors that are orthogonal (at right angles) to one another. In an n-dimensional data space, the process of orthogonalization takes a set of vectors and yields a set of orthogonal vectors.

- **Orthonormalization** is an orthogonalization process that also normalizes the product.

- **Eigenvalue** (roughly corresponding to the length of the eigenvector) is used to calculate the proportion of variance represented by each eigenvector. This is done by dividing the eigenvalue for each eigenvector by the sum of eigenvalues for all eigenvectors.

In summary, the covariance matrix is used to calculate Eigenvectors. An orthonormalization process is undertaken that produces orthogonal, normalized vectors from the Eigenvectors. The eigenvector with the greatest eigenvalue is the first principal component with successive components having smaller eigenvalues. In this way, the PCA algorithm has the effect of taking a dataset and transforming it into a new, lower-dimensional coordinate system.

Employing PCA

Now that we've reviewed the PCA algorithm at a high level, we're going to jump straight in and apply PCA to a key Python dataset — the UCI handwritten `digits` dataset, distributed as part of **scikit-learn**.

This dataset is composed of *1,797* instances of handwritten digits gathered from *44* different writers. The input (pressure and location) from these authors' writing is resampled twice across an *8 x 8* grid so as to yield maps of the kind shown in the following image:

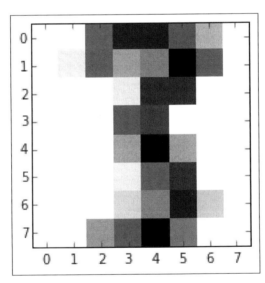

These maps can be transformed into feature vectors of length 64, which are then readily usable as analysis input. With an input dataset of 64 features, there is an immediate appeal to using a technique like PCA to reduce the set of variables to a manageable amount. As it currently stands, we cannot effectively explore the dataset with exploratory visualization!

We will begin applying PCA to the handwritten `digits` dataset with the following code:

```
import numpy as np
from sklearn.datasets import load_digits
import matplotlib.pyplot as plt
from sklearn.decomposition import PCA
from sklearn.preprocessing import scale
from sklearn.lda import LDA
import matplotlib.cm as cm

digits = load_digits()
data = digits.data

n_samples, n_features = data.shape
n_digits = len(np.unique(digits.target))
labels = digits.target
```

This code does several things for us:

1. First, it loads up a set of necessary libraries, including numpy, a set of components from scikit-learn, including the `digits` dataset itself, PCA and data scaling functions, and the plotting capability of matplotlib.

2. The code then begins preparing the `digits` dataset. It does several things in order:
    ○ First, it loads the dataset before creating helpful variables
    ○ The `data` variable is created for subsequent use, and the number of distinct `digits` in the `target` vector (*0* through to *9*, so `n_digits` = `10`) is saved as a variable that we can easily access for subsequent analysis
    ○ The `target` vector is also saved as labels for later use
    ○ All of this variable creation is intended to simplify subsequent analysis

3. With the dataset ready, we can initialize our PCA algorithm and apply it to the dataset:

```
pca = PCA(n_components=10)
data_r = pca.fit(data).transform(data)

print('explained variance ratio (first two components): %s' %
str(pca.explained_variance_ratio_))
print('sum of explained variance (first two components): %s' %
str(sum(pca.explained_variance_ratio_)))
```

4. This code outputs the variance explained by each of the first ten principal components ordered by explanatory power.

In the case of this set of 10 principal components, they collectively explain *0.589* of the overall dataset variance. This isn't actually too bad, considering that it's a reduction from *64* variables to 10 components. It does, however, illustrate the potential lossiness of PCA. The key question, though, is whether this reduced set of components makes subsequent analysis or classification easier to achieve; that is, whether many of the remaining components contained variance that disrupts classification attempts.

Having created a data_r object containing the output of pca performed over the digits dataset, let's visualize the output. To do so, we'll first create a vector of colors for class coloration. We then simply create a scatterplot with colorized classes:

```
X = np.arange(10)
ys = [i+x+(i*x)**2 for i in range(10)]

plt.figure()
colors = cm.rainbow(np.linspace(0, 1, len(ys)))
for c, i target_name in zip(colors, [1,2,3,4,5,6,7,8,9,10], labels):
    plt.scatter(data_r[labels == I, 0], data_r[labels == I, 1],
    c=c, alpha = 0.4)
    plt.legend()
    plt.title('Scatterplot of Points plotted in first \n'
    '10 Principal Components')
    plt.show()
```

The resulting scatterplot looks as follows:

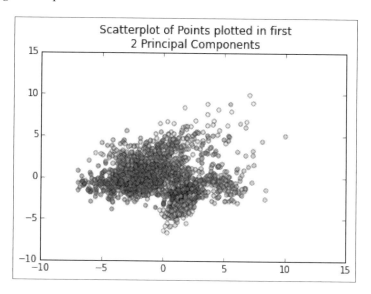

This plot shows us that, while there is some separation between classes in the first two principal components, it may be tricky to classify highly accurately with this dataset. However, classes do appear to be clustered and we may be able to get reasonably good results by employing a clustering analysis. In this way, PCA has given us some insight into how the dataset is structured and has informed our subsequent analysis.

At this point, let's take this insight and move on to examine clustering by the application of the k-means clustering algorithm.

Introducing k-means clustering

In the previous section, you learned that unsupervised machine learning algorithms are used to extract key structural or information content from large, possibly complex datasets. These algorithms do so with little or no manual input and function without the need for training data (sets of labeled explanatory and response variables needed to train an algorithm in order to recognize the desired classification boundaries). This means that unsupervised algorithms are effective tools to generate information about the structure and content of new or unfamiliar datasets. They allow the analyst to build a strong understanding in a fraction of the time.

Clustering – a primer

Clustering is probably the archetypal unsupervised learning technique for several reasons.

A lot of development time has been sunk into optimizing clustering algorithms, with efficient implementations available in most data science languages including Python.

Clustering algorithms tend to be very fast, with smoothed implementations running in polynomial time. This makes it uncomplicated to run multiple clustering configurations, even over large datasets. Scalable clustering implementations also exist that parallelize the algorithm to run over **TB-scale** datasets.

Clustering algorithms are frequently easily understood and their operation is thus easy to explain if necessary.

The most popular clustering algorithm is k-means; this algorithm forms k-many clusters by first randomly initiating the clusters as k-many points in the data space. Each of these points is the mean of a cluster. An iterative process then occurs, running as follows:

- Each point is assigned to a cluster based on the least (within cluster) sum of squares, which is intuitively the nearest mean.

- The center (centroid) of each cluster becomes the new mean. This causes each of the means to shift.

Over enough iterations, the centroids move into positions that minimize a performance metric (the performance metric most commonly used is the "within cluster least sum of squares" measure). Once this measure is minimized, observations are no longer reassigned during iteration; at this point the algorithm has converged on a solution.

Kick-starting clustering analysis

Now that we've reviewed the clustering algorithm, let's run through the code and see what clustering can do for us:

```
from time import time
import numpy as np
import matplotlib.pyplot as plt

np.random.seed()


digits = load_digits()
```

```
data = scale(digits.data)

n_samples, n_features = data.shape
n_digits = len(np.unique(digits.target))
labels = digits.target

sample_size = 300

print("n_digits: %d, \t n_samples %d, \t n_features %d"
    % (n_digits, n_samples, n_features))


print(79 * '_')
print('% 9s' % 'init'            time    inertia    homo    compl    v-meas
ARI      AMI   silhouette')

def bench_k_means(estimator, name, data):
    t0 = time()
    estimator.fit(data)
    print('% 9s %.2fs %i %.3f %.3f %.3f %.3f %.3f %.3f'
        % (name, (time() - t0), estimator.inertia_,
           metrics.homogeneity_score(labels, estimator.labels_),
           metrics.completeness_score(labels, estimator.labels_),
           metrics.v_measure_score(labels, estimator.labels_),
           metrics.adjusted_rand_score(labels, estimator.labels_),
           metrics.silhouette_score(data, estimator.labels_,
              metric='euclidean',
              sample_size=sample_size)))
```

One critical difference between this code and the PCA code we saw previously is that this code begins by applying a scale function to the `digits` dataset. This function scales values in the dataset between *0* and *1*. It's critically important to scale data wherever needed, either on a log scale or bound scale, so as to prevent the magnitude of different feature values to have disproportionately powerful effects on the dataset. The key to determining whether the data needs scaling at all (and what kind of scaling is needed, within which range, and so on) is very much tied to the shape and nature of the data. If the distribution of the data shows outliers or variation within a large range, it may be appropriate to apply log-scaling. Whether this is done manually through visualization and exploratory analysis techniques or through the use of summary statistics, decisions around scaling are tied to the data under inspection and the analysis techniques to be used. A further discussion of scaling decisions and considerations may be found in *Chapter 7, Feature Engineering Part II*.

Helpfully, scikit-learn uses the k-means++ algorithm by default, which improves over the original k-means algorithm in terms of both running time and success rate in avoiding poor clusterings.

The algorithm achieves this by running an initialization procedure to find cluster centroids that approximate minimal variance within classes.

You may have spotted from the preceding code that we're using a set of performance estimators to track how well our k-means application is performing. It isn't practical to measure the performance of a clustering algorithm based on a single correctness percentage or using the same performance measures that are commonly used with other algorithms. The definition of success for clustering algorithms is that they provide an interpretation of how input data is grouped that trades off between several factors, including class separation, in-group similarity, and cross-group difference.

The **homogeneity score** is a simple, zero-to-one-bounded measure of the degree to which clusters contain only assignments of a given class. A score of one indicates that all clusters contain measurements from a single class. This measure is complimented by the **completeness score**, which is a similarly bounded measure of the extent to which all members of a given class are assigned to the same cluster. As such, a completeness score and homogeneity score of one indicates a perfect clustering solution.

The **validity measure (v-measure)** is a harmonic mean of the homogeneity and completeness scores, which is exactly analogous to the F-measure for binary classification. In essence, it provides a single, 0-1-scaled value to monitor both homogeneity and completeness.

The **Adjusted Rand Index (ARI)** is a similarity measure that tracks the consensus between sets of assignments. As applied to clustering, it measures the consensus between the true, pre-existing observation labels and the labels predicted as an output of the clustering algorithm. The Rand index measures labeling similarity on a *0-1* bound scale, with one equaling perfect prediction labels.

The main challenge with all of the preceding performance measures as well as other similar measures (for example, Akaike's mutual information criterion) is that they require an understanding of the ground truth, that is, they require some or all of the data under inspection to be labeled. If labels do not exist and cannot be generated, these measures won't work. In practice, this is a pretty substantial drawback as very few datasets come prelabeled and the creation of labels can be time-consuming.

One option to measure the performance of a k-means clustering solution without labeled data is the **Silhouette Coefficient**. This is a measure of how well-defined the clusters within a model are. The Silhouette Coefficient for a given dataset is the mean of the coefficient for each sample, where this coefficient is calculated as follows:

$$s = \frac{b-a}{\max(a,b)}$$

The definitions of each term are as follows:

- *a*: The mean distance between a sample and all other points in the same cluster
- *b*: The mean distance between a sample and all other points in the next nearest cluster

This score is bounded between *-1* and *1*, with *-1* indicating incorrect clustering, *1* indicating very dense clustering, and scores around *0* indicating overlapping clusters. This tends to fit our expectations of how a good clustering solution is composed.

In the case of the `digits` dataset, we can employ all of the performance measures described here. As such, we'll complete the preceding example by initializing our `bench_k_means` function over the `digits` dataset:

```
bench_k_means(KMeans(init='k-means++', n_clusters=n_digits, n_
init=10), name="k-means++", data=data)
print(79 * '_')
```

This yields the following output (note that the random seed means your results will vary from mine!):

n_digits: 10,		n_samples 1797,			n_features 64			
init	time	inertia	homo	compl	v-meas	ARI	AMI	silhouette
k-means++	0.25s	69517	0.596	0.643	0.619	0.465	0.592	0.123

Lets take a look at these results in more detail.

The Silhouette score at `0.123` is fairly low, but not surprisingly so, given that the handwritten digits data is inherently noisy and does tend to overlap. However, some of the other scores are not that impressive. The V-measure at `0.619` is reasonable, but in this case is held back by a poor homogeneity measure, suggesting that the cluster centroids did not resolve perfectly. Moreover, the ARI at `0.465` is not great.

Let's put this in context. The worst case classification attempt, random assignment, would give at best 10% classification accuracy. All of our performance measures would be accordingly very low. While we're definitely doing a lot better than that, we're still trailing far behind the best computational classification attempts. As we'll see in *Chapter 4, Convolutional Neural Networks*, convolutional nets achieve results with extremely low classification errors on handwritten digit datasets. We're unlikely to achieve this level of accuracy with traditional k-means clustering!

All in all, it's reasonable to think that we could do better.

To give this another try, we'll apply an additional stage of processing. To learn how to do this, we'll apply PCA—the technique we previously walked through—to reduce the dimensionality of our input dataset. The code to achieve this is very simple, as follows:

```
pca = PCA(n_components=n_digits).fit(data)
bench_k_means(KMeans(init=pca.components_, n_clusters=10),
name="PCA-based",
data=data)
```

This code simply applies PCA to the digits dataset, yielding as many principal components as there are classes (in this case, digits). It can be sensible to review the output of PCA before proceeding as the presence of any small principal components may suggest a dataset that contains collinearity or otherwise merits further inspection.

This instance of clustering shows noticeable improvement:

n_digits: 10,		n_samples 1797,			n_features 64		
init	time	inertia	homo	compl	v-meas	ARI	silhouette
PCA-based	0.02s	71820	0.673	0.715	0.693	0.567	0.121

The V-measure and ARI have increased by approximately *0.08* points, with the V-measure reading a fairly respectable 0.693. The Silhouette Coefficient did not change significantly. Given the complexity and interclass overlap within the digits dataset, these are good results, particularly stemming from such a simple code addition!

Inspection of the `digits` dataset with clusters superimposed shows that some meaningful clusters appear to have been formed. It is also apparent from the following plot that actually detecting the character from the input feature vectors may be a challenging task:

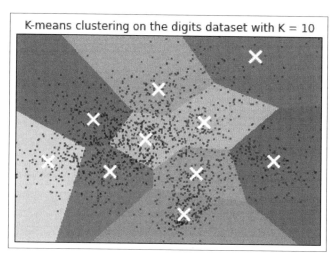

K-means clustering on the digits dataset with K = 10

Tuning your clustering configurations

The previous examples described how to apply k-means, walked through relevant code, showed how to plot the results of a clustering analysis, and identified appropriate performance metrics. However, when applying k-means to real-world datasets, there are some extra precautions that need to be taken, which we will discuss.

Another critical practical point is how to select an appropriate value for k. Initializing k-means clustering with a specific k value may not be harmful, but in many cases it is not clear initially how many clusters you might find or what values of k may be helpful.

We can rerun the preceding code for multiple values of k in a batch and look at the performance metrics, but this won't tell us which instance of k is most effectively capturing structure within the data. The risk is that as k increases, the Silhouette Coefficient or unexplained variance may decrease dramatically, without meaningful clusters being formed. The extreme case of this would be if $k = o$, where o is the number of observations in the sample; every point would have its own cluster, the Silhouette Coefficient would be low, but the results wouldn't be meaningful. There are, however, many less extreme cases in which overfitting may occur due to an overly high k value.

To mitigate this risk, it's advisable to use supporting techniques to motivate a selection of *k*. One useful technique in this context is the **elbow method**. The elbow method is a very simple technique; for each instance of *k*, plot the percentage of explained variance against *k*. This typically leads to a plot that frequently looks like a bent arm.

For the PCA-reduced dataset, this code looks like the following snippet:

```
import numpy as np
from sklearn.cluster import KMeans
from sklearn.datasets import load_digits
from scipy.spatial.distance import cdist
import matplotlib.pyplot as plt
from sklearn.decomposition import PCA
from sklearn.preprocessing import scale

digits = load_digits()
data = scale(digits.data)

n_samples, n_features = data.shape
n_digits = len(np.unique(digits.target))
labels = digits.target

K = range(1,20)
explainedvariance= []
for k in K:
    reduced_data = PCA(n_components=2).fit_transform(data)
    kmeans = KMeans(init = 'k-means++', n_clusters = k, n_init = k)
    kmeans.fit(reduced_data)
    explainedvariance.append(sum(np.min(cdist(reduced_data,
    kmeans.cluster_centers_, 'euclidean'), axis =
    1))/data.shape[0])
    plt.plot(K, meandistortions, 'bx-')
    plt.show()
```

This application of the elbow method takes the PCA reduction from the previous code sample and applies a test of the explained variance (specifically, a test of the variance within clusters). The result is output as a measure of unexplained variance for each value of k in the range specified. In this case, as we're using the digits dataset (which we know to have ten classes), the range specified was 1 to 20:

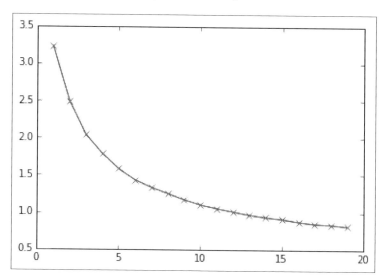

The elbow method involves selecting the value of k that maximizes explained variance while minimizing κ; that is, the value of k at the crook of the elbow. The technical sense underlying this is that a minimal gain in explained variance at greater values of k is offset by the increasing risk of overfitting.

Elbow plots may be more or less pronounced and the elbow may not always be clearly identifiable. This example shows a more gradual progression than may be observable in other cases with other datasets. It's worth noting that, while we know the number of classes within the dataset to be ten, the elbow method starts to show diminishing returns on k increases almost immediately and the elbow is located at around five classes. This has a lot to do with the substantial overlap between classes, which we saw in previous plots. While there are ten classes, it becomes increasingly difficult to clearly identify more than five or so.

With this in mind, it's worth noting that the elbow method is intended for use as a heuristic rather than as some kind of objective principle. The use of PCA as a preprocess to improve clustering performance also tends to smooth the graph, delivering a more gradual curve than otherwise.

In addition to making use of the elbow method, it can be valuable to look at the clusters themselves, as we did earlier in the chapter, using PCA to reduce the dimensionality of the data. By plotting the dataset and projecting cluster assignation onto the data, it is sometimes very obvious when a k-means implementation has fitted to a local minima or has overfit the data. The following plot demonstrates extreme overfitting of our previous k-means clustering algorithm to the `digits` dataset, artificially prompted by using **K = 150**. In this example, some clusters contain a single observation; there's really no way that this output would generalize to other samples well:

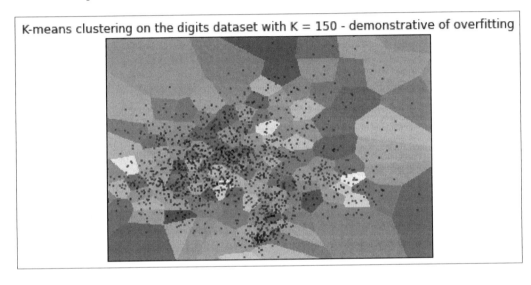

Plotting the elbow function or cluster assignments is quick to achieve and straightforward to interpret. However, we've spoken of these techniques in terms of being heuristics. If a dataset contains a deterministic number of classes, we may not be sure that a heuristic method will deliver generalizable results.

Another drawback is that visual plot checking is a very manual technique, which makes it poorly-suited for production environments or automation. In such circumstances, it's ideal to find a code-based, automatable method. One solid option in this case is **v-fold cross-validation**, a widely-used validation technique.

Cross-validation is simple to undertake. To make it work, one splits the dataset into *v* parts. One of the parts is set aside individually as a test set. The model is trained against the training data, which is all parts except the test set. Let's try this now, again using the `digits` dataset:

```
import numpy as np
from sklearn import cross_validation
from sklearn.cluster import KMeans
```

```
from sklearn.datasets import load_digits
from sklearn.preprocessing import scale


digits = load_digits()
data = scale(digits.data)

n_samples, n_features = data.shape
n_digits = len(np.unique(digits.target))
labels = digits.target



kmeans = KMeans(init='k-means++', n_clusters=n_digits, n_init=n_
digits)
cv = cross_validation.ShuffleSplit(n_samples, n_iter = 10, test_size =
0.4, random_state = 0)
scores = cross_validation.cross_val_score(kmeans, data, labels, cv =
cv, scoring = 'adjusted_rand_score')
print(scores)
print(sum(scores)/cv.n_iter)
```

This code performs some now familiar data loading and preparation and initializes the k-means clustering algorithm. It then defines cv, the cross-validation parameters. This includes specification of the number of iterations, n_iter, and the amount of data that should be used in each fold. In this case, we're using 60% of the data samples as training data and 40% as test data.

We then apply the k-means model and cv parameters that we've specified within the cross-validation scoring function and print the results as scores. Let's take a look at these scores now:

```
[ 0.39276606  0.49571292  0.43933243  0.53573558  0.42459285
  0.55686854  0.4573401   0.49876358  0.50281585  0.4689295 ]


0.4772857426
```

This output gives us, in order, the adjusted Rand score for cross-validated, k-means++ clustering performed across each of the 10 folds in order. We can see that results do fluctuate between around 0.4 and 0.55; the earlier ARI score for k-means++ without PCA fell within this range (at 0.465). What we've created, then, is code that we can incorporate into our analysis in order to check the quality of our clustering automatically on an ongoing basis.

As noted earlier in this chapter, your choice of success measure is contingent on what information you already have. In most cases, you won't have access to ground truth labels from a dataset and will be obliged to use a measure such as the Silhouette Coefficient that we discussed previously.

Sometimes, even using both cross-validation and visualizations won't provide a conclusive result. Especially with unfamiliar datasets, it's not unheard of to run into issues where some noise or secondary signal resolves better at a different k value than the signal you're attempting to analyze.

As with every other algorithm discussed in this book, it is imperative to understand the dataset one wishes to work with. Without this insight, it's entirely possible for even a technically correct and rigorous analysis to deliver inappropriate conclusions. *Chapter 6, Text Feature Engineering* will discuss principles and techniques for the inspection and preparation of unfamiliar datasets more thoroughly.

Self-organizing maps

A SOM is a technique to generate topological representations of data in reduced dimensions. It is one of a number of techniques with such applications, with a better-known alternative being PCA. However, SOMs present unique opportunities, both as dimensionality reduction techniques and as a visualization format.

SOM – a primer

The SOM algorithm involves iteration over many simple operations. When applied at a smaller scale, it behaves similarly to k-means clustering (as we'll see shortly). At a larger scale, SOMs reveal the topology of complex datasets in a powerful way.

An SOM is made up of a grid (commonly rectangular or hexagonal) of nodes, where each node contains a weight vector that is of the same dimensionality as the input dataset. The nodes may be initialized randomly, but an initialization that roughly approximates the distribution of the dataset will tend to train faster.

The algorithm iterates as observations are presented as input. Iteration takes the following form:

- Identifying the winning node in the current configuration — the **Best Matching Unit (BMU)**. The BMU is identified by measuring the Euclidean distance in the data space of all the weight vectors.
- The BMU is adjusted (moved) towards the input vector.
- Neighboring nodes are also adjusted, usually by lesser amounts, with the magnitude of neighboring movement being dictated by a neighborhood function. (Neighborhood functions vary. In this chapter, we'll use a Gaussian neighborhood function.)

This process repeats over potentially many iterations, using sampling if appropriate, until the network converges (reaching a position where presenting a new input does not provide an opportunity to minimize loss).

A node in an SOM is not unlike that of a neural network. It typically possesses a weight vector of length equal to the dimensionality of the input dataset. This means that the topology of the input dataset can be preserved and visualized through a lower-dimensional mapping.

The code for this SOM class implementation is available in the book repository in the som.py script. For now, let's start working with the SOM algorithm in a familiar context.

Employing SOM

As discussed previously, the SOM algorithm is iterative, being based around Euclidean distance comparisons of vectors.

This mapping tends to form a fairly readable 2D grid. In the case of the commonly-used Iris tutorial dataset, an SOM will map it out pretty cleanly:

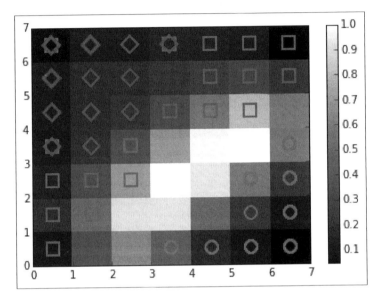

In this diagram, the classes have been separated and also ordered spatially. The background coloring in this case is a clustering density measure. There is some minimal overlap between the blue and green classes, where the SOM performed an imperfect separation. On the Iris dataset, an SOM will tend to approach a converged solution on the order of 100 iterations, with little visible improvement after 1,000. For more complex datasets containing less clearly divisible cases, this process can take tens of thousands of iterations.

Awkwardly, there aren't implementations of the SOM algorithm within pre-existing Python packages like scikit-learn. This makes it necessary for us to use our own implementation.

The SOM code we'll be working with for this purpose is located in the associated GitHub repository. For now, let's take a look at the relevant script and get an understanding of how the code works:

```
import numpy as np
from sklearn.datasets import load_digits
from som import Som
```

```
from pylab import plot,axis,show,pcolor,colorbar,bone


digits = load_digits()
data = digits.data
labels = digits.target
```

At this point, we've loaded the `digits` dataset and identified `labels` as a separate set of data. Doing this will enable us to observe how the SOM algorithm separates classes when assigning them to `map`:

```
som = Som(16,16,64,sigma=1.0,learning_rate=0.5)
som.random_weights_init(data)
print("Initiating SOM.")
som.train_random(data,10000)
print("\n. SOM Processing Complete")


bone()
pcolor(som.distance_map().T)
colorbar()
```

At this point, we have utilized a `Som` class that is provided in a separate file, `Som.py`, in the repository. This class contains the methods required to deliver the SOM algorithm we discussed earlier in the chapter. As arguments to this function, we provide the dimensions of the map (After trialing a range of options, we'll start out with 16 x 16 in this case — this grid size gave the feature map enough space to spread out while retaining some overlap between groups.) and the dimensionality of the input data. (This argument determines the length of the weight vector within the SOM's nodes.) We also provide values for sigma and learning rate.

Sigma, in this case, defines the spread of the neighborhood function. As noted previously, we're using a Gaussian neighborhood function. The appropriate value for sigma varies by grid size. For an *8 x 8* grid, we would typically want to use a value of *1.0* for Sigma, while in this case we're using *1.3* for a *16 x 16* grid. It is fairly obvious when one's value for sigma is off; if the value is too small, values tend to cluster near the center of the grid. If the values are too large, the grid typically ends up with several large, empty spaces towards the center.

The *learning rate* self-explanatorily defines the initial learning rate for the SOM. As the map continues to iterate, the learning rate adjusts according to the following function:

$$learning\ rate(t) = learning\ rate/\left(1 + t/(0.5 * t)\right)$$

Here, *t* is the iteration index.

We follow up by first initializing our SOM with random weights.

 As with k-means clustering, this initialization method is slower than initializing based on an approximation of the data distribution. A preprocessing step similar to that employed by the k-means++ algorithm would accelerate the SOM's runtime. Our SOM runs sufficiently quickly over the `digits` dataset to make this optimization unnecessary for now.

Next, we set up label and color assignations for each class, so that we can distinguish classes on the plotted SOM. Following this, we iterate through each data point.

On each iteration, we plot a class-specific marker for the BMU as calculated by our SOM algorithm.

When the SOM finishes iteration, we add a **U-Matrix** (a colorized matrix of relative observation density) as a monochrome-scaled plot layer:

```
labels[labels == '0'] = 0
labels[labels == '1'] = 1
labels[labels == '2'] = 2
labels[labels == '3'] = 3
labels[labels == '4'] = 4
labels[labels == '5'] = 5
labels[labels == '6'] = 6
labels[labels == '7'] = 7
labels[labels == '8'] = 8
labels[labels == '9'] = 9

markers = ['o', 'v', '1', '3', '8', 's', 'p', 'x', 'D', '*']
colors = ["r", "g", "b", "y", "c", (0,0.1,0.8), (1,0.5,0), (1,1,0.3),
"m", (0.4,0.6,0)]
for cnt,xx in enumerate(data):
    w = som.winner(xx)
    plot(w[0]+.5,w[1]+.5,markers[labels[cnt]],
    markerfacecolor='None', markeredgecolor=colors[labels[cnt]],
    markersize=12, markeredgewidth=2)
    axis([0,som.weights.shape[0],0,som.weights.shape[1]])
    show()
```

This code generates a plot similar to the following:

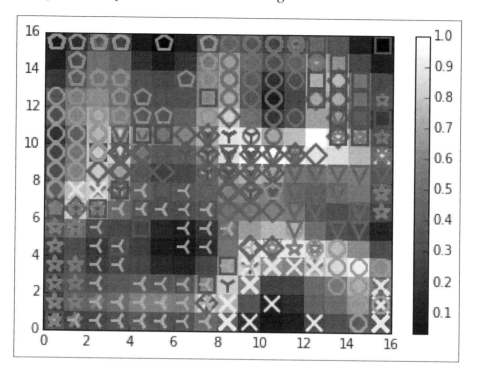

This code delivers a 16 x 16 node SOM plot. As we can see, the map has done a reasonably good job of separating each cluster into topologically distinct areas of the map. Certain classes (particularly the digits five in cyan circles and nine in green stars) have been located over multiple parts of the SOM space. For the most part, though, each class occupies a distinct region and it's fair to say that the SOM has been reasonably effective. The U-Matrix shows that regions with a high density of points are co-habited by data from multiple classes. This isn't really a surprise as we saw similar results with k-means and PCA plotting.

Further reading

Victor Powell and Lewis Lehe provide a fantastic interactive, visual explanation of PCA at `http://setosa.io/ev/principal-component-analysis/`, this is ideal for readers who are new to the core concepts of PCA or who are not quite getting it.

For a lengthier and more mathematically-involved treatment of PCA, touching on underlying matrix transformations, Jonathon Shlens from Google research provides a clear and thorough explanation at `http://arxiv.org/abs/1404.1100`.

For a thorough worked example that translates Jonathon's description into clear Python code, consider Sebastian Raschka's demonstration using the Iris dataset at `http://sebastianraschka.com/Articles/2015_pca_in_3_steps.html`.

Finally, consider the sklearn documentation for more details on arguments to the PCA class at `http://scikit-learn.org/stable/modules/generated/sklearn.decomposition.PCA.html`.

For a lively and expert treatment of k-means, including detailed investigations of the conditions that cause it to fail, and potential alternatives in such cases, consider David Robinson's fantastic blog, variance explained at `http://varianceexplained.org/r/kmeans-free-lunch/`.

A specific discussion of the Elbow method is provided by Rick Gove at `https://bl.ocks.org/rpgove/0060ff3b656618e9136b`.

Finally, consider sklearn's documentation for another view on unsupervised learning algorithms, including k-means at `http://scikit-learn.org/stable/tutorial/statistical_inference/unsupervised_learning.html`.

Much of the existing material on Kohonen's SOM is either rather old, very high-level, or formally expressed. A decent alternative to the description in this book is provided by John Bullinaria at `http://www.cs.bham.ac.uk/~jxb/NN/l16.pdf`.

For readers interested in a deeper understanding of the underlying mathematics, I'd recommend reading the work of Tuevo Kohonen directly. The 2012 edition of self-organising maps is a great place to start.

The concept of multicollinearity, referenced in the chapter, is given a clear explanation for the unfamiliar at `https://onlinecourses.science.psu.edu/stat501/node/344`.

Summary

In this chapter, we've reviewed three techniques with a broad range of applications for preprocessing and dimensionality reduction. In doing so, you learned a lot about an unfamiliar dataset.

We started out by applying PCA, a widely-utilized dimensionality reduction technique, to help us understand and visualize a high-dimensional dataset. We then followed up by clustering the data using k-means clustering, identifying means of improving and measuring our k-means analysis through performance metrics, the elbow method, and cross-validation. We found that k-means on the `digits` dataset, taken as is, didn't deliver exceptional results. This was due to class overlap that we spotted through PCA. We overcame this weakness by applying PCA as a preprocess to improve our subsequent clustering results.

Finally, we developed an SOM algorithm that delivered a cleaner separation of the `digit` classes than PCA.

Having learned some key basics around unsupervised learning techniques and analytical methodology, let's dive into the use of some more powerful unsupervised learning algorithms.

Deep Belief Networks

2

In the preceding chapter, we looked at some widely-used dimensionality reduction techniques, which enable a data scientist to get greater insight into the nature of datasets.

The next few chapters will focus on some more sophisticated techniques, drawing from the area of deep learning. This chapter is dedicated to building an understanding of how to apply the **Restricted Boltzmann Machine (RBM)** and manage the deep learning architecture one can create by chaining RBMs — the **deep belief network (DBN)**. DBNs are trainable to effectively solve complex problems in text, image, and sound recognition. They are used by leading companies for object recognition, intelligent image search, and robotic spatial recognition.

The first thing that we're going to do is get a solid grounding in the algorithm underlying DBN; unlike clustering or PCA, this code isn't widely-known by data scientists and we're going to review it in some depth to build a strong working knowledge. Once we've worked through the theory, we'll build upon it by stepping through code that brings the theory into focus and allows us to apply the technique to real-world data. The diagnosis of these techniques is not trivial and needs to be rigorous, so we'll emphasize the thought processes and diagnostic techniques that enable us to effectively watch and control the success of your implementation.

By the end of this chapter, you'll understand how the RBM and DBN algorithms work, know how to use them, and feel confident in your ability to improve the quality of the results you get out of them. To summarize, the contents of this chapter are as follows:

- Neural networks – a primer
- Restricted Boltzmann Machines
- Deep belief networks

Neural networks – a primer

The RBM is a form of recurrent neural network. In order to understand how the RBM works, it is necessary to have a more general understanding of neural networks. Readers with an understanding of artificial neural network (hereafter neural network, for the sake of simplicity) algorithms will find familiar elements in the following description.

There are many accounts that cover neural networks in great theoretical detail; we won't go into great detail retreading this ground. For the purposes of this chapter, we will first describe the components of a neural network, common architectures, and prevalent learning processes.

The composition of a neural network

For unfamiliar readers, neural networks are a class of mathematical models that train to produce and optimize a definition for a function (or distribution) over a set of input features. The specific objective of a given neural network application can be defined by the operator using a performance measure (typically a cost function); in this way, neural networks may be used to classify, predict, or transform their inputs.

The use of the word neural in neural networks is the product of a long tradition of drawing from heavy-handed biological metaphors to inspire machine learning research. Hence, artificial neural networks algorithms originally drew (and frequently still draw) from biological neuronal structures.

A neural network is composed of the following elements:

- A learning process: A neural network learns by adjusting parameters within the weight function of its nodes. This occurs by feeding the output of a performance measure (as described previously, in supervised learning contexts this is frequently a cost function, some measure of inaccuracy relative to the target output of the network) into the learning function of the network. This learning function outputs the required weight adjustments (Technically, it typically calculates the partial derivatives—terms required by gradient descent.) to minimize the cost function.

- A set of neurons or weights: Each contains a weight function (the activation function) that manipulates input data. The activation function may vary substantially between networks (with one well-known example being the hyperbolic tangent). The key requirement is that the weights must be adaptive, that is,, adjustable based on updates from the learning process. In order to model non-parametrically (that is, to model effectively without defining details of the probability distribution), it is necessary to use both visible and hidden units. Hidden units are never observed.

- Connectivity functions: They control which nodes can relay data to which other nodes. Nodes may be able to freely relay input to one another in an unrestricted or restricted fashion, or they may be more structured in layers through which input data must flow in a directed fashion. There is a broad range of interconnection patterns, with different patterns producing very different network properties and possibilities.

Utilizing this set of elements enables us to build a broad range of neural networks, ranging from the familiar directed acyclic graph (with perhaps the best-known example being the **Multi-Layer Perceptron (MLP)**) to creative alternatives. The **Self-Organizing Map (SOM)** that we employed in the preceding chapter was a type of neural network, with a unique learning process. The algorithm that we'll examine later in this chapter, that of the RBM, is another neural network algorithm with some unique properties.

Network topologies

There are many variations on how the neurons in a neural network are connected, with structural decisions being an important factor in determining the network's learning capabilities. Common topologies in unsupervised learning tend to differ from those common to supervised learning. One common and now familiar unsupervised learning topology is that of the SOM that we discussed in the last chapter.

The SOM, as we saw, directly projects individual input cases onto a weight vector contained by each node. It then proceeds to reorder these nodes until an appropriate mapping of the dataset is converged on. The actual structure of the SOM was a variant based on the details of training, specific outcome of a given instance of training, and design decisions taken in structuring the network, but square or hexagonal grid structures are becoming increasingly common.

A very common topology type in supervised learning is that of a three-layer, feedforward network, with the classical case being the MLP. In this network topology model, the neurons in the network are split into layers, with each layer communicating to the layer "beyond" it. The first layer contains inputs that are fed to a hidden layer. The hidden layer develops a representation of the data using weight activations (with the right activation function, for example, sigmoid or gauss, an MLP can act as a universal function approximator) and activation values are communicated to the output layer. The output layer typically delivers network results. This topology, therefore, looks as follows:

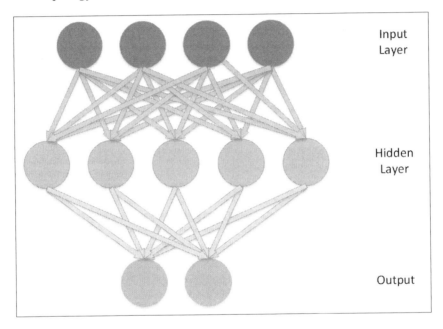

Other network topologies deliver different capabilities. The topology of a Boltzmann Machine, for instance, differs from those described previously. The Boltzmann machine contains hidden and visible neurons, like those of a three-layer network, but all of these neurons are connected to one another in a directed, cyclic graph:

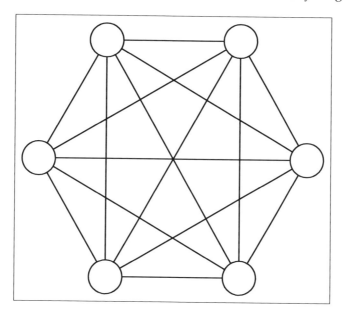

This topology makes Boltzmann machines stochastic—probabilistic rather than deterministic—and able to develop in one of several ways given a sufficiently complex problem. The Boltzmann machine is also generative, which means that it is able to fully (probabilistically) model all of the input variables, rather than using the observed variables to specifically model the target variables.

Which network topology is appropriate depends to a large extent on your specific challenge and the desired output. Each tends to be strong in certain areas. Furthermore, each of the topologies described here will be accompanied by a learning process that enables the network to iteratively converge on an (ideally optimal) solution.

There are a broad range of learning processes, with specific processes and topologies being more or less compatible with one another. The purpose of a learning process is to enable the network to adjust its weights, iteratively, in such a way as to create an increasingly accurate representation of the input data.

As with network topologies, there are a great many learning processes to consider. Some familiarity is assumed and a great many excellent resources on learning processes exist (some good examples are given at the end of this chapter). This section will focus on delivering a common characterization of learning processes, while later in the chapter, we'll look in greater detail at a specific example.

As noted, the objective of learning in a neural network is to iteratively improve the distribution of weights across the model so that it approximates the function underlying input data with increasing accuracy. This process requires a performance measure. This may be a classification error measure, as is commonly used in supervised, classification contexts (that is, with the backpropagation learning algorithm in MLP networks). In stochastic networks, it may be a probability maximization term (such as energy in energy-based networks).

In either case, once there is a measure to increase probability, the network is effectively attempting to reduce that measure using an optimization method. In many cases, the optimization of the network is achieved using **gradient descent**. As far as the gradient descent algorithm method is concerned, the size of your performance measure value on a given training iteration is analogous to the slope of your gradient. Minimizing the performance measure is therefore a question of descending that gradient to the point at which the error measure is at its lowest for that set of weights.

The size of the network's updates for the next iteration (the learning rate of your algorithm) may be influenced by the magnitude of your performance measure, or it may be hard-coded.

The weight updates by which your network adjusts may be derived from the error surface itself; if so, your network will typically have a means of calculating the gradient, that is, deriving the values to which updates need to adjust the parameters on your network's activated weight functions so as to continue to reduce the performance measure.

Having reviewed the general concepts underlying network topologies and learning methods, let's move into the discussion of a specific neural network, the RBM. As we'll see, the RBM is a key part of a powerful deep learning algorithm.

Restricted Boltzmann Machine

The RBM is a fundamental part of this chapter's subject deep learning architecture—the DBN. The following sections will begin by introducing the theory behind an RBM, including the architectural structure and learning processes.

Following that, we'll dive straight into the code for an RBM class, making links between the theoretical elements and functions in code. We'll finish by touching on the applications of RBMs and the practical factors associated with implementing an RBM.

Introducing the RBM

A Boltzmann machine is a particular type of stochastic, recurrent neural network. It is an energy-based model, which means that it uses an energy function to associate an energy value with each configuration of the network.

We briefly discussed the structure of a Boltzmann machine in the previous section. As mentioned, a Boltzmann machine is a directed cyclic graph, where every node is connected to all other nodes. This property enables it to model in a recurrent fashion, such that the model's outputs evolve and can be viewed over time.

The learning loop in a Boltzmann machine involves maximizing the probability of the training dataset, X. As noted, the specific performance measure used is energy, which is characterized as the negative log of the probability for a dataset X, given a vector of model parameters, Θ. This measure is calculated and used to update the network's weights in such a way as to minimize the free energy in the network.

The Boltzmann machine has seen particular success in processing image data, including photographs, facial features, and handwriting classification contexts.

Unfortunately, the Boltzmann machine is not practical for more challenging ML problems. This is due to the fact that there are challenges with the machine's ability to scale; as the number of nodes increases, the compute time grows exponentially, eventually leaving us in a position where we're unable to compute the free energy of the network.

For those with an interest in the underlying formal reasoning, this happens because the probability of a data point, x, $p(x; \Theta)$, must integrate to *1* over all x. Achieving this requires that we use a partition function, Z, used as a normalizing constant. (Z is a constant such that multiplying a non-negative function by Z will make the non-negative function integrate to *1* over all inputs; in this case, over all x.)

The probability model function is a function of a set of normal distributions. In order to get the energy for our model, we need to differentiate for each of the model's parameters; however, this becomes complicated because of the partition function. Each model parameter produces equations dependent on other model parameters and we ultimately find ourselves unable to calculate the energy without (potentially) hugely expensive calculations, whose cost increases as the network scales.

In order to overcome the weaknesses of the Boltzmann machine, it is necessary to make adjustments to both the network topology and training process.

Topology

The main topological change that delivers efficiency improvements is the restriction of connectivity between nodes. First, one must prevent connection between nodes within the same layer. Additionally, all skip-layer connections (that is, direct connections between non-consecutive layers) must be prevented. A Boltzmann machine with this architecture is referred to as an RBM and appears as shown in the following diagram:

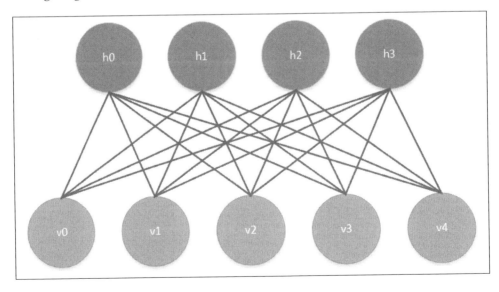

One advantage of this topology is that the hidden and visible layers are conditionally independent given one another. As such, it is possible to sample from one layer using the activations of the other.

Training

We observed previously that, for Boltzmann machines, the training time of the machine scales extremely poorly as the machine is scaled up to additional nodes, putting us in a position where we cannot evaluate the energy function that we're attempting to use in training.

The RBM is typically trained using a procedure with a different learning algorithm at its heart, the **Permanent Contrastive Divergence (PCD)** algorithm, which provides an approximation of maximum likelihood. PCD doesn't evaluate the energy function itself, but instead allows us to estimate the gradient of the energy function. With this information, we can proceed by making very small adjustments in the direction of the steepest gradient via which we may progress, as desired, toward the local minimum.

The PCD algorithm is made up of two phases. These are referred to as the positive and negative phases, and each phase has a corresponding effect on the energy of the model. The positive phase increases the probability of the training dataset, X, thus reducing the energy of the model. Following this, the negative phase uses a sampling approach from the model to estimate the negative phase gradient. The overall effect of the negative phase is to decrease the probability of samples generated by the model.

Sampling in the negative phase and throughout the update process is achieved using a form of sampling called **Gibbs sampling**.

Gibbs sampling is a variant of the **Markov Chain Monte Carlo (MCMC)** family of algorithms, and samples from an approximated multivariate probability distribution. What this means is, rather than using a summed calculation in building our probabilistic model (just as we might do, for instance, when we flip a coin a certain number of times; in such cases, we may sum the number of heads attempts as a proportion of the sum of all attempts), we approximate the value of an integral instead. The subject of how to create a probabilistic model by approximating an integral deserves more time than this book can give it. As such the *Further reading* section of this chapter provides an excellent paper reference. The key points to bear in mind for now (and stripping out a lot of important detail!) are that, instead of summing each case exactly once, we sample based on the (often non-uniform) distribution of the data in question. Gibbs sampling is a probabilistic sampling method for each parameter in a model, based on all of the other parameter values in that model. As soon as a new parameter value is obtained, it is immediately used in sampling calculations for other parameters.

Some of you may be asking at this point why PCD is necessary. Why not use a more familiar method, such as gradient descent with line search? To put it simply, we cannot easily calculate the free energy of our network as this calculation involves an integration across all the network's nodes. We recognized this limitation when we called out the big weakness of the Boltzmann machine—that the compute time grows exponentially as the number of nodes increases, leaving us in a situation where we're trying to minimize a function whose value we cannot calculate!

What PCD provides is a way to estimate the gradient of the energy function. This enables an approximation of the network's free energy, which is fast enough to be viable for application and has shown to be generally accurate. (Refer to the *Further reading* section for a performance comparison.)

As we saw previously, the RBM's probability model function is the joint distribution of our model parameters, making Gibbs sampling appropriate!

The training loop in an initialized RBM involves several steps:

1. We obtain the current iteration's activated hidden layer weight values.

2. We perform the positive phase of PCD, using the state of the Gibbs chain from the previous iteration as input.

3. We perform the negative phase of PCD using the pre-existing state of the Gibbs chain. This gives us the free energy value.

4. We update the activated weights on the hidden layer using the energy value we've calculated.

This algorithm allows the RBM to iteratively step toward a decreased free energy value. The RBM continues to train until both the probability of the training dataset integrates to one and free energy is equal to zero, at which point the RBM has converged.

Now that we've had a chance to review the RBM's topology and training process, let's apply the algorithm to classify a substantial real dataset.

Applications of the RBM

Now that we have a general working knowledge of the RBM algorithm, let's walk through code to create an RBM. We'll be working with an RBM class that will allow us to classify the MNIST handwritten digits dataset. The code we're about to review does the following:

- It sets up the initial parameters of an RBM, including layer size, shareable bias vectors, and shareable weight matrix for connectivity with external network structures (this enables deep belief networks)

- It defines functions for communication and inference between hidden and visible layers

- It defines functions that allow us to update the parameters of network nodes

- It defines functions that handle efficient sampling for the learning process, using PCD-k to accelerate sampling (making it possible to compute in a reasonable frame of time)

- It defines functions that compute the free energy of the model (used to calculate the gradient required for PCD-k updates)

- It identifies the **Psuedo-Likelihood (PL)**, usable as a log-likelihood proxy to guide the selection of appropriate hyperparameters

Let's begin examining our RBM class:

```
class RBM(object):
    def __init__(
        self,
        input=None,
        n_visible=784,
        n_hidden=500,
        w=None,
        hbias=None,
        vbias=None,
        numpy_rng=None,
        theano_rng=None
    ):
```

The first element that we need to build is an RBM constructor, which we can use to define the parameters of the model, such as the number of visible and hidden nodes (n_visible and n_hidden) as well as additional parameters that can be used to adjust how the RBM's inference functions and CD updates are performed.

The w parameter can be used as a pointer to a shared weight matrix. This becomes more relevant when implementing a DBN, as we'll see later in the chapter; in such architectures, the weight matrix needs to be shared between different parts of the network.

The hbias and vbias parameters are used similarly as optional references to shared hidden and visible (respectively) units' bias vectors. Again, these are used in DBNs.

The input parameter enables the RBM to be connected, top-to-tail, to other graph elements. This allows one to, for instance, chain RBMs.

Having set up this constructor, we next need to flesh out each of the preceding parameters:

```
self.n_visible = n_visible
self.n_hidden = n_hidden

if numpy_rng is None:
    numpy_rng = numpy.random.RandomState(1234)

if theano_rng is None:
    theano_rng = RandomStreams(numpy_rng.randint(2 ** 30))
```

This is fairly straightforward stuff; we set the visible and hidden nodes for our RBM and set up two random number generators. The theano_rng parameter will be used later in our code to sample from the RBM's hidden units:

```
if W is None:
    initial_W = numpy.asarray(
        numpy_rng.uniform(
            low=-4 * numpy.sqrt(6. / (n_hidden + n_visible)),
            high=4 * numpy.sqrt(6. / (n_hidden + n_visible)),
            size=(n_visible, n_hidden)
        ),
        dtype=theano.config.floatX
    )
```

This code switches up the data type for W so that it can be run over the GPU. Next, we set up shared variables using theano.shared, which allows a variable's storage to be shared between functions that it appears in. Within the current example, the shared variables that we create will be the weight vector (W) and bias variables for hidden and visible units (hbias and vbias, respectively). When we move on to creating deep networks with multiple components, the following code will allow us to share components between parts of our networks:

```
W = theano.shared(value=initial_W, name='W', borrow=True)

if hbias is None:
    hbias = theano.shared(
        value=numpy.zeros(
            n_hidden,
            dtype=theano.config.floatX
        ),
        name='hbias',
        borrow=True
    )

if vbias is None:
    vbias = theano.shared(
        value=numpy.zeros(
            n_visible,
            dtype=theano.config.floatX
        ),
        name='vbias',
        borrow=True
    )
```

At this point, we're ready to initialize the input layer as follows:

```
self.input = input
if not input:
    self.input = T.matrix('input')

self.W = W
self.hbias = hbias
self.vbias = vbias
self.theano_rng = theano_rng
self.params = [self.W, self.hbias, self.vbias]
```

As we now have an initialized `input` layer, our next task is to create the symbolic graph that we described earlier in the chapter. Achieving this is a matter of creating functions to manage the interlayer propagation and activation computation operations of the network:

```
def propup(self, vis):
        pre_sigmoid_activation = T.dot(vis, self.W) + self.hbias
        return [pre_sigmoid_activation, T.nnet.sigmoid(pre_sigmoid_
activation)]


    def propdown(self, hid):
        pre_sigmoid_activation = T.dot(hid, self.W.T) + self.vbias
        return [pre_sigmoid_activation, T.nnet.sigmoid(pre_sigmoid_
activation)]
```

These two functions pass the activation of one layer's units to the other layer. The first function passes the visible units' activation upward to the hidden units so that the hidden units can compute their activation conditional on a sample of the visible units. The second function does the reverse—propagating the hidden layer's activation downward to the visible units.

It's probably worth asking why we're creating both `propup` and `propdown`. As we reviewed it, PCD only requires that we perform sampling from the hidden units. So what's the value of `propup`?

In a nutshell, sampling from the visible layer becomes useful when we want to sample from the RBM to review its progress. In most applications where our RBM is processing visual data, it is immediately valuable to periodically take the output of sampling from the visible layer and plot it, as shown in the following example:

As we can see here, over the course of iteration, our network begins to change its labeling; in the first case, 7 morphs into 9, while elsewhere 9 becomes 6 and the network gradually reaches a definition of 3-ness.

As we discussed earlier, it's helpful to have as many views on the operation of your RBM as possible to ensure that it's delivering meaningful results. Sampling from the outputs it generates is one way to improve this visibility.

Armed with information about the visible layer's activation, we can deliver a sample of the unit activations from the hidden layer, given the activation of the hidden nodes:

```
def sample_h_given_v(self, v0_sample):

pre_sigmoid_h1, h1_mean = self.propup(v0_sample)
    h1_sample = self.theano_rng.binomial(size=h1_mean.shape,
    n=1, p=h1_mean, dtype=theano.config.floatX)


    return [pre_sigmoid_h1, h1_mean, h1_sample]
```

Likewise, we can now sample from the visible layer given hidden unit activation information:

```
def sample_v_given_h(self, h0_sample):
    pre_sigmoid_v1, v1_mean = self.propdown(h0_sample)
      v1_sample = self.theano_rng.binomial(size=v1_mean.shape,
      n=1, p=v1_mean, dtype=theano.config.floatX)

    return [pre_sigmoid_v1, v1_mean, v1_sample]
```

We've now achieved the connectivity and update loop required to perform a Gibbs sampling step, as described earlier in this chapter. Next, we should define this sampling step!

```
def gibbs_hvh(self, h0_sample):

    pre_sigmoid_v1, v1_mean, v1_sample =
    self.sample_v_given_h(h0_sample)
    pre_sigmoid_h1, h1_mean, h1_sample =
    self.sample_h_given_v(v1_sample)
    return [pre_sigmoid_v1, v1_mean, v1_sample,
            pre_sigmoid_h1, h1_mean, h1_sample]
```

As discussed, we need a similar function to sample from the visible layer:

```
def gibbs_vhv(self, v0_sample):

    pre_sigmoid_h1, h1_mean, h1_sample =
    self.sample_h_given_v(v0_sample)
    pre_sigmoid_v1, v1_mean, v1_sample =
    self.sample_v_given_h(h1_sample)
    return [pre_sigmoid_h1, h1_mean, h1_sample,
            pre_sigmoid_v1, v1_mean, v1_sample]
```

The code that we've written so far gives us some of our model. It set up the nodes and layers and connections between layers. We've written the code that we need in order to update the network based on Gibbs sampling from the hidden layer.

What we're still missing is code that allows us to perform the following:

- Compute the free energy of the model. As we discussed, the model uses energy as the term to do the following:
  - Implement PCD using our Gibbs sampling step code, and setting the Gibbs step count parameter, $k = 1$, to compute the parameter gradient for gradient descent
  - Create a means to feed the output of PCD (the computed gradient) to our previously defined network update code

- Develop the means to track the progress and success of our RBM throughout the training.

First off, we'll create the means to calculate the free energy of our RBM. Note that this is the inverse log of the probability distribution for the hidden layer, which we discussed earlier:

```
def free_energy(self, v_sample):

    wx_b = T.dot(v_sample, self.W) + self.hbias
    vbias_term = T.dot(v_sample, self.vbias)
    hidden_term = T.sum(T.log(1 + T.exp(wx_b)), axis=1)
    return -hidden_term - vbias_term
```

Next, we'll implement PCD. At this point, we'll be setting a couple of interesting parameters. The lr, short for learning rate, is an adjustable parameter used to adjust learning speed. The k parameter points to the number of steps to be performed by PCD (remember the PCD-k notation from earlier in the chapter?).

We discussed the PCD as containing two phases, positive and negative. The following code computes the positive phase of PCD:

```
def get_cost_updates(self, lr=0.1, persistent = , k=1):

        pre_sigmoid_ph, ph_mean, ph_sample =
        self.sample_h_given_v(self.input)



        chain_start = persistent
```

Meanwhile, the following code implements the negative phase of PCD. To do so, we scan the `gibbs_hvh` function `k` times, using Theano's scan operation, performing one Gibbs sampling step with each scan. After completing the negative phase, we acquire the free energy value:

```
        (
            [
                pre_sigmoid_nvs,
                nv_means,
                nv_samples,
                pre_sigmoid_nhs,
                nh_means,
                nh_samples
            ],
            updates
        ) = theano.scan(
            self.gibbs_hvh,
            outputs_info=[None, None, None, None, None, chain_start],
            n_steps=k
        )



        chain_end = nv_samples[-1]

        cost = T.mean(self.free_energy(self.input)) - T.mean(
            self.free_energy(chain_end))

        gparams = T.grad(cost, self.params,
        consider_constant=[chain_end])
```

Having written code that performs the full PCD process, we need a way to feed the outputs to our network. At this point, we're able to connect our PCD learning process to the code to update the network that we reviewed earlier. The preceding updates dictionary points to `theano.scan` of the `gibbs_hvh` function. As you may recall, `gibbs_hvh` currently contains rules for random states of `theano_rng`. What we need to do now is add the new parameter values and variable containing the state of the Gibbs chain to the dictionary (the `updates` variable):

```
for gparam, param in zip(gparams, self.params):
    updates[param] = param - gparam * T.cast(
        lr,
        dtype=theano.config.floatX
    )

updates = nh_samples[-1]
monitoring_cost =
self.get_pseudo_likelihood_cost(updates)


    return monitoring_cost, updates
```

We now have almost all the parts that we need to make our RBM work. What's clearly missing is a means to inspect training, either during or after completion, to ensure that our RBM is learning an appropriate representation of the data.

We talked previously about how to train an RBM, specifically about challenges posed by the partition function. Furthermore, earlier in the code, we implemented one means by which we can inspect an RBM during training; we created the `gibbs_vhv` function to perform Gibbs sampling from the model.

In our previous discussion around how to validate an RBM, we discussed visually plotting the filters that the RBM has created. We'll review how this can be achieved shortly.

The final possibility is to use the inverse log of the PL as a more tractable proxy to the likelihood itself. Technically, the log-PL is the sum of the log-probabilities of each data point (each x) conditioned on all other data points. As discussed, this becomes too expensive with larger-dimensional datasets, so a stochastic approximation to log-PL is used.

We referenced a function that will enable us to get PL cost during the `get_cost_` `updates` function, specifically the `get_pseudo_likelihood_cost` function. Now it's time to flesh out this function and obtain the pseudo-likelihood:

```
def get_pseudo_likelihood_cost(self, updates):

        bit_i_idx = theano.shared(value=0, name='bit_i_idx')
        xi = T.round(self.input)

        fe_xi = self.free_energy(xi)

        xi_flip = T.set_subtensor(xi[:, bit_i_idx], 1 - xi[:,
        bit_i_idx])

        fe_xi_flip = self.free_energy(xi_flip)

        cost = T.mean(self.n_visible *
        T.log(T.nnet.sigmoid(fe_xi_flip - fe_xi)))


        updates[bit_i_idx] = (bit_i_idx + 1) % self.n_visible

        return cost
```

We've now filled out each element on the list of missing components and have completely reviewed the RBM class. We've explored how each element ties into the theory behind the RBM and should now have a thorough understanding of how the RBM algorithm works. We understand what the outputs of our RBM will be and will soon be able to review and assess them. In short, we're ready to train our RBM. Beginning the training of the RBM is a matter of running the following code, which triggers the `train_set_x` function. We'll discuss this function in greater depth later in this chapter:

```
    train_rbm = theano.function(
        [index],
        cost,
        updates=updates,
        givens={
            x: train_set_x[index * batch_size: (index + 1) *
            batch_size]
        },
        name='train_rbm'
    )

    plotting_time = 0.
    start_time = time.clock()
```

Having updated the RBM's updates and training set, we run through training epochs. Within each epoch, we train over the training data before plotting the weights as a matrix (as described earlier in the chapter):

```
for epoch in xrange(training_epochs):

    mean_cost = []
    for batch_index in xrange(n_train_batches):
        mean_cost += [train_rbm(batch_index)]

    print 'Training epoch %d, cost is ' % epoch,
    numpy.mean(mean_cost)

    plotting_start = time.clock()
    image = Image.fromarray(
        tile_raster_images(
            X=rbm.W.get_value(borrow=True).T,
            img_shape=(28, 28),
            tile_shape=(10, 10),
            tile_spacing=(1, 1)
        )
    )
    image.save('filters_at_epoch_%i.png' % epoch)
    plotting_stop = time.clock()
    plotting_time += (plotting_stop - plotting_start)

end_time = time.clock()

pretraining_time = (end_time - start_time) - plotting_time

print ('Training took %f minutes' % (pretraining_time / 60.))
```

The weights tend to plot fairly recognizably and resemble Gabor filters (linear filters commonly used for edge detection in images). If your dataset is handwritten characters on a fairly low-noise background, you tend to find that the weights trace the strokes used. For photographs, the filters will approximately trace edges in the image. The following image shows an example output:

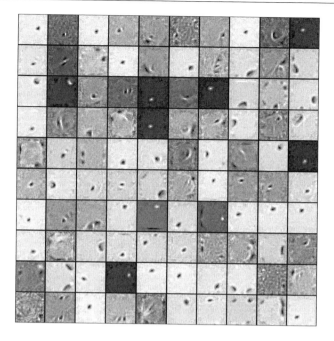

Finally, we create the persistent Gibbs chains that we need to derive our samples. The following function performs a single Gibbs step, as discussed previously, then updates the chain:

```
plot_every = 1000

    (
        [
            presig_hids,
            hid_mfs,
            hid_samples,
            presig_vis,
            vis_mfs,
            vis_samples
        ],
        updates
    ) = theano.scan(
        rbm.gibbs_vhv,
        outputs_info=[None, None, None, None, None, persistent_vis_
chain],
        n_steps=plot_every
    )
```

This code runs the `gibbs_vhv` function we described previously, plotting network output samples for our inspection:

```
updates.update({persistent_vis_chain: vis_samples[-1]})
sample_fn = theano.function(
    [],
    [
        vis_mfs[-1],
        vis_samples[-1]
    ],
    updates=updates,
    name='sample_fn'
)

image_data = numpy.zeros(
    (29 * n_samples + 1, 29 * n_chains - 1),
    dtype='uint8'
)
for idx in xrange(n_samples):

    vis_mf, vis_sample = sample_fn()
    print ' ... plotting sample ', idx
    image_data[29 * idx:29 * idx + 28, :] = tile_raster_images(
        X=vis_mf,
        img_shape=(28, 28),
        tile_shape=(1, n_chains),
        tile_spacing=(1, 1)
    )

image = Image.fromarray(image_data)
image.save('samples.png')
```

At this point, we have an entire RBM. We have the PCD algorithm and the ability to update the network using this algorithm and Gibbs sampling. We have several visible output methods so that we can assess how well our RBM has trained.

However, we're not done yet! Next, we'll begin to see what the most frequent and powerful application of the RBM is.

Further applications of the RBM

We can use the RBM as an ML algorithm in and of itself. It functions comparably well with other algorithms. Advantageously, it can be scaled up to a point where it can learn high-dimensional datasets. However, this isn't where the real strength of the RBM lies.

The RBM is most commonly used as a pretraining mechanism for a highly effective deep network architecture called a DBN. DBNs are extremely powerful tools to learn and classify a range of image datasets. They possess a very good ability to generalize to unknown cases and are among the best image-learning tools available. For this reason, DBNs are in use at many of the world's top tech and data science companies, primarily in image search and recognition contexts.

Deep belief networks

A DBN is a graphical model, constructed using multiple stacked RBMs. While the first RBM trains a layer of features based on input from the pixels of the training data, subsequent layers treat the activations of preceding layers as if they were pixels and attempt to learn the features in subsequent hidden layers. This is frequently described as learning the representation of data and is a common theme in deep learning.

How many multiple RBMs there should be depends on what is needed for the problem at hand. From a practical perspective, it's a trade-off between increasing accuracy and increasing computational cost. It is the case that each layer of RBMs will improve the lower bound of the log probability of the training data. In other words; the DBN almost inevitably becomes less bad with each additional layer of features.

As far as layer size is concerned, it is generally advantageous to reduce the number of nodes in the hidden layers of successive RBMs. One should avoid contexts in which an RBM has at least as many visible units as the RBM preceding it has hidden units (which raises the risk of simply learning the identity function of the network).

It can be advantageous (but is by no means necessary) when successive RBMs decrease in layer size until the final RBM has a layer size approximating the dimensionality of variance in the data. Affixing an MLP to the end of a DBN whose layers have too many nodes will harm classification performance; it's like trying to affix a drinking straw to the end of a hosepipe! Even an MLP with many neurons may not successfully train in such contexts. On a related note, it has been noted that even if the layers don't contain very many nodes, with enough layers, more or less any function can be modeled.

Determining what the dimensionality of variance in the data is, is not a simple task. One tool that can support this task is PCA; as we saw in the preceding chapter, PCA can enable us to get a reasonable idea as to how many components of meaningful size exist in the input data.

Training a DBN

Training a DBN is typically done greedily, which is to say that it trains to optimize locally at each layer, rather than attempting to reach a global optimum. The learning process is as follows:

- The first layer of the DBN is trained using the method that we saw in our earlier discussion of RBM learning. As such, the first layer converts its data distribution to a posterior distribution using Gibbs sampling over the hidden units.

- This distribution is far more conducive for RBM training than the input data itself so the next RBM layer learns that distribution!

- Successive RBM layers continue to train on the samples output by preceding layers.

- All of the parameters within this architecture are tuned using a performance measure.

This performance measure may vary. It may be a log-likelihood proxy used in gradient descent, as discussed earlier in the chapter. In supervised contexts, a classifier (for example, an MLP) can be added as the final layer of the architecture and prediction accuracy can be used as the performance measure to fine-tune the deep architecture.

Let's move on to using the DBN in practice.

Applying the DBN

Having discussed the DBN and theory surrounding it, it's time to set up our own. We'll be working in a similar way to the RBM, by walking through a DBN class and connecting the code to the theory, discussing what to expect and how to review the network's performance, before initializing and training our network to see it in action.

Let's take a look at our DBN class:

```
class DBN(object):

    def __init__(self, numpy_rng, theano_rng=None, n_ins=784,
```

```
        hidden_layers_sizes=[500, 500], n_outs=10):

    self.sigmoid_layers = []
    self.rbm_layers = []
    self.params = []
    self.n_layers = len(hidden_layers_sizes)

    assert self.n_layers > 0

    if not theano_rng:
        theano_rng = RandomStreams(numpy_rng.randint(2 ** 30))


    self.x = T.matrix('x')
    self.y = T.ivector('y')
```

The DBN class contains a number of parameters that bear further explanation. The numpy_rng and theano_rng parameters, used to determine initial weights, are already familiar from our examination of the RBM class. The n_ins parameter is a pointer to the dimension (in features) of the DBN's input. The hidden_layers_sizes parameter is a list of hidden layer sizes. Each value in this list will guide the DBN constructor in creating an RBM layer of the relevant size; as you'll note, the n_layers parameter refers to the number of layers in the network and is set by hidden_layers_sizes. Adjustment of values in this list enables us to make DBNs whose layer sizes taper down from the input layer size, to increasingly succinct representations, as discussed earlier in the chapter.

It's also worth noting that self.sigmoid_layers will store the MLP component (the final layer of the DBN), while self.rbm_layers stores the RBM layers used to pretrain the MLP.

With this done, we do the following to complete our DBN architecture:

- We create n_layers sigmoid layers
- We connect the sigmoid layers to form an MLP
- We construct an RBM for each sigmoid layer with a shared weight matrix and hidden bias between each sigmoid layer and RBM

The following code creates n_layers many layers with sigmoid activations; first creating the input layer, then creating hidden layers whose size corresponds to the values in our hidden_layers_sizes list:

```
    for i in xrange(self.n_layers):

        if i == 0:
```

```
        input_size = n_ins
    else:
            input_size = hidden_layers_sizes[i - 1]
    if i == 0:
        layer_input = self.x
    else:
        layer_input = self.sigmoid_layers[-1].output

    sigmoid_layer = HiddenLayer(rng=numpy_rng,
                                input=layer_input,
                                n_in=input_size,
                                n_out=hidden_layers_sizes[i],
                                activation=T.nnet.sigmoid)
    self.sigmoid_layers.append(sigmoid_layer)

    self.params.extend(sigmoid_layer.params)
```

Next up, we create an RBM that shares weights with the sigmoid layers. This directly leverages the RBM class that we described previously:

```
    rbm_layer = RBM(numpy_rng=numpy_rng,
                    theano_rng=theano_rng,
                    input=layer_input,
                    n_visible=input_size,
                    n_hidden=hidden_layers_sizes[i],
                    W=sigmoid_layer.W,
                    hbias=sigmoid_layer.b)
    self.rbm_layers.append(rbm_layer)
```

Finally, we add a logistic regression layer to the end of the DBN so as to form an MLP:

```
    self.logLayer = LogisticRegression(
        input=self.sigmoid_layers[-1].output,
        n_in=hidden_layers_sizes[-1],
        n_out=n_outs)
    self.params.extend(self.logLayer.params)

    self.finetune_cost = self.logLayer.negative_log_
likelihood(self.y)

    self.errors = self.logLayer.errors(self.y)
```

Now that we've put together our MLP class, let's construct DBN. The following code constructs the network with 28 * 28 inputs (that is, 28*28 pixels in the MNIST image data), three hidden layers of decreasing size, and 10 output values (for each of the 10 handwritten number classes in the MNIST dataset):

```
numpy_rng = numpy.random.RandomState(123)
print '... building the model'
dbn = DBN(numpy_rng=numpy_rng, n_ins=28 * 28,
          hidden_layers_sizes=[1000, 800, 720],
          n_outs=10)
```

As discussed earlier in this section, a DBN trains in two stages — a layer-wise pretraining in which each layer takes the output of the preceding layer to train on, which is followed by a fine-tuning step (backpropagation) that allows for weight adjustment across the whole network. The first stage, pretraining, is achieved by performing one step of PCD within each layer's RBM. The following code will perform this pretraining step:

```
print '... getting the pretraining functions'
pretraining_fns =
dbn.pretraining_functions(train_set_x=train_set_x,
batch_size=batch_size, k=k)

print '... pre-training the model'
start_time = time.clock()

for i in xrange(dbn.n_layers):
    for epoch in xrange(pretraining_epochs):
        c = []
        for batch_index in xrange(n_train_batches):
            c.append(pretraining_fns[i](index=batch_index,
                                        lr=pretrain_lr))
        print 'Pre-training layer %i, epoch %d, cost ' % (i,
epoch),
        print numpy.mean(c)

end_time = time.clock()
```

Running the pretrained DBN is then achieved by the following command:

`python code/DBN.py`

 Note that even with GPU acceleration, this code will spend quite a lot of time pretraining, and it is therefore suggested that you run it overnight.

Validating the DBN

Validation of a DBN as a whole is done in a very familiar way. We can use the minimal validation error from cross-validation as one error measure. However, the minimal cross-validation error can underestimate the error expected on cross-validation data as the meta-parameters may overfit to the new data.

As such, we should use our cross-validation error to adjust our metaparameters until the cross-validation error is minimized. Then we should expose our DBN to the held-out test set, using test error as our validation measure. Our DBN class performs exactly this training process.

However, this doesn't tell us exactly what to do if the network fails to train adequately. What do we do if our DBN is underperforming?

The first thing to do is recognize the potential causes and, in this area, there are some usual culprits. We know that the training of underlying RBMs is also quite tricky and any individual layer may fail to train. Thankfully, our RBM class gives us the ability to tap into and view the weights (filters) being generated by each layer, and we can plot these to get a view on what our network is attempting to represent.

Additionally, we want to ask whether our network is overfitting, or else, underfitting. Either is entirely possible and it's useful to recognize how and why this might be happening. In the case of underfitting, the training process may simply be unable to find good parameters for the model. This is particularly common when you are using a larger network to resolve a large problem space, but can be seen even with some smaller models. If you think that underfitting might be happening with your DBN, you have a couple of options. The first is to simply reduce the size of your hidden layers. This may, or may not, work well. A better alternative is to gradually taper your hidden layers such that each layer learns a refined version of the preceding layer's representation. How to do this, how sharply to taper, and when to stop is a matter of trial and error in the first case and of experience-based learning over the long term.

Overfitting is a well-known phenomenon where your algorithm trains overly specifically on the training data provided. This class of problem is typically identified at the point of cross-validation (where your error rate will increase dramatically), but can be quite pernicious. Means of resolving an overfitting issue do exist; one can increase the training dataset size. A more heavy-handed Bayesian approach would be to attach an additional criterion (for example, a prior) that is used to reduce the value of fitting the training data. Some of the most effective methods to improve classification performance are preprocessing methods, which we'll discuss in *Chapters 6, Text Feature Engineering* and *Chapter 7, Feature Engineering Part II*.

Though this code will initialize from a predefined position (given a seed value), the stochastic nature of the model means that it will quickly diverge and results may vary. When running on my system, this DBN achieved a minimal cross-validation error of 1.19%. More importantly, it achieved a test error of 1.30% after 46 supervised epochs. These are good results; indeed, they are comparable with field-leading examples!

Further reading

For a primer on neural networks, it makes sense to read from a range of sources. There are many concerns to be aware of and different authors emphasize on different material. A solid introduction is provided by Kevin Gurney in An Introduction to Neural Networks.

An excellent piece on the intuitions underlying Markov Chain Monte Carlo is available at `http://twiecki.github.io/blog/2015/11/10/mcmc-sampling/`.

For readers with a specific interest in the intuitions supporting Gibbs Sampling, Philip Resnik, and Eric Hardisty's paper, *Gibbs Sampling for the Uninitiated*, provides a technical, but clear description of how Gibbs works. It's particularly notable to have some really first-rate analogies! Find them at `https://www.umiacs.umd.edu/~resnik/pubs/LAMP-TR-153.pdf`.

There aren't many good explanations of Contrastive Divergence, one I like is provided by Oliver Woodford at `http://www.robots.ox.ac.uk/~ojw/files/NotesOnCD.pdf`. If you're a little daunted by the heavy use of formal expressions, I would still recommend that you read it for its articulate description of theory and practical concerns involved.

This chapter used the Theano documentation available at `http://deeplearning.net/tutorial/contents.html` as a base for discussion and implementation of RBM and DBN classes.

Summary

We've covered a lot of ground in this chapter! We began with an overview of Neural Networks, focusing on the general properties of topology and learning method before taking a deep dive into the RBM algorithm and RBM code itself. We took this solid understanding forward to create a DBN. In doing so, we linked the DBN theory and code together, before firing up our DBN to work over the MNIST dataset. We performed image classification in a 10-class problem and achieved an extremely competitive result, with classification error below 2%!

In the next chapter, we'll continue to build on your mastery of deep learning by introducing you to another deep learning architecture—**Stacked Denoising Autoencoders (SDA)**.

3
Stacked Denoising Autoencoders

In this chapter, we'll continue building our skill with deep architectures by applying **Stacked Denoising Autoencoders (SdA)** to learn feature representations for high-dimensional input data.

We'll start, as before, by gaining a solid understanding of the theory and concepts that underpin autoencoders. We'll identify related techniques and call out the strengths of autoencoders as part of your data science toolkit. We'll discuss the use of **Denoising Autoencoders (dA)**, a variation of the algorithm that introduces stochastic corruption to the input data, obliging the autoencoder to decorrupt the input and, in so doing, build a more effective feature representation.

We'll follow up on theory, as before, by walking through the code for a dA class, linking theory and implementation details to build a strong understanding of the technique.

At this point, we'll take a journey very similar to that taken in the preceding chapter—by stacking dA, we'll create a deep architecture that can be used to pretrain an MLP network, which offers substantial performance improvements in a range of unsupervised learning applications including speech data processing.

Autoencoders

The autoencoder (also called the **Diabolo network**) is another crucial component of deep architectures. The autoencoder is related to the RBM, with autoencoder training resembling RBM training; however, autoencoders can be easier to train than RBMs with contrastive divergence and are thus preferred in contexts where RBMs train less effectively.

Introducing the autoencoder

An autoencoder is a simple three-layer neural network whose output units are directly connected back to the input units. The objective of the autoencoder is to encode the **i-dimensional** input into an **h-dimensional** representation, where $h < i$, before reconstructing (decoding) the input at the output layer. The training process involves iteration over this process until the reconstruction error is minimized — at which point one should have arrived at the most efficient representation of input data (should, barring the possibility of arriving at local minima!).

In a preceding chapter, we discussed PCA as being a powerful dimensionality reduction technique. This description of autoencoders as finding the most efficient reduced-dimensional representation of input data will no doubt be familiar and you may be asking why we're exploring another technique that fulfils the same role.

The simple answer is that like the SOM, autoencoders can provide nonlinear reductions, which enables them to process high-dimensional input data more effectively than PCA. This revives a form of our earlier question — why discuss autoencoders if they deliver what an SOM does, without even providing the illuminating visual presentation?

Simply put, autoencoders are a more developed and sophisticated set of techniques; the use of denoising and stacking techniques enable reductions of high-dimensional, multimodal data that can be trained with relative ease to greater accuracy, at greater scale, than the techniques that we discussed in *Chapter 1, Unsupervised Machine Learning*.

Having discussed the capabilities of autoencoders at a high level, let's dig in a little further to understand the topology of autoencoders as well as what their training involves.

Topology

As described earlier in this chapter, an autoencoder has a relatively simple structure. It is a three-layer neural network, with **input**, **hidden**, and **output** layers. The **input** feeds forward into the **hidden** layer, then the **output** layer, as with most neural network architectures. One topological feature worth mentioning is that the **hidden** layer is typically of fewer nodes than the **input** or **output** layers. (However, as intimated previously, the required number of **hidden** nodes is really a function of the complexity of the **input** data; the goal of the **hidden** layer is to bottleneck the information content from the **input** and force the network to identify a representation that captures underlying statistical properties. Representing very complex input accurately might require a large quantity of hidden nodes.)

The key feature of an autoencoder is that the **output** is typically set to be the **input**; the performance measure for an autoencoder is its accuracy in reconstructing the **input** after encoding it within the **hidden** layer. Autoencoder topology tends to take the following form:

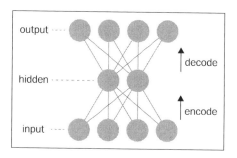

The encoding function that occurs between the **input** and **hidden** layers is a mapping of an input (x) to a new form (y). A simple example mapping function might be a nonlinear (in this case sigmoid, s) function of the input as follows:

$$y = s\left(Wx + b\right)$$

However, more sophisticated encodings may exist or be developed to accommodate specific subject domains. In this case, of course, W represents the weight values assigned to x and b is an adjustable variable that can be tuned to enable the minimization of reconstruction error.

The autoencoder then decodes to deliver its output. This reconstruction is intended to take the same shape as x and will occur through a similar transformation as follows:

$$z = s\left(W'y + b'\right)$$

Here, b' and W' are typically also configurable to allow network optimization.

Training

The network trains, as discussed, by minimizing the reconstruction error. One popular method to measure this error is a simple squared error measure, as shown in the following formula:

$$E = \frac{1}{2}\left\|z - x\right\|^2$$

However, different and more appropriate error measures exist for cases where the input is in a less generic format (such as a set of bit probabilities).

While the intention is that autoencoders capture the main axes of variation in the input dataset, it is possible for an autoencoder to learn something far less useful—the identity function of the input.

Denoising autoencoders

While autoencoders can work well in some applications, they can be challenging to apply to problems where the input data contains a complex distribution that must be modeled in high dimensionality. The major challenge is that, with autoencoders that have **n-dimensional** input and an encoding of at least *n*, there is a real likelihood that the autoencoder will just learn the identity function of the input. In such cases, the encoding is a literal copy of the input. Such autoencoders are called **overcomplete**.

One of the most important properties when training a machine learning technique is to understand how the dimensionality of hidden layers affects the quality of the resulting model. In cases where the input data is complex and the hidden layer has too few nodes to capture that complexity effectively, the result is obvious—the network fails to train as well as it might with more nodes.

To capture complex distributions in input data, then, you may wish to use a large number of hidden nodes. In cases where the hidden layer has at least as many nodes as the input, there is a strong possibility that the network will learn the identity of the input; in such cases, each element of the input is learned as a specific unique case. Naturally, a model that has been trained to do this will work very well over training data, but as it has learned a trivial pattern that cannot be generalized to unfamiliar data, it is liable to fail catastrophically when validated.

This is particularly relevant when modeling complex data, such as speech data. Such data is frequently complex in distribution, so the classification of speech signals requires multimodal encoding and a high-dimensional hidden layer. Of course, this brings an increased risk of the autoencoder (or any of a large number of models as this is not an autoencoder-specific problem) learning the identity function.

While (rather surprisingly) overcomplete autoencoders can and do learn error-minimizing representations under certain configurations (namely, ones in which the first hidden layer needs very small weights so as to force the hidden units into a linear orientation and subsequent weights have large values), such configurations are difficult to optimize for, and it has been desirable to find another way to prevent overcomplete autoencoders from learning the identity function.

There are several different ways that an overcomplete autoencoder can be prevented from learning the identity function while still capturing something useful within its representation. By far, the most popular approach is to introduce noise to the input data and force the autoencoder to train on the noisy data by learning distributions and statistical regularities rather than identity. This can be effectively achieved by multiple methods, including using sparseness constraints or dropout techniques (wherein input values are randomly set to zero).

The process that we'll be using to introduce noise to the input in this chapter is dropout. Via this method, up to half of the inputs are randomly set to zero. To achieve this, we create a stochastic corruption process that operates on our input data:

```
def get_corrupted_input(self, input, corruption_level):

    return self.theano_rng.binomial(size=input.shape, n=1, p=1 -
    corruption_level, dtype=theano.config.floatX) * input
```

In order to accurately model the input data, the autoencoder has to predict the corrupted values from the uncorrupted values, thus learning meaningful statistical properties (that is, distribution).

In addition to preventing an autoencoder from learning the identity values of data, adding a denoising process also tends to produce models that are substantially more robust to input variations or distortion. This proves to be particularly useful for input data that is inherently noisy, such as speech or image data. One commonly recognized advantage of deep learning techniques, mentioned in the preface to this book, is that deep learning algorithms minimize the need for feature engineering. Where many learning algorithms require lengthy and complicated preprocessing of input data (filtering of images or manipulation of audio signals) to reconstruct the denoised input and enable the model to train, a dA can work effectively with minimal preprocessing. This can dramatically decrease the time it takes to train a model over your input data to practical levels of accuracy.

Finally, it's worth observing that an autoencoder that learns the identity function of the input dataset is probably misconfigured in a fundamental way. As the main added value of the autoencoder is to find a lower-dimensional representation of the feature set, an autoencoder that has learned the identity function of the input data may simply have too many nodes. If in doubt, consider reducing the number of nodes in your hidden layer.

Now that we've discussed the topology of an autoencoder—the means by which one might be effectively trained and the role of denoising in improving autoencoder performance—let's review **Theano** code for a dA so as to carry the preceding theory into practice.

Applying a dA

At this point, we're ready to step through the implementation of a dA. Once again, we're leveraging the Theano library to apply a dA class.

Unlike the RBM class that we explored in the previous chapter, the DenoisingAutoencoder is relatively simple and tying the functionality of the dA to the theory and math that we examined earlier in this chapter is relatively simple.

In *Chapter 2, Deep Belief Networks*, we applied an RBM class that had a number of elements that, while not necessary for the correct functioning of the RBM in itself, enabled shared parameters within multilayer, deep architectures. The dA class we'll be using possesses similar shared elements that will provide us with the means to build a multilayer autoencoder architecture later in the chapter.

We begin by initializing a dA class. We specify the number of visible units, n_visible, as well as the number of hidden units, n_hidden. We additionally specify variables for the configuration of the input (input) as well as the weights (W) and the hidden and visible bias values (bhid and bvis respectively). The four additional variables enable autoencoders to receive configuration parameters from other elements of a deep architecture:

```
class dA(object):

    def __init__(
        self,
        numpy_rng,
        theano_rng=None,
        input=None,
        n_visible=784,
        n_hidden=500,
        W=None,
        bhid=None,
        bvis=None
    ):

        self.n_visible = n_visible
        self.n_hidden = n_hidden
```

We follow up by initialising the weight and bias variables. We set the weight vector, W to an initial value, `initial_W`, which we obtain using random, uniform sampling from the range:

$$-4 * \sqrt{\frac{6.}{(n\_hidden+n\_visible)}} \quad to \quad 4 * \sqrt{\frac{6.}{\left(n_{hidden}+n_{visible}\right)}}.$$

We then set the visible and hidden bias variables to arrays of zeroes using `numpy.zeros`:

```
    if not theano_rng:
        theano_rng = RandomStreams(numpy_rng.randint(2 ** 30))

    if not W:
        initial_W = numpy.asarray(
            numpy_rng.uniform(
                low=-4 * numpy.sqrt(6. / (n_hidden + n_visible)),
                high=4 * numpy.sqrt(6. / (n_hidden + n_visible)),
                size=(n_visible, n_hidden)
            ),
            dtype=theano.config.floatX
        )
        W = theano.shared(value=initial_W, name='W', borrow=True)

    if not bvis:
        bvis = theano.shared(
            value=numpy.zeros(
                n_visible,
                dtype=theano.config.floatX
            ),
            borrow=True
        )

    if not bhid:
        bhid = theano.shared(
            value=numpy.zeros(
                n_hidden,
                dtype=theano.config.floatX
            ),
            name='b',
            borrow=True
        )
```

Earlier in the chapter, we described how the autoencoder translates between visible and hidden layers via mappings such as $y = s(Wx + b)$. To enable such translation, it is necessary to define W, b, W', and b' in relation to the previously described autoencoder parameters, bhid, bvis, and W. W' and b' are referred to as W_prime and b_prime in the following code:

```
self.W = W
self.b = bhid
self.b_prime = bvis
self.W_prime = self.W.T
self.theano_rng = theano_rng
if input is None:
    self.x = T.dmatrix(name='input')
else:
    self.x = input

self.params = [self.W, self.b, self.b_prime]
```

The preceding code sets b and b_prime to bhid and bvis respectively, while W_prime is set as the transpose of W; in other words, the weights are tied. Tied weights are sometimes, but not always, used in autoencoders for several reasons:

- Tying weights improves the quality of results in several contexts (albeit often in contexts where the optimal solution is PCA, which is the solution an autoencoder with tied weights will tend to reach)
- Tying weights improves the memory consumption of the autoencoder by reducing the number of parameters that need be stored
- Most importantly, tied weights provide a regularization effect; they require one less parameter to be optimized (thus one less thing that can go wrong!)

However, in other contexts, it's both common and appropriate to use untied weights. This is true, for instance, in cases where the input data is multimodal and the optimal decoder models a nonlinear set of statistical regularities. In such cases, a linear model, such as PCA, will not effectively model the nonlinear trends and you will tend to obtain better results using untied weights.

Having configured the parameters to our autoencoder, the next step is to define the functions that enable it to learn. Earlier in this chapter, we determined that autoencoders learn effectively by adding noise to input data, then attempting to learn an encoded representation of that input that can in turn be reconstructed into the input. What we need next, then, are functions that deliver this functionality. We begin by corrupting the input data:

```
def get_corrupted_input(self, input, corruption_level):

    return self.theano_rng.binomial(size=input.shape, n=1, p=1 -
    corruption_level, dtype=theano.config.floatX) * input
```

The degree of corruption is configurable using a `corruption_level` parameter; as we recognized earlier, the corruption of the input through dropout typically does not exceed 50% of cases, or 0.5. The function takes a random set of cases, where the number of cases is that proportion of the `input` whose `size` is equal to `corruption_level`. The function produces a corruption vector of $0's$ and $1's$ equal in length to the input, where a `corruption_level` sized proportion of the vector is 0. The corrupted input vector is then simply a multiple of the autoencoder's input vector and corruption vector:

```
def get_hidden_values(self, input):
    return T.nnet.sigmoid(T.dot(input, self.W) + self.b)
```

Next, we obtain the hidden values. This is done via code that performs the equation $y = s(Wx + b)$ to obtain y (the hidden values). To get the autoencoder's output (z), we reconstruct the hidden layer via code that uses the previously defined b_prime and W_prime to perform $z = s(W'y + b')$:

```
defget_reconstructed_input(self, hidden):
    returnT.nnet.sigmoid(T.dot(hidden, self.W_prime) +
    self.b_prime)
```

The final missing piece is the calculation of cost updates. We reviewed one cost function previously, a simple squared error measure: $E = \frac{1}{2}\|z - x\|^2$. Let's use this cost function to calculate our cost updates, based on the input (x) and reconstruction (z):

```
def get_cost_updates(self, corruption_level, learning_rate):

    tilde_x = self.get_corrupted_input(self.x, corruption_level)
    y = self.get_hidden_values(tilde_x)
```

```
z = self.get_reconstructed_input(y)
E = (0.5 * (T.z - T.self.x)) ^ 2
cost = T.mean(E)

gparams = T.grad(cost, self.params)
updates = [
    (param, param - learning_rate * gparam)
    for param, gparam in zip(self.params, gparams)
]


return (cost, updates)
```

At this point, we have a functional dA! It may be used to model nonlinear properties of input data and can work as an effective tool to learn valid and lower-dimensional representations of input data. However, the real power of autoencoders comes from the properties that they display when stacked together, as the building blocks of a deep architecture.

Stacked Denoising Autoencoders

While autoencoders are valuable tools in themselves, significant accuracy can be obtained by stacking autoencoders to form a deep network. This is achieved by feeding the representation created by the encoder on one layer into the next layer's encoder as the input to that layer.

Stacked denoising autoencoders (SdAs) are currently in use in many leading data science teams for sophisticated natural language analyses as well as a hugely broad range of signals, image, and text analysis.

The implementation of a SdA will be very familiar after the previous chapter's discussion of deep belief networks. The SdA is used in much the same way as the RBMs in our deep belief networks were used. Each layer of the deep architecture will have a dA and sigmoid component, with the autoencoder component being used to pretrain the sigmoid network. The performance measure used by a stacked denoising autoencoder is the training set error, with an intensive period of layer-to-layer (layer-wise) pretraining used to gradually align network parameters before a final period of fine-tuning. During fine-tuning, the network is trained using validation and test data, over fewer epochs but with larger update steps. The goal is to have the network converge at the end of the fine-tuning in order to deliver an accurate result.

In addition to delivering on the typical advantages of deep networks (the ability to learn feature representations for complex or high-dimensional datasets, and the ability to train a model without extensive feature engineering), stacked autoencoders have an additional, interesting property.

Correctly configured stacked autoencoders can capture a **hierarchical grouping** of their input data. Successive layers of a stacked denoised autoencoder may learn increasingly high-level features. Where the first layer might learn some first-order features from input data (such as learning edges in a photo image), a second layer may learn some grouping of first-order features (for instance, by learning given configurations of edges that correspond to contours or structural elements in the input image).

There's no golden rule to determine how many layers or how large layers should be for a given problem. The best solution is usually to experiment with these model parameters until you find an optimal point. This experimentation is best done with a hyperparameter optimization technique or genetic algorithm (subjects we'll discuss in later chapters of this book).

Higher layers may learn increasingly high-order configurations, enabling a stacked denoised autoencoder to learn to recognize facial features, alphanumerical characters, or generalized forms of objects (such as a bird). This is what gives SdAs their unique capability to learn very sophisticated, high-level abstractions of their input data.

Autoencoders can be stacked indefinitely, and it has been demonstrated that continuing to stack autoencoders can improve the effectiveness of the deep architecture (with the main constraint becoming compute cost in time). In this chapter, we'll look at stacking three autoencoders to solve a natural language processing challenge.

Applying the SdA

Now that we've had a chance to understand the advantages and power of the SdA as a deep learning architecture, let's test our skills on a real-world dataset.

For this chapter, let's step away from image datasets and work with the **OpinRank Review** dataset, a text dataset of around 259,000 hotel reviews from TripAdvisor — accessible via the UCI machine learning dataset repository. This freely-available dataset provides review scores (as floating point numbers from 1 to 5) and review text for a broad range of hotels; we'll be applying our stacked dA to attempt to identify the scoring of each hotel from its review text.

We'll be applying our autoencoder to analyze a preprocessed version of this data, which is accessible from the GitHub share accompanying this chapter. We'll be discussing the techniques by which we prepare text data in an upcoming chapter. For the interested reader, the source data is available at `https://archive.ics.uci.edu/ml/datasets/OpinRank+Review+Dataset`.

In order to get started, we're going to need a stacked denoising autoencoder (hereafter SdA) class:

```
class SdA(object):



    def __init__(
        self,
        numpy_rng,
        theano_rng=None,
        n_ins=280,
        hidden_layers_sizes=[500, 500],
        n_outs=5,
        corruption_levels=[0.1, 0.1]
    ):
```

As we previously discussed, the SdA is created by feeding the encoding from one layer's autoencoder as the input to the subsequent layer. This class supports the configuration of the layer count (reflected in, but not set by, the length of the hidden_layers_sizes and corruption_levels vectors). It also supports differentiated layer sizes (in nodes) at each layer, which can be set using hidden_layers_sizes. As we discussed, the ability to configure successive layers of the autoencoder is critical to developing successful representations.

Next, we need parameters to store the MLP (self.sigmoid_layers) and dA (self.dA_layers) elements of the SdA. In order to specify the depth of our architecture, we use the self.n_layers parameter to specify the number of sigmoid and dA layers required:

```
self.sigmoid_layers = []
self.dA_layers = []
self.params = []
self.n_layers = len(hidden_layers_sizes)

assertself.n_layers> 0
```

Next, we need to construct our sigmoid and dA layers. We begin by setting the hidden layer size to be set either from the input vector size or by the activation of the preceding layer. Following this, `sigmoid_layer` and `dA_layer` components are created, with the dA layer drawing from the dA class that we discussed earlier in this chapter:

```
for i in xrange(self.n_layers):
    if i == 0:
        input_size = n_ins
    else:
        input_size = hidden_layers_sizes[i - 1]

    if i == 0:
        layer_input = self.x
    else:
        layer_input = self.sigmoid_layers[-1].output

    sigmoid_layer = HiddenLayer(rng=numpy_rng,
    input=layer_input,
    n_in=input_size,
    n_out=hidden_layers_sizes[i],
    activation=T.nnet.sigmoid)

    self.sigmoid_layers.append(sigmoid_layer)
    self.params.extend(sigmoid_layer.params)

    dA_layer = dA(numpy_rng=numpy_rng,
    theano_rng=theano_rng,
    input=layer_input,
    n_visible=input_size,
    n_hidden=hidden_layers_sizes[i],
    W=sigmoid_layer.W,
    bhid=sigmoid_layer.b)

    self.dA_layers.append(dA_layer)
```

Having implemented the layers of our stacked dA, we'll need a final, logistic regression layer to complete the MLP component of the network:

```
self.logLayer = LogisticRegression(
    input=self.sigmoid_layers[-1].output,
    n_in=hidden_layers_sizes[-1],
    n_out=n_outs
)

self.params.extend(self.logLayer.params)
self.finetune_cost = self.logLayer.negative_log_likelihood(self.y)
self.errors = self.logLayer.errors(self.y)
```

This completes the architecture of our SdA. Next up, we need to generate the training functions used by the SdA class. Each function will the minibatch index (index) as an argument, together with several other elements—the corruption_level and learning_rate are enabled here so that we can adjust them (for example, gradually increase or decrease them) during training. Additionally, we identify variables that help identify where the batch starts and ends—batch_begin and batch_end, respectively:

> The ability to dynamically adjust the learning rate is particularly very helpful and may be applied in one of two ways. Once a technique has begun to converge on an appropriate solution, it is very helpful to be able to reduce the learning rate. If you do not do this, you risk creating a situation in which the network oscillates between values located around the optimum without ever hitting it. In some contexts, it can be helpful to tie the learning rate to the network's performance measure. If the error rate is high, it makes sense to make larger adjustments until the error rate begins to decrease!

```python
def pretraining_functions(self, train_set_x, batch_size):
    index = T.lscalar('index')
    corruption_level = T.scalar('corruption')
    learning_rate = T.scalar('lr')
    batch_begin = index * batch_size
    batch_end = batch_begin + batch_size

    pretrain_fns = []
    for dA in self.dA_layers:
        cost, updates = dA.get_cost_updates(corruption_level,
          learning_rate)
        fn = theano.function(
            inputs=[
                index,
                theano.Param(corruption_level, default=0.2),
                theano.Param(learning_rate, default=0.1)
            ],
            outputs=cost,
            updates=updates,
            givens={
                self.x: train_set_x[batch_begin: batch_end]
            }
        )
        pretrain_fns.append(fn)

    return pretrain_fns
```

The pretraining functions that we've created takes the minibatch `index` and can optionally take the corruption level or learning rate. It performs one step of pretraining and outputs the cost value and vector of weight updates.

In addition to pretraining, we need to build functions to support the fine-tuning stage, wherein the network is run iteratively over the validation and test data to optimize network parameters. The training function (`train_fn`) seen in the code below implements a single step of fine-tuning. The `valid_score` is a Python function that computes a validation score using the error measure produced by the SdA over validation data. Similarly, `test_score` computes the error score over test data.

To get this process off the ground, we first need to set up training, validation, and test datasets. Each stage requires two datasets (set x and set y) containing the features and class labels, respectively. The required number of minibatches for validation and test is determined, and an index is created to track the batch size (and provide a means of identifying at which entries a batch starts and ends). Training, validation, and testing occurs for each batch and afterward, both `valid_score` and `test_score` are calculated across all batches:

```
def build_finetune_functions(self, datasets, batch_size,
    learning_rate):

    (train_set_x, train_set_y) = datasets[0]
    (valid_set_x, valid_set_y) = datasets[1]
    (test_set_x, test_set_y) = datasets[2]

    n_valid_batches = valid_set_x.get_value(borrow=True).shape[0]
    n_valid_batches /= batch_size
    n_test_batches = test_set_x.get_value(borrow=True).shape[0]
    n_test_batches /= batch_size

    index = T.lscalar('index')


    gparams = T.grad(self.finetune_cost, self.params)


    updates = [
        (param, param - gparam * learning_rate)
        For param, gparam in zip(self.params, gparams)
]

train_fn = theano.function(
    inputs=[index],
```

```python
        outputs=self.finetune_cost,
        updates=updates,
        givens={
            self.x: train_set_x[
                index * batch_size: (index + 1) * batch_size
            ],
            self.y: train_set_y[
                index * batch_size: (index + 1) * batch_size
            ]
        },
        name='train'
    )

    test_score_i = theano.function(
        [index],
        self.errors,
        givens={
            self.x: test_set_x[
            index * batch_size: (index + 1) * batch_size
        ],
            self.y: test_set_y[
            index * batch_size: (index + 1) * batch_size
        ]
    },
        name='test'
    )

    valid_score_i = theano.function(
        [index],
        self.errors,
        givens={
            self.x: valid_set_x[
                index * batch_size: (index + 1) * batch_size
            ],
            self.y: valid_set_y[
                index * batch_size: (index + 1) * batch_size
            ]
        },
        name='valid'
    )


    def valid_score():
```

```
    return [valid_score_i(i) for i inxrange(n_valid_batches)]

def test_score():
    return [test_score_i(i) for i inxrange(n_test_batches)]

return train_fn, valid_score, test_score
```

With the training functionality in place, the following code initiates our stacked dA:

```
numpy_rng = numpy.random.RandomState(89677)
print '... building the model'
    sda = SdA(
        numpy_rng=numpy_rng,
        n_ins=280,
        hidden_layers_sizes=[240, 170, 100],
        n_outs=5
    )
```

It should be noted that, at this point, we should be trying an initial configuration of layer sizes to see how we do. In this case, the layer sizes used are the product of some initial testing. As we discussed, training the SdA occurs in two stages. The first is a layer-wise pretraining process that loops over all of the SdA's layers. The second is a process of fine-tuning over validation and test data.

To pretrain the SdA, we provide the required corruption levels to train each layer and iterate over the layers using our previously defined pretraining_fns:

```
print '... getting the pretraining functions'
pretraining_fns = sda.pretraining_functions(train_set_x=train_set_x,
batch_size=batch_size)

print '... pre-training the model'
start_time = time.clock()
corruption_levels = [.1, .2, .2]
for i in xrange(sda.n_layers):

    for epoch in xrange(pretraining_epochs):
        c = []
        for batch_index in xrange(n_train_batches):
            c.append(pretraining_fns[i](index=batch_index,
            corruption=corruption_levels[i],
            lr=pretrain_lr))
```

```
print 'Pre-training layer %i, epoch %d, cost ' % (i, epoch),

print numpy.mean(c)

end_time = time.clock()

print(('The pretraining code for file ' +
os.path.split(__file__)[1] + ' ran for %.2fm' % ((end_time - start_
time) / 60.)), file = sys.stderr)
```

At this point, we're able to initialize our `SdA` class via calling the preceding code stored within this book's GitHub repository: `MasteringMLWithPython/Chapter3/SdA.py`

Assessing SdA performance

The SdA will take a significant length of time to run. With 15 epochs per layer and each layer typically taking an average of 11 minutes, the network will run for around 500 minutes on a modern desktop system with GPU acceleration and a single-threaded GotoBLAS.

On a system without GPU acceleration, the network will take substantially longer to train, and it is recommended that you use the alternative, which runs over a significantly smaller input dataset: `MasteringMLWithPython/Chapter3/SdA_no_blas.py`

The results are of high quality, with a validation error score of 3.22% and test error score of 3.14%. These results are particularly impressive given the ambiguous and sometimes challenging nature of natural language processing applications.

It was noticeable that the network classified more correctly for the 1-star and 5-star rating cases than for the intermediate levels. This is largely due to the ambiguous nature of unpolarized or unemotional language.

Part of the reason that this input data was classifiable was via significant feature engineering. While time-consuming and sometimes problematic, we've seen that well-executed feature engineering combined with an optimized model can deliver an excellent level of accuracy. In *Chapter 6, Text Feature Engineering*, we'll be applying the techniques used to prepare this dataset ourselves.

Further reading

A well-informed overview of autoencoders (amongst other subjects) is provided by Quoc V. Le from the Google Brain team. Read about it at `https://cs.stanford.edu/~quocle/tutorial2.pdf`.

This chapter used the Theano documentation available at `http://deeplearning.net/tutorial/contents.html` as a base for discussion as Theano was the main library used in this chapter.

Summary

In this chapter, we introduced the autoencoder, an effective dimensionality reduction technique with some unique applications. We focused on the theory behind the stacked denoised autoencoder, an extension of autoencoders whereby any number of autoencoders are stacked in a deep architecture. We were able to apply the stacked denoised autoencoder to a challenging natural language processing problem and met with great success, delivering highly accurate sentiment analysis of hotel reviews.

In the next chapter, we will discuss supervised deep learning methods, including **Convolutional Neural Networks (CNN)**.

4
Convolutional Neural Networks

In this chapter, you'll be learning how to apply the convolutional neural network (also referred to as the CNN or convnet), perhaps the best-known deep architecture, via the following steps:

- Taking a look at the convnet's topology and learning processes, including convolutional and pooling layers

- Understanding how we can combine convnet components into successful network architectures

- Using Python code to apply a convnet architecture so as to solve a well-known image classification task

Introducing the CNN

In the field of machine learning, there is an enduring preference for developing structures in code that parallel biological structures. One of the most obvious examples is that of the MLP neural network, whose topology and learning processes are inspired by the neurons of the human brain.

This preference has turned out to be highly efficient; the availability of specialized, optimized biological structures that excel at specific sets of tasks gives us a wealth of templates and clues from which to design and create effective learning models.

The design of convolutional neural networks takes inspiration from the visual cortex—the area of the brain that processes visual input. The visual cortex has several specializations that enable it to effectively process visual data; it contains many receptor cells that detect light in overlapping regions of the visual field. All receptor cells are subject to the same convolution operation, which is to say that they all process their input in the same way. These specializations were incorporated into the design of convnets, making their topology noticeably distinct from that of other neural networks.

It's safe to say that CNN (convnets for short) are underpinning many of the most impactful current advances in artificial intelligence and machine learning. Variants of CNN are applied to some of the most sophisticated visual, linguistic, and problem-solving applications in existence. Some examples include the following:

- Google has developed a range of specialized convnet architectures, including **GoogLeNet**, a 22-layer convnet architecture. In addition, Google's DeepDream program, which became well-known for its overtrained, hallucinogenic imagery, also uses a convolutional neural network.

- Convolutional nets have been taught to play the game **Go** (a long-standing AI challenge), achieving win-rates ranging between 85% and 91% against highly-ranked players.

- Facebook uses convolutional nets in face verification (**DeepFace**).

- Baidu, Microsoft research, IBM, and Twitter are among the many other teams using convnets to tackle the challenges around trying to deliver next-generation intelligent applications.

In recent years, object recognition challenges, such as the 2014 **ImageNet** challenge, have been dominated by winners employing specialized convnet implementations or multiple-model ensembles that combine convnets with other architectures.

While we'll cover how to create and effectively apply ensembles in *Chapter 8, Ensemble Methods*, this chapter focuses on the successful application of convolutional neural networks to large-scale visual classification contexts.

Understanding the convnet topology

The convolutional neural network's architecture should be fairly familiar; the network is an acyclic graph composed of layers of increasingly few nodes, where each layer feeds into the next. This will be very familiar from many well-known network topologies such as the MLP.

Perhaps the most immediate difference between a convolutional neural network and most other networks is that all of the neurons in a convnet are identical! All neurons possess the same parameters and weight values. As you can see, this will immediately reduce the number of parameter values controlled by the network, bringing substantial efficiency savings. It also typically improves network learning rate as there are fewer free parameters to be managed and computed over. As we'll see later in this chapter, shared weights also enable a convnet to learn features irrespective of their position in the input (for example, the input image or audio signal).

Another big difference between convolutional networks and other architectures is that the connectivity between nodes is limited such as to develop a spatially local connectivity pattern. In other words, the inputs to a given node will be limited to only those nodes whose receptor fields are contiguous. This may be spatially contiguous, as in the case of image data; in such cases, each neuron's inputs will ultimately draw from a continuous subset of the image. In the case of audio signal data, the input might instead be a continuous window of time.

To illustrate this more clearly, let's take an example input image and discuss how a convolutional network might process parts of that image across specific nodes. Nodes in the first layer of a convolutional neural network will be assigned subsets of the input image. In this case, let's say that they take a 3 x 3 pixel subset of the image each. Our coverage covers the entire image without any overlap between the areas taken as input by nodes and without any gaps. (Note that none of these conditions are automatically true for convnet implementations.) Each node is assigned a 3 x 3 pixel subset of the image (the receptive field of the node) and outputs a transformed version of that input. We'll disregard the specifics of that transformation for now.

This output is usually then picked up by a second layer of nodes. In this case, let's say that our second layer is taking a subset of all of the outputs from nodes in the first layer. For example, it might be taking a contiguous 6 x 6 pixel subset of the original image; that is, it has a receptive field that covers the outputs of exactly four nodes from the preceding layer. This becomes a little more intuitive when explained visually:

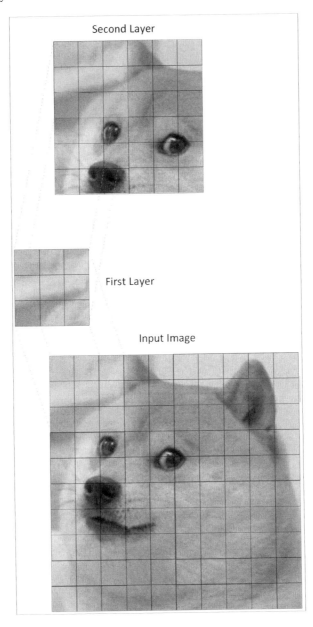

Each layer is **composable**; the output of one convolutional layer may be fed into the next layer as an input. This provides the same effect that we saw in the *Chapter 3, Stacked Denoising Autoencoders*; successive layers develop representations of increasingly high-level, abstract features. Furthermore, as we build downward — adding layers — the representation becomes responsive to a larger region of pixel space. Ultimately, by stacking layers, we can work our way toward global representations of the entire input.

Understanding convolution layers

As described, in order to prevent each node from learning an unpredictable (and difficult to tune!) set of very local, free parameters, weights in a layer are shared across the entire layer. To be completely precise, the filters applied in a convolutional layer are a single set of filters, which are slid (convolved) across the input dataset. This produces a two-dimensional activation map of the input, which is referred to as the feature map.

The filter itself is subject to four hyperparameters: size, depth, stride, and zero-padding. The size of the filter is fairly self-explanatory, being the area of the filter (obviously, found by multiplying height and width; a filter need not be square!). Larger filters will tend to overlap more, and as we'll see, this can improve the accuracy of classification. Crucially, however, increasing the filter size will create increasingly large outputs. As we'll see, managing the size of outputs from convolutional layers is a huge factor in controlling the efficiency of a network.

Depth defines the number of nodes in the layer that connect to the same region of the input. The trick to understanding depth is to recognize that looking at an image (for people or networks) involves processing multiple different types of property. Anyone who has ever looked at all the image adjustment sliders in Photoshop has an idea of what this might entail. Depth is sometimes referred to as a dimension in its own right; it almost relates to the complexity of an image, not in terms of its contents but in terms of the number of channels needed to accurately describe it.

It's possible that the depth might describe color channels, with nodes mapped to recognize green, blue, or red in the input. This, incidentally, leads to a common convention where depth is set to three (particularly at the first convolution layer). It's very important to recognize that some nodes commonly learn to express less easily-described properties of input images that happen to enable a convnet to learn that image more accurately. Increasing the depth hyperparameter tends to enable nodes to encode more information about inputs, with the attendant problems and benefits that you might expect.

As a result, setting the depth parameter to too small a value tends to lead to poor results because the network doesn't have the expressive depth (in terms of channel count) required to accurately characterize input data. This is a problem analogous to not having enough features, except that it's more easily fixed; one can tune the depth of the network upward to improve the expressive depth of the convnet.

Equally, setting the depth parameter to too small a value can be redundant or harmful to performance, thereafter. If in doubt, consider testing the appropriate depth value during network configuration via hyperparameter optimization, the elbow method, or another technique.

Stride is a measure of spacing between neurons. A stride value of one will lead every element of the input (for an image, potentially every pixel) to be the center of a filter instance. This naturally leads to a high degree of overlap and very large outputs. Increasing the stride causes less of an overlap in the receptive fields and the output's size is reduced. While tuning the stride of a convnet is a question of weighing accuracy against output size, it can generally be a good idea to use smaller strides, which tend to work better. In addition, a stride value of one enables us to manage down-sampling and scale reduction at pooling layers (as we'll discuss later in the chapter).

The following diagram graphically displays both **Depth** and **Stride**:

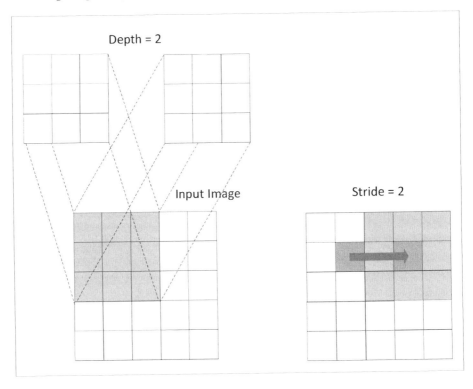

The final hyperparameter, zero-padding, offers an interesting convenience. Zero-padding is the process of setting the outer values (the border) of each receptive field to zero, which has the effect of reducing the output size for that layer. It's possible to set one, or multiple, pixels around the border of the field to zero, which reduces the output size accordingly. There are, of course, limits; obviously, it's not a good idea to set zero-padding and stride such that areas of the input are not touched by a filter! More generally, increasing the degree of zero-padding can cause a decrease in effectiveness, which is tied to the increased difficulty of learning features via coarse coding. (Refer to the *Understanding pooling layers* section in this chapter.)

However, zero-padding is very helpful because it enables us to adjust the input and output sizes to be the same. This is a very common practice; using zero-padding to ensure that the size of the input layer and output layer are equal, we are able to easily manage the stride and depth values. Without using zero-padding in this way, we would need to do a lot of work tracking input sizes and managing network parameters simply to make the network function correctly. In addition, zero-padding also improves performance as, without it, a convnet will tend to gradually degrade content at the edges of the filter.

In order to calibrate the number of nodes, appropriate stride, and padding for successive layers when we define our convnet, we need to know the size of the output from the preceding layer. We can calculate the spatial size of a layer's output (O) as a function of the input image size (W), filter size (F), stride (S), and the amount of zero-padding applied (P), as follows:

$$O = \frac{W - F + 2P}{S + 1}$$

If O is not an integer, the filters do not tile across the input neatly and instead extend over the edge of the input. This can cause some problematic issues when training (normally involving thrown exceptions)! By adjusting the stride value, one can find a whole-number solution for O and train effectively. It is normal for the stride to be constrained to what is possible given the other hyperparameter values and size of the input.

We've discussed the hyperparameters involved in correctly configuring the convolutional layer, but we haven't yet discussed the convolution process itself. Convolution is a mathematical operator, like addition or derivation, which is heavily used in signal processing applications and in many other contexts where its application helps simplify complex equations.

Loosely speaking, convolution is an operation over two functions, such as to produce a third function that is a modified version of one of the two original functions. In the case of convolution within a convnet, the first component is the network's input. In the case of convolution applied to images, convolution is applied in two dimensions (the width and height of the image). The input image is typically three matrices of pixels—one for each of the red, blue, and green color channels, with values ranging between *0* and *255* in each channel.

> At this point, it's worth introducing the concept of a **tensor**. Tensor is a term commonly used to refer to an n-dimensional array or matrix of input data, commonly applied in deep learning contexts. It's effectively analogous to a matrix or array. We'll be discussing tensors in more detail, both in this chapter and in *Chapter 9, Additional Python Machine Learning Tools* (where we review the **TensorFlow** library). It's worth noting that the term tensor is noticing a resurgence of use in the machine learning community, largely through the influence of Google machine intelligence research teams.

The second input to the convolution operation is the convolution kernel, a single matrix of floating point numbers that acts as a filter on the input matrices. The output of this convolution operation is the feature map. The convolution operation works by sliding the filter across the input, computing the dot product of the two arguments at each instance, which is written to the feature map. In cases where the stride of the convolutional layer is one, this operation will be performed across each pixel of the input image.

The main advantage of convolution is that it reduces the need for feature engineering. Creating and managing complex kernels and performing the highly specialized feature engineering processes needed is a demanding task, made more challenging by the fact that feature engineering processes that work well in one context can work poorly in most others. While we discuss feature engineering in detail in *Chapter 7, Feature Engineering Part II*, convolutional nets offer a powerful alternative.

CNN, however, incrementally improve their kernel's ability to filter a given input, thus automatically optimizing their kernel. This process is accelerated by learning multiple kernels in parallel at once. This is feature learning, which we've encountered in previous chapters. Feature learning can offer tremendous advantages in time and in increasing the accessibility of many problems. As with our earlier SDA and DBN implementations, we would look to pass our learned features to a much simpler, shallow neural network, which uses these features to classify the input image.

Understanding pooling layers

Stacking convolutional layers allows us to create a topology that effectively creates features as feature maps for complex, noisy input data. However, convolutional layers are not the only component of a deep network. It is common to weave convolutional layers in with pooling layers. Pooling is an operation over feature maps, where multiple feature values are aggregated into a single value—mostly using a max (**max-pooling**), mean (**mean-pooling**), or summation (**sum-pooling**) operation.

Pooling is a fairly natural approach that offers substantial advantages. If we do not aggregate feature maps, we tend to find ourselves with a huge amount of features. The **CIFAR-10** dataset that we'll be classifying later in this chapter contains 60,000 32 x 32 pixel images. If we hypothetically learned *200* features for each image—over 8 x 8 inputs—then at each convolution, we'd find ourselves with an output vector of size *(32 – 8+1) * (32 – 8+1) * 200*, or *125,000* features per image. Convolution produces a huge amount of features that tend to make computation very expensive and can also introduce significant overfitting problems.

The other major advantage provided by a pooling operation is that it provides a level of robustness against the many, small deviations and variances that occur in modeling noisy, high-dimensional data. Specifically, pooling prevents the network learning the position of features too specifically (overfitting), which is obviously a critical requirement in image processing and recognition settings. With pooling, the network no longer fixates on the precise location of features in the input and gains a greater ability to generalize. This is called **translation-invariance**.

Max-pooling is the most commonly applied pooling operation. This is because it focuses on the most responsive features in question that should, in theory, make it the best candidate for image recognition and classification purposes. By a similar logic, min-pooling tends to be applied in cases where it is necessary to take additional steps to prevent an overly sensitive classification or overfitting from occurring.

For obvious reasons, it's prudent to begin modeling using a quickly applied and straightforward pooling method such as max-pooling. However, when seeking additional gains in network performance during later iterations, it's important to look at whether your pooling operations can be improved on. There isn't any real restriction in terms of defining your own pooling operation. Indeed, finding a more effective subsampling method or alternative aggregation can substantially improve the performance of your model.

In terms of `theano` code, a max-pooling implementation is pretty straightforward and may look like this:

```
from theano.tensor.signal import downsample

input = T.dtensor4('input')
maxpool_shape = (2, 2)
pool_out = downsample.max_pool_2d(input, maxpool_shape, ignore_
border=True)
f = theano.function([input],pool_out)
```

The `max_pool_2d` function takes an n-dimensional `tensor` and downscaling factor, in this case, `input` and `maxpool_shape`, with the latter being a tuple of length 2, containing width and height downscaling factors for the input image. The `max_pool_2d` operation then performs max-pooling over the two trailing dimensions of the vector:

```
invals = numpy.random.RandomState(1).rand(3, 2, 5, 5)

pool_out = downsample.max_pool_2d(input, maxpool_shape, ignore_
border=False)
f = theano.function([input],pool_out)
```

The `ignore_border` determines whether the border values are considered or discarded. This max-pooling operation produces the following, given that `ignore_border = True`:

```
[[ 0.72032449   0.39676747]
 [ 0.6852195    0.87811744]]
```

As you can see, pooling is a straightforward operation that can provide dramatic results (in this case, the input was a 5 x 5 matrix, reduced to 2 x 2). However, pooling is not without critics. In particular, *Geoffrey Hinton* offered this pretty delightful soundbite:

> *"The pooling operation used in convolutional neural networks is a big mistake and the fact that it works so well is a disaster.*
>
> *If the pools do not overlap, pooling loses valuable information about where things are. We need this information to detect precise relationships between the parts of an object. Its true that if the pools overlap enough, the positions of features will be accurately preserved by "coarse coding" (see my paper on "distributed representations" in 1986 for an explanation of this effect). But I no longer believe that coarse coding is the best way to represent the poses of objects relative to the viewer (by pose I mean position, orientation, and scale)."*

This is a bold statement, but it makes sense. Hinton's telling us that the pooling operation, as an aggregation, does what any aggregation necessarily does — it reduces the data to a simpler and less informationally-rich format. This wouldn't be too damaging, except that Hinton goes further.

Even if we'd reduced the data down to single values for each pool, we could still hope that the fact that multiple pools overlap spatially would still present feature encodings. (This is the coarse coding referred to by Hinton.) This is also quite an intuitive concept. Imagine that you're listening in to a signal on a noisy radio frequency. Even if you only caught one word in three, it's probable that you'd be able to distinguish a distress signal from the shipping forecast!

However, Hinton follows up by observing that coarse coding is not as effective in learning pose (position, orientation, and scale). There are so many permutations in viewpoint relative to an object that it's unlikely two images would be alike and the sheer variety of possible poses becomes a challenge for a convolutional network using pooling. This suggests that an architecture that does not overcome this challenge may not be able to break past an upper limit for image classification.

However, the general consensus, at least for now, is that even after acknowledging all of this, it is still highly advantageous in terms of efficiency and translation-invariance to continue using pooling operations in convnets. Right now, the argument goes that it's the best we have!

Meanwhile, Hinton proposed an alternative to convnets in the form of the **transforming autoencoder**. The transforming autoencoder offers accuracy improvements on learning tasks that require a high level of precision (such as facial recognition), where pooling operations would cause a reduction in precision. The *Further reading* section of this chapter contains recommendations if you are interested in learning more about the transforming autoencoder.

So, we've spent quite a bit of time digging into the convolutional neural network — its components, how they work, and their hyperparameters. Before we move on to put the theory into action, it's worth discussing how all of these theoretical components fit together into a working architecture. To do this, let's discuss what training a convnet looks like.

Training a convnet

The means of training a convolutional network will be familiar to readers of the preceding chapters. The convolutional architecture itself is used to pretrain a simpler network structure (for example, an MLP). The backpropagation algorithm is the standard method to compute the gradient when pretraining. During this process, every layer undertakes three tasks:

- **Forward pass**: Each feature map is computed as a sum of all feature maps convolved with the corresponding weight kernel

- **Backward pass**: The gradients respective to inputs are calculated by convolving the transposed weight kernel with the gradients, with respect to the outputs

- The loss for each kernel is calculated, enabling the individual weight adjustment of every kernel as needed

Repetition of this process allows us to achieve increasing kernel performance until we reach a point of convergence. At this point, we will hope to have developed a set of features sufficient that the capping network is able to effectively classify over these features.

This process can execute slowly, even on a fairly advanced GPU. Some recent developments have helped accelerate the training process, including the use of the Fast **Fourier Transform** to accelerate the convolution process (for cases where the convolution kernel is of roughly equal size to the input image).

Putting it all together

So far, we've discussed some of the elements required to create a CNN. The next subject of discussion should be how we go about combining these components to create capable convolutional nets as well as which combinations of components can work well. We'll draw guidance from a number of forerunning convnet implementations as we build an understanding of what is commonly done as well as what is possible.

Probably the best-known convolutional network implementation is Yann LeCun's **LeNet**. LeNet has gone through several iterations since LeNet-1 in late 1980, but has been increasingly effective at performing tasks including handwritten digit and image classification. LeNet is structured using alternating convolution and pooling layers capped by an MLP, as follows:

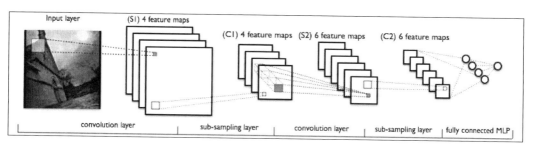

Each layer is partially-connected, as we discussed earlier, with the MLP being a fully connected layer. At each layer, multiple feature maps (channels) are employed; this gives us the advantage of being able to create more complex sets of filters. As we'll see, using multiple channels within a layer is a powerful technique employed in advanced use cases.

It's common to use max-pooling layers to reduce the dimensionality of the output to match the input as well as generally manage output volumes. How pooling is implemented, particularly in regard to the relative position of convolutional and pooling layers, is an element that tends to vary between implementations. It's generally common to develop a layer as a set of operations that feed into, and are fed into, a single **Fully Connected** layer, as shown in the following example:

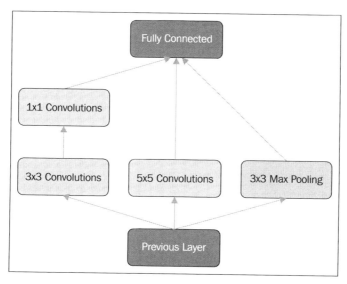

While this network structure wouldn't work in practice, it's a helpful illustration of the fact that a network can be constructed from the components you've learned about in a number of ways. How this network is structured and how complex it becomes should be motivated by the challenge the network is intended to solve. Different problems can call for very different solutions.

In the case of the LeNet implementation that we'll be working with later in this chapter, each layer contains multiple convolutional layers in parallel with a max-pooling layer following each. Diagrammatically, a LeNet layer looks like the following image:

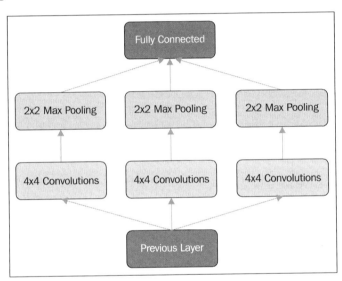

This architecture will enable us to start looking at some initial use cases quickly and easily, but in general won't perform well for some of the state-of-the-art applications we'll run into later in this book. Given this fact, there are some more extensive deep learning architectures designed to tackle the most challenging problems, whose topologies are worth discussing. One of the best-known convnet architectures is Google's **Inception** network, now more commonly known as GoogLeNet.

GoogLeNet was designed to tackle computer vision challenges involving Internet-quality image data, that is, images that have been captured in real contexts where the pose, lighting, occlusion, and clutter of images vary significantly. GoogLeNet was applied to the 2014 ImageNet challenge with noteworthy success, achieving only 6.7% error rate on the test dataset. ImageNet images are small, high-granularity images taken from many, varied classes. Multiple classes may appear very similar (such as varieties of tree) and the network architecture must be able to find increasingly challenging class distinctions to succeed. For a concrete example, consider the following ImageNet image:

Given the demands of this problem, the GoogLeNet architecture used to win ImageNet 14 departs from the LeNet model in several key ways. GoogLeNet's basic layer design is known as the Inception module and is made up of the following components:

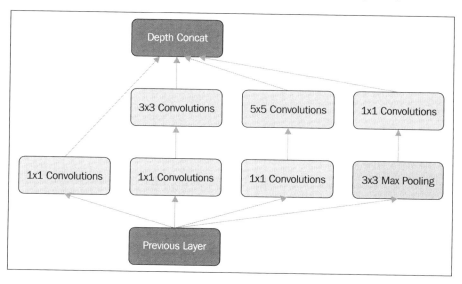

The 1 x 1 convolutional layers used here are followed by **Rectified Linear Units (ReLU)**. This approach is heavily used in speech and audio modeling contexts as ReLU can be used to effectively train deep models without pretraining and without facing some of the gradient vanishing problems that challenge other activation types. More information on ReLU is provided in the *Further reading* section of this chapter. The **DepthConcat** element provides a concatenation function, which consolidates the outputs of multiple units and substantially improves training time.

GoogLeNet chains layers of this type to create a full network. Indeed, the repetition of inception modules through GoogLeNet (nine times!) suggests that **Network In Network (NIN)** (deep architectures created from chained network modules) approaches are going to continue to be a serious contender in deep learning circles. The paper describing GoogLeNet and demonstrating how inception models were integrated into the network is provided in the Further reading section of this chapter.

Beyond the regularity of Inception module stacking, GoogLeNet has a few further surprises to throw at us. The first few layers are typically more straightforward with single-channel convolutional and max-pooling layers used at first. Additionally, at several points, GoogLeNet introduced a branch off the main structure using an average-pool layer, feeding into auxiliary softmax classifiers. The purpose of these classifiers was to improve the gradient signal that gets propagated back in lower layers of the network, enabling stronger performance at the early and middle network layers. Instead of one huge and potentially vague backpropagation process stemming from the final layer of the network, GoogLeNet instead has several intermediary update sources.

What's really important to take from this implementation is that GoogLeNet and other top convnet architectures are mainly successful because they are able to find effective configurations using the highly available components that we've discussed in this chapter. Now that we've had a chance to discuss the architecture and components of a convolutional net and the opportunity to discuss how these components are used to construct some highly advanced networks, it's time to apply the techniques to solve a problem of our own!

Applying a CNN

We'll be working with image data to try out our convnet. The image data that we worked with in earlier chapters, including the MNIST digit dataset, was a useful training dataset (with many valuable real-world applications such as automated check reading!). However, it differs from almost all photographic or video data in an important way; most visual data is highly noisy.

Problem variables can include pose, lighting, occlusion, and clutter, which may be expressed independently or in conjunction in huge variety. This means that the task of creating a function that is invariant to all properties of noise in the dataset is challenging; the function is typically very complex and nonlinear. In *Chapter 7, Feature Engineering Part II*, we'll discuss how techniques such as whitening can help mitigate some of these challenges, but as we'll see, even such techniques by themselves are insufficient to yield good classification (at least, without a very large investment of time!). By far, the most efficient solution to the problem of noise in image data, as we've already seen in multiple contexts, is to use a deep architecture rather than a broad one (that is, a neural network with few, high-dimensional layers, which is vulnerable to problematic overfitting and generalizability problems).

From discussions in previous chapters, the reasons for a deep architecture may already be clear; successive layers of a deep architecture reuse the reasoning and computation performed in preceding layers. Deep architectures can thus build a representation that is sequentially improved by successive layers of the network without performing extensive recalculation on any individual layer. This makes the challenging task of classifying large datasets of noisy photograph data achievable to a high level of accuracy in a relatively short time, without extensive feature engineering.

Now that we've discussed the challenges of modeling image data and advantages of a deep architecture in such contexts, let's apply a convnet to a real-world classification problem.

As in preceding chapters, we're going to start out with a toy example, which we'll use to familiarize ourselves with the architecture of our deep network. This time, we're going to take on a classic image processing challenge, CIFAR-10. CIFAR-10 is a dataset of 60,000 32 x 32 color images in 10 classes, with each class containing 6,000 images. The data is already split into five training batches, with one test batch. The classes and some images from each dataset are as follows:

While the industry has — to an extent — moved on to tackle other datasets such as ImageNet, CIFAR-10 was long regarded as the bar to reach in terms of image classification, with a great many data scientists attempting to create architectures that classify the dataset to human levels of accuracy, where human error rate is estimated at around 6%.

In November 2014, Kaggle ran a contest whose objective was to classify CIFAR-10 as accurately as possible. This contest's highest-scoring entry produced 95.55% classification accuracy, with the result using convolutional networks and a Network-in-Network approach. We'll discuss the challenge of classifying this dataset, as well as some of the more advanced techniques we can bring to bear, in *Chapter 8, Ensemble Methods*; for now, let's begin by having a go at classification with a convolutional network.

For our first attempt, we'll apply a fairly simple convolutional network with the following objectives:

- Applying a filter to the image and view the output
- Seeing the weights that our convnet created
- Understanding the difference between the outputs of effective and ineffective networks

In this chapter, we're going to take an approach that we haven't taken before, which will be of huge importance to you when you come to use these techniques in the wild. We saw earlier in this chapter how the deep architectures developed to solve different problems may differ structurally in many ways.

It's important to be able to create problem-specific network architectures so that we can adapt our implementation to fit a range of real-world problems. To do this, we'll be constructing our network using components that are modular and can be recombined in almost any way necessary, without too much additional effort. We saw the impact of modularity earlier in this chapter, and it's worth exploring how to apply this effect to our own networks.

As we discussed earlier in the chapter, convnets become particularly powerful when tasked to classify very large and varied datasets of up to tens or hundreds of thousands of images. As such, let's be a little ambitious and see whether we can apply a convnet to classify CIFAR-10.

In setting up our convolutional network, we'll begin by defining a useable class and initializing the relevant network parameters, particularly weights and biases. This approach will be familiar to readers of the preceding chapters.

```
class LeNetConvPoolLayer(object):

    def __init__(self, rng, input, filter_shape, image_shape,
    poolsize=(2, 2)):

        assert image_shape[1] == filter_shape[1]
        self.input = input

        fan_in = numpy.prod(filter_shape[1:])
        fan_out = (filter_shape[0] * numpy.prod(filter_shape[2:])
                numpy.prod(poolsize))

        W_bound = numpy.sqrt(6. / (fan_in + fan_out))
        self.W = theano.shared(
            numpy.asarray(
                rng.uniform(low=-W_bound, high=W_bound,
                size=filter_shape),
                dtype=theano.config.floatX
            ),
            borrow=True
        )
```

Before moving on to create the biases, it's worth reviewing what we have thus far. The LeNetConvPoolLayer class is intended to implement one full convolutional and pooling layer as per the LeNet layer structure. This class contains several useful initial parameters.

From previous chapters, we're familiar with the rng parameter used to initialize weights to random values. We can also recognize the input parameter. As in most cases, image input tends to take the form of a symbolic image tensor. This image input is shaped by the image_shape parameter; this is a tuple or list of length 4 describing the dimensions of the input. As we move through successive layers, image_shape will reduce increasingly. As a tuple, the dimensions of image_shape simply specify the height and width of the input. As a list of length 4, the parameters, in order, are as follows:

* The batch size
* The number of input feature maps
* The height of the input image
* The width of the input image

While `image_shape` specifies the size of the input, `filter_shape` specifies the dimensions of the filter. As a list of length 4, the parameters, in order, are as follows:

- The number of filters (channels) to be applied
- The number of input feature maps
- The height of the filter
- The width of the filter

However, the height and width may be entered without any additional parameters. The final parameter here, `poolsize`, describes the downsizing factor. This is expressed as a list of length 2, the first element being the number of rows and the second—the number of columns.

Having defined these values, we immediately apply them to define the `LeNetConvPoolLayer` class better. In defining `fan_in`, we set the inputs to each hidden unit to be a multiple of the number of input feature maps—the filter height and width. Simply enough, we also define `fan_out`, a gradient that's calculated as a multiple of the number of output feature maps—the feature height and width—divided by the pooling size.

Next, we move on to defining the bias as a set of one-dimensional tensors, one for each output feature map:

```
b_values = numpy.zeros((filter_shape[0],),
dtype=theano.config.floatX)
self.b = theano.shared(value=b_values, borrow=True)

conv_out = conv.conv2d(
    input=input,
    filters=self.W,
    filter_shape=filter_shape,
    image_shape=image_shape
)
```

With this single function call, we've defined a convolution operation that uses the filters we previously defined. At times, it can be a little staggering to see how much theory needs to be known to effectively apply a single function! The next step is to create a similar pooling operation using `max_pool_2d`:

```
pooled_out = downsample.max_pool_2d(
    input=conv_out,
    ds=poolsize,
```

```
            ignore_border=True
    )


    self.output = T.tanh(pooled_out + self.b.dimshuffle('x',
                 0, 'x', 'x'))

    self.params = [self.W, self.b]

    self.input = input
```

Finally, we add the bias term, first reshaping it to be a tensor of shape (1, n_filters, 1, 1). This has the simple effect of causing the bias to affect every feature map and minibatch. At this point, we have all of the components we need to build a basic convnet. Let's move on to create our own network:

```
    x = T.matrix('x')
    y = T.ivector('y')
```

This process is fairly simple. We build the layers in order, passing parameters to the class that we previously specified. Let's start by building our first layer:

```
    layer0_input = x.reshape((batch_size, 1, 32, 32))

    layer0 = LeNetConvPoolLayer(
        rng,
        input=layer0_input,
        image_shape=(batch_size, 1, 32, 32),
        filter_shape=(nkerns[0], 1, 5, 5),
        poolsize=(2, 2)
    )
```

We begin by reshaping the input to spread it across all of the intended minibatches. As the CIFAR-10 images are of a 32 x 32 dimension, we've used this input size for the height and width dimensions. The filtering process reduces the size of this input to 32- 5+1 in each dimension, or 28. Pooling reduces this by half in each dimension to create an output layer of shape (batch_size, nkerns[0], 14, 14).

This is a completed first layer. Next, we can attach a second layer to this using the same code:

```
layer1 = LeNetConvPoolLayer(
    rng,
    input=layer0.output,
    image_shape=(batch_size, nkerns[0], 14, 14),
    filter_shape=(nkerns[1], nkerns[0], 5, 5),
    poolsize=(2, 2)
)
```

As per the previous layer, the output shape for this layer is (batch_size, nkerns[1], 5, 5). So far, so good! Let's feed this output to the next, fully-connected sigmoid layer. To begin with, we need to flatten the input shape to two dimensions. With the values that we've fed to the network so far, the input will be a matrix of shape *(500, 1250)*. As such, we'll set up an appropriate layer2:

```
layer2_input = layer1.output.flatten(2)

layer2 = HiddenLayer(
    rng,
    input=layer2_input,
    n_in=nkerns[1] * 5 * 5
    n_out=500,
    activation=T.tanh
)
```

This leaves us in a good place to finish this network's architecture, by adding a final, logistic regression layer that calculates the values of the fully-connected sigmoid layer.

Let's try out this code:

```
x = T.matrix(CIFAR-10_train)
y = T.ivector(CIFAR-10_test)
```

```
Chapter_4/convolutional_mlp.py
```

The results that we obtained were as follows:

```
Optimization complete.
Best validation score of 0.885725 % obtained at iteration 17400, with
test performance 0.902508 %
The code for file convolutional_mlp.py ran for 26.50m
```

This accuracy score, at validation, is reasonably good. It's not at a human level of accuracy, which, as we established, is roughly 94%. Equally, it is not the best score that we could achieve with a convnet.

For instance, the Further Reading section of this chapter refers to a convnet implemented in Torch using a combination of dropout (which we studied in *Chapter 3, Stacked Denoising Autoencoders*) and **Batch Normalization** (a normalization technique intended to reduce covariate drift during the training process; refer to the Further Reading section for further technical notes and papers on this technique), which scored 92.45% validation accuracy.

A score of 88.57% is, however, in the same ballpark and can give us confidence that we're within striking distance of an effective network architecture for the CIFAR-10 problem. More importantly, you've learned a lot about how to configure and train a convolutional neural network effectively.

Further Reading

The glut of recent interest in Convolutional Networks means that we're spoiled for choice for further reading. One good option for an unfamiliar reader is the course notes from Andrej Karpathy's course: `http://cs231n.github.io/convolutional-networks/`.

For readers with an interest in the deeper details of specific best-in-class implementations, some of the networks referenced in this chapter were the following:

Google's GoogLeNet (`http://www.cs.unc.edu/~wliu/papers/GoogLeNet.pdf`)

Google Deepmind's Go-playing program AlphaGo (`https://gogameguru.com/i/2016/03/deepmind-mastering-go.pdf`)

Facebook's DeepFace architecture for facial recognition (`https://www.cs.toronto.edu/~ranzato/publications/taigman_cvpr14.pdf`)

The ImageNet LSVRC-2010 contest winning network, described here by Krizhevsky, Sutskever and Hinton (`http://www.cs.toronto.edu/~fritz/absps/imagenet.pdf`)

Finally, Sergey Zagoruyko's Torch implementation of a ConvNet with Batch normalization is available here: `http://torch.ch/blog/2015/07/30/cifar.html`.

Summary

In this chapter, we covered a lot of ground. We began by introducing a new kind of neural network, the convnet. We explored the theory and architecture of a convnet in the most ubiquitous form and also by discussing some state-of the-art network design principles that have been developing as recently as mid-2015 in organizations such as Google and Baidu. We built an understanding of the topology and also of how the network operates.

Following this, we began to work with the convnet itself, applying it to the CIFAR-10 dataset. We used modular convnet code to create a functional architecture that reached a reasonable level of accuracy in classifying 10-class image data. While we're definitely still at some distance from human levels of accuracy, we're gradually closing the gap! *Chapter 8, Ensemble Methods* will pick up from what you learned here, taking these techniques and their application to the next level.

5
Semi-Supervised Learning

Introduction

In previous chapters, we've tackled a range of data challenges using advanced techniques. In each case, we've applied our techniques to datasets with reasonable success.

In many regards, though, we've had it pretty easy. Our data has been largely derived from canonical and well-prepared sources so we haven't had to do a great deal of preparation. In the real world, though, there are few datasets like this (except, perhaps, the ones that we're able to specify ourselves!). In particular, it is rare and improbable to come across a dataset in the wild, which has class labels available. Without labels on a sufficient portion of the dataset, we find ourselves unable to build a classifier that can accurately predict labels on validation or test data. So, what do we do?

The common solution is attempt to tag our data manually; not only is this time-consuming, but it also suffers from certain types of human error (which are especially common with high-dimensional datasets, where a human observer is unable to identify class boundaries as well as a computational approach might).

A fairly new and quite exciting alternative approach is to use **semi-supervised learning** to apply labels to unlabeled data via capturing the shape of underlying distributions. Semi-supervised learning has been growing in popularity over the last decade for its ability to save large amounts of annotation time, where annotation, if possible, may potentially require human expertise or specialist equipment. Contexts where this has proven to be particularly valuable have been natural language parsing and speech signal analysis; in both areas, manual annotation has proven to be complex and time-consuming.

In this chapter, you're going to learn how to apply several semi-supervised learning techniques, including, **Contrastive Pessimistic Likelihood Estimation (CPLE)**, self learning, and S3VM. These techniques will enable us to label training data in a range of otherwise problematic contexts. You'll learn to identify the capabilities and limitations of semi-supervised techniques. We'll use a number of recent Python libraries developed on top of scikit-learn to apply semi-supervised techniques to several use cases, including audio signal data.

Let's get started!

Understanding semi-supervised learning

The most persistent cost in performing machine learning is the creation of tagged data for training purposes. Datasets tend not to come with class labels provided due to the circularity of the situation; one needs a trained classification technique to generate class labels, but cannot train the technique without labeled training and test data. As mentioned, tagging data manually or via test processes is one option, but this can be prohibitively time-consuming, costly (particularly for medical tests), challenging to organize, and prone to error (with large or complex datasets). Semi-supervised techniques suggest a better way to break this deadlock.

Semi-supervised learning techniques use both unlabeled and labeled data to create better learning techniques than can be created with either unlabeled or labeled data individually. There is a family of techniques that exists in a space between supervised (with labeled data) and unsupervised (with unlabeled data) learning.

The main types of technique that exist in this group are semi-supervised techniques, transductive techniques, and active learning techniques, as well as a broad set of other methods.

Semi-supervised techniques leave a set of test data out of the training process so as to perform testing at a later stage. Transductive techniques, meanwhile, are purely intended to develop labels for unlabeled data. There may not be a test process embedded in a transductive technique and there may not be labeled data available for use.

In this chapter, we'll focus on a set of semi-supervised techniques that deliver powerful dataset labeling capability in very familiar formats. A lot of the techniques that we'll be discussing are useable as wrappers around familiar, pre-existing classifiers, from linear regression classifiers to SVMs. As such, many of them can be run using estimators from Scikit-learn. We'll begin by applying a linear regression classifier to test cases before moving on to apply an SVM with semi-supervised extensions.

Semi-supervised algorithms in action

We've discussed what semi-supervised learning is, why we want to engage in it, and what some of the general realities of employing semi-supervised algorithms are. We've gone about as far as we can with general descriptions. Over the next few pages, we'll move from this general understanding to develop an ability to use a semi-supervised application effectively.

Self-training

Self-training is the simplest semi-supervised learning method and can also be the fastest. Self-training algorithms see an application in multiple contexts, including NLP and computer vision; as we'll see, they can present both substantial value and significant risks.

The objective of self-training is to combine information from unlabeled cases with that of labeled cases to iteratively identify labels for the dataset's unlabeled examples. On each iteration, the labeled training set is enlarged until the entire dataset is labeled.

The self-training algorithm is typically applied as a wrapper to a base model. In this chapter, we'll be using an SVM as the base for our self-training model. The self-training algorithm is quite simple and contains very few steps, as follows:

1. A set of labeled data is used to predict labels for a set of unlabeled data. (This may be all unlabeled data or part of it.)
2. Confidence is calculated for all newly labeled cases.
3. Cases are selected from the newly labeled data to be kept for the next iteration.

4. The model trains on all labeled cases, including cases selected in previous iterations.

5. The model iterates through steps 1 to 4 until it successfully converges.

Presented graphically, this process looks as follows:

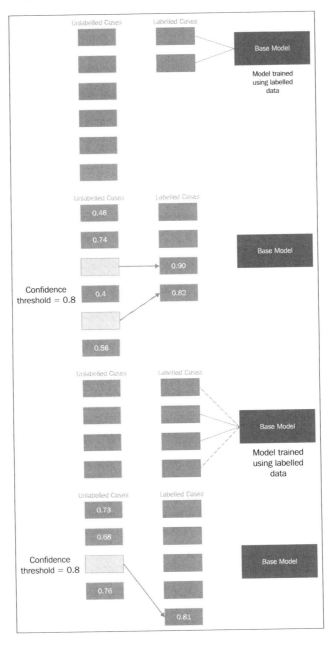

Upon completing training, the self-trained model would be tested and validated. This may be done via cross-validation or even using held-out, labeled data, should this exist.

Self-training provides real power and time saving, but is also a risky process. In order to understand what to look out for and how to apply self-training to your own classification algorithms, let's look in more detail at how the algorithm works.

To support this discussion, we're going to work with code from the semisup-learn GitHub repository. In order to use this code, we'll need to clone the relevant GitHub repository. Instructions for this are located in *Appendix A*.

Implementing self-training

The first step in each iteration of self-training is one in which class labels are generated for unlabeled cases. This is achieved by first creating a SelfLearningModel class, which takes a base supervised model (basemodel) and an iteration limit as arguments. As we'll see later in this chapter, an iteration limit can be explicitly specified or provided as a function of classification accuracy (that is, convergence). The prob_threshold parameter provides a minimum quality bar for label acceptance; any projected label that scores at less than this level will be rejected. Again, we'll see in later examples that there are alternatives to providing a hardcoded threshold value.

```
class SelfLearningModel(BaseEstimator):


    def __init__(self, basemodel, max_iter = 200, prob_threshold = 0.8):
        self.model = basemodel
        self.max_iter = max_iter
        self.prob_threshold = prob_threshold
```

Having defined the shell of the SelfLearningModel class, the next step is to define functions for the process of semi-supervised model fitting:

```
def fit(self, X, y):
    unlabeledX = X[y==-1, :]
    labeledX = X[y!=-1, :]
    labeledy = y[y!=-1]

    self.model.fit(labeledX, labeledy)
    unlabeledy = self.predict(unlabeledX)
    unlabeledprob = self.predict_proba(unlabeledX)
    unlabeledy_old = []

    i = 0
```

The x parameter is a matrix of input data, whose shape is equivalent to [n_samples, n_features]. X is used to create a matrix of [n_samples, n_samples] size. The y parameter, meanwhile, is an array of labels. Unlabeled points are marked as -1 in y. From X, the unlabeledX and labeledX parameters are created quite simply by operations over X that select elements in X whose position corresponds to a -1 label in y. The labeledy parameter performs a similar selection over y. (Naturally, we're not that interested in the unlabeled samples of y as a variable, but we need the labels that do exist for classification attempts!)

The actual process of label prediction is achieved, first, using sklearn's predict operation. The unlabeledy parameter is generated using sklearn's predict method, while the predict_proba method is used to calculate probabilities for each projected label. These probabilities are stored in unlabeledprob.

Scikit-learn's predict and predict_proba methods work to predict class labels and the probability of class labeling being correct, respectively. As we'll be applying both of these methods within several of our semi-supervised algorithms, it's informative to understand how they actually work.

The predict method produces class predictions for input data. It does so via a set of binary classifiers (that is, classifiers that attempt to differentiate only two classes). A full model with n-many classes contains a set of binary classifiers as follows:

$$\frac{n*(n-1)}{2}$$

In order to make a prediction for a given case, all classifiers whose scores exceed zero, vote for a class label to apply to that case. The class with the most votes (and not, say, the highest sum classifier score) is identified. This is referred to as a one-versus-one prediction method and is a fairly common approach.

Meanwhile, `predict_proba` works by invoking **Platt calibration**, a technique that allows the outputs of a classification model to be transformed into a probability distribution over the classes. This involves first training the base model in question, fitting a regression model to the classifier's scores:

$$P(y \mid X) = \frac{1}{\left(1 + \exp\left(A * f(X) + B\right)\right)}$$

This model can then be optimized (through scalar parameters A and B) using a maximum likelihood method. In the case of our self-training model, `predict_proba` allows us to fit a regression model to the classifier's scores and thus calculate probabilities for each class label. This is extremely helpful!

Next, we need a loop for iteration. The following code describes a `while` loop that executes until there are no cases left in `unlabeledy_old` (a copy of `unlabeledy`) or until the max iteration count is reached. On each iteration, a labeling attempt is made for each case that does not have a label whose probability exceeds the probability threshold (`prob_threshold`):

```
while (len(unlabeledy_old) == 0 or
    numpy.any(unlabeledy!=unlabeledy_old)) and i < self.max_iter:
    unlabeledy_old = numpy.copy(unlabeledy)
    uidx = numpy.where((unlabeledprob[:, 0] > self.prob_threshold)
    | (unlabeledprob[:, 1] > self.prob_threshold))[0]
```

The `self.model.fit` method then attempts to fit a model to the unlabeled data. This unlabeled data is presented in a matrix of size `[n_samples, n_samples]` (as referred to earlier in this chapter). This matrix is created by appending (with `vstack` and `hstack`) the unlabeled cases:

```
self.model.fit(numpy.vstack((labeledX, unlabeledX[uidx, :])),
    numpy.hstack((labeledy, unlabeledy_old[uidx])))
```

Finally, the iteration performs label predictions, followed by probability predictions for those labels.

```
unlabeledy = self.predict(unlabeledX)
unlabeledprob = self.predict_proba(unlabeledX)
i += 1
```

On the next iteration, the model will perform the same process, this time taking the newly labeled data whose probability predictions exceeded the threshold as part of the dataset used in the `model.fit` step.

If one's model does not already include a classification method that can generate label predictions (like the `predict_proba` method available in sklearn's SVM implementation), it is possible to introduce one. The following code checks for the `predict_proba` method and introduces `Platt scaling` of generated labels if this method is not found:

```
if not getattr(self.model, "predict_proba", None):
    self.plattlr = LR()
    preds = self.model.predict(labeledX)
    self.plattlr.fit( preds.reshape( -1, 1 ), labeledy )


return self



def predict_proba(self, X):
        if getattr(self.model, "predict_proba", None):
        return self.model.predict_proba(X)
        else:
            preds = self.model.predict(X)
            return self.plattlr.predict_proba(preds.reshape( -1, 1 ))
```

Once we have this much in place, we can begin applying our self-training architecture. To do so, let's grab a dataset and start working!

For this example, we'll use a simple linear regression classifier, with **Stochastic Gradient Descent (SGD)** as our learning component as our base model (`basemodel`). The input dataset will be the statlog `heart` dataset, obtained from `www.mldata.org`. This dataset is provided in the GitHub repository accompanying this chapter.

The `heart` dataset is a two-class dataset, where the classes are the absence or presence of a heart disease. There are no missing values across the 270 cases for any of its 13 features. This data is unlabeled and many of the variables needed are usually captured via expensive and sometimes inconvenient tests. The variables are as follows:

- age
- sex
- chest pain type (4 values)
- resting blood pressure
- serum cholestoral in mg/dl
- fasting blood sugar > 120 mg/dl
- resting electrocardiographic results (values 0,1,2)
- maximum heart rate achieved
- exercise induced angina
- 10. oldpeak = ST depression induced by exercise relative to rest
- the slope of the peak exercise ST segment
- number of major vessels (0-3) colored by flourosopy
- thal: 3 = normal; 6 = fixed defect; 7 = reversable defect

Lets get started with the `Heart` dataset by loading in the data, then fitting a model to it:

```
heart = fetch_mldata("heart")
X = heart.data
ytrue = np.copy(heart.target)
ytrue[ytrue==-1]=0

labeled_N = 2
ys = np.array([-1]*len(ytrue)) # -1 denotes unlabeled point
random_labeled_points = random.sample(np.where(ytrue == 0)[0],
labeled_N/2)+\random.sample(np.where(ytrue == 1)[0], labeled_N/2)
ys[random_labeled_points] = ytrue[random_labeled_points]

basemodel = SGDClassifier(loss='log', penalty='l1')

basemodel.fit(X[random_labeled_points, :], ys[random_labeled_points])
print "supervised log.reg. score", basemodel.score(X, ytrue)

ssmodel = SelfLearningModel(basemodel)
ssmodel.fit(X, ys)
print "self-learning log.reg. score", ssmodel.score(X, ytrue)
```

Attempting this yields moderate, but not excellent, results:

```
self-learning log.reg. score 0.470347
```

However, over 1,000 trials, we find that the quality of our outputs is quite variant:

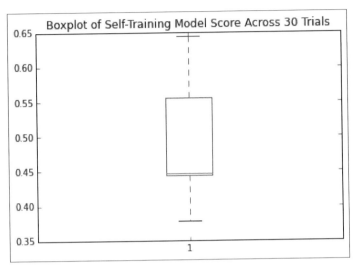

Given that we're looking at classification accuracy scores for sets of real-world and unlabeled data, this isn't a terrible result, but I don't think we should be satisfied with it. We're still labeling more than half of our cases incorrectly!

We need to understand the problem a little better; right now, it isn't clear what's going wrong or how we can improve on our results. Let's figure this out by returning to the theory around self-training to understand how we can diagnose and improve our implementation.

Finessing your self-training implementation

In the previous section, we discussed the creation of self-training algorithms and tried out an implementation. However, what we saw during our first trial was that our results, while demonstrating the potential of self-training, left room for growth. Both the accuracy and variance of our results were questionable.

Self-training can be a fragile process. If an element of the algorithm is ill-configured or the input data contains peculiarities, it is very likely that the iterative process will fail once and continue to compound that error by reintroducing incorrectly labeled data to future labeling steps. As the self-training algorithm iteratively feeds itself, garbage in, garbage out is a very real concern.

There are several quite common flavors of risk that should be called out. In some cases, labeled data may not add more useful information. This is particularly common in the first few iterations, and understandably so! In general, unlabeled cases that are most easily labeled are the ones that are most similar to existing labeled cases. However, while it's easy to generate high-probability labels for these cases, there's no guarantee that their addition to the labeled set will make it easier to label during subsequent iterations.

Unfortunately, this can sometimes lead to a situation in which cases are being added that have no real effect on classification while classification accuracy in general deteriorates. Even worse, adding cases that are similar to pre-existing cases in enough respects to make them easy to label, but that actually misguide the classifier's decision boundary, can introduce misclassification increases.

Diagnosing what went wrong with a self-training model can sometimes be difficult, but as always, a few well-chosen plots add a lot of clarity to the situation. As this type of error occurs particularly often within the first few iterations, simply adding an element to the label prediction loop that writes the current classification accuracy allows us to understand how accuracy trended during early iterations.

Once the issue has been identified, there are a few possible solutions. If enough labeled data exists, a simple solution is to attempt to use a more diverse set of labeled data to kick-start the process.

While the impulse might be to use all of the labeled data, we'll see later in this chapter that self-training models are vulnerable to overfitting—a risk that forces us to hold on to some data for validation purposes. A promising option is to use multiple subsets of our dataset to train multiple self-training model instances. Doing so, particularly over several trials, can help us understand the impact of our input data on our self-training models performance.

In *Chapter 8, Ensemble Methods*, we'll explore some options around ensembles that will enable us to use multiple self-training models together to yield predictions. When ensembling is accessible to us, we can even consider applying multiple sampling techniques in parallel.

If we don't want to solve this problem with quantity, though, perhaps we can solve it by improving quality. One solution is to create an appropriately diverse subset of the labeled data through selection. There isn't a hard limit on the number of labeled cases that works well as a minimum amount to start up a self-training implementation. While you could hypothetically start working with even one labeled case per class (as we did in our preceding training example), it'll quickly become obvious that training against a more diverse and overlapping set of classes benefits from more labeled data.

Another class of error that a self-training model is particularly vulnerable to is biased selection. Our naïve assumption is that the selection of data during each iteration is, at worst, only slightly biased (favoring one class only slightly more than others). The reality is that this is not a safe assumption. There are several factors that can influence the likelihood of biased selection, with the most likely culprit being disproportionate sampling from one class.

If the dataset as a whole, or the labeled subsets used, are biased toward one class, then the risk increases that your self-training classifier will overfit. This only compounds the problem as the cases provided for the next iteration are liable to be insufficiently diverse to solve the problem; whatever incorrect decision boundary was set up by the self-training algorithm will be set where it is—overfit to a subset of the data. Numerical disparity between each class' count of cases is the main symptom here, but the more usual methods to spot overfitting can also be helpful in diagnosing problems around selection bias.

This reference to the usual methods of spotting overfitting is worth expanding on because techniques to identify overfitting are highly valuable! These techniques are typically referred to as validation techniques. The fundamental concept underpinning validation techniques is that one has two sets of data—one that is used to build a model, and the other is used to test it.

The most effective validation technique is independent validation, the simplest form of which involves waiting to determine whether predictions are accurate. This obviously isn't always (or even, often) possible!

Given that it may not be possible to perform independent validation, the best bet is to hold out a subset of your sample. This is referred to as sample splitting and is the foundation of modern validation techniques. Most machine learning implementations refer to training, test, and validation datasets; this is a case of multilayered validation in action.

A third and critical validation tool is resampling, where subsets of the data are iteratively used to repeatedly validate the dataset. In *Chapter 1, Unsupervised Machine Learning*, we saw the use of v-fold cross-validation; cross-validation techniques are perhaps the best examples of resampling in action.

Beyond applicable techniques, it's a good idea to be mindful of the needed sample size required for the effective modeling of your data. There are no universal principles here, but I always rather liked the following rule of thumb:

If m points are required to determine a univariate regression line with sufficient precision, then it will take at least mn observations and perhaps $n!mn$ observations to appropriately characterize and evaluate a regression model with n variables.

Note that there is some tension between the suggested solutions to this problem (resampling, sample splitting, and validation techniques including cross-validation) and the preceding one. Namely, overfitting requires a more restrained use of subsets of the labeled training data, while bad starts are less likely to occur using more training data. For each specific problem, depending on the complexity of the data under analysis, there will be an appropriate balance to strike. By monitoring for signs of either type of problem, the appropriate action (whether that is an increase or decrease in the amount of labeled data used simultaneously in an iteration) can be taken at the right time.

A further class of risk introduced by self-training is that the introduction of unlabeled data almost always introduces noise. If dealing with datasets where part or all of the unlabeled cases are highly noisy, the amount of noise introduced may be sufficient to degrade classification accuracy.

The idea of using data complexity and noise measures to understand the degree of noise in one's dataset is not new. Fortunately for us, quite a lot of good estimators already exist that we can take advantage of.

There are two main groups of relative complexity measures. Some attempt to measure the overlap of values of different classes, or separability; measures in this group attempt to describe the degree of ambiguity of each class relative to the other classes. One good measure for such cases is the maximum **Fisher's discriminant ratio**, though maximum individual feature efficiency is also effective.

Alternatively (and sometimes more simply), one can use the error function of a linear classifier to understand how separable the dataset's classes are from one another. By attempting to train a simple linear classifier on your dataset and observing the training error, one can immediately get a good understanding as to how linearly separable the classes are. Furthermore, measures related to this classifier (such as the fraction of points in the class boundary or the ratio of average intra/inter class nearest neighbor distance) can also be extremely helpful.

There are other data complexity measures that specifically measure the density or geometry of the dataset. One good example is the fraction of maximum covering spheres. Again, helpful measures can be accessed by applying a linear classifier and including the nonlinearity of that classifier.

Improving the selection process

The key to the self-training algorithm working correctly is the accurate calculation of confidence for each label projection. Confidence calculation is the key to successful self-training.

During our first explanation of self-training, we used some simplistic values for certain parameters, including a parameter closely tied to confidence calculation. In selecting our labeled cases, we used a fixed confidence level for comparison against predicted probabilities, where we could've adopted any one of several different strategies:

- Adding all of the projected labels to the set of labeled data
- Using a confidence threshold to select only the few most confident labels to the set
- Adding all the projected labels to the labeled dataset and weighing each label by confidence

All in all, we've seen that self-training implementations present quite a lot of risk. They're prone to a number of training failures and are also subject to overfitting. To make matters worse, as the amount of unlabeled data increases, the accuracy of a self-training classifier becomes increasingly at risk.

Our next step will be to look at a very different self-training implementation. While conceptually similar to the algorithm that we worked with earlier in this chapter, the next technique we'll be looking at operates under different assumptions to yield very different results.

Contrastive Pessimistic Likelihood Estimation

In our preceding discovery and application of self-training techniques, we found self-training to be a powerful technique with significant risks. Particularly, we found a need for multiple diagnostic tools and some quite restrictive dataset conditions. While we can work around these problems by subsetting, identifying optimal labeled data, and attentively tracking performance for some datasets, some of these actions continue to be impossible for the very data that self-training would bring the most benefit to—data where labeling requires expensive tests, be those medical or scientific, with specialist knowledge and equipment.

In some cases, we end up with some self-training classifiers that are outperformed by their supervised counterparts, which is a pretty terrible state of affairs. Even worse, while a supervised classifier with labeled data will tend to improve in accuracy with additional cases, semi-supervised classifier performance can degrade as the dataset size increases. What we need, then, is a less naïve approach to semi-supervised learning. Our goal should be to find an approach that harnesses the benefits of semi-supervised learning while maintaining performance at least comparable with that of the same classifier under a supervised approach.

A very recent (May 2015) approach to self-supervised learning, CPLE, provides a more general way to perform semi-supervised parameter estimation. CPLE provides a rather remarkable advantage: it produces label predictions that have been demonstrated to consistently outperform those created by equivalent semi-supervised classifiers or by supervised classifiers working from the labeled data! In other words, when performing a linear discriminant analysis, for instance, it is advised that you perform a CPLE-based, semi-supervised analysis instead of a supervised one, as you will always obtain at least equivalent performance.

This is a pretty big claim and it needs substantiating. Let's start by building an understanding of how CPLE works before moving on to demonstrate its superior performance in real cases.

CPLE uses the familiar measure of maximized log-likelihood for parameter optimization. This can be thought of as the success condition; the model we'll develop is intended to optimize the maximized log-likelihood of our model's parameters. It is the specific guarantees and assumptions that CPLE incorporates that make the technique effective.

In order to create a better semi-supervised learner—one that improves on it's supervised alternative—CPLE takes the supervised estimates into account explicitly, using the loss incurred between the semi-supervised and supervised models as a training performance measure:

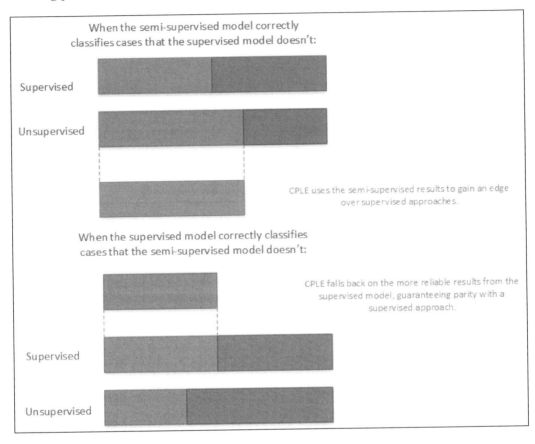

CPLE calculates the relative improvement of any semi-supervised estimate over the supervised solution. Where the supervised solution outperforms the semi-supervised estimate, the loss function shows this and the model can train to adjust the semi-supervised model to reduce this loss. Where the semi-supervised solution outperforms the supervised solution, the model can learn from the semi-supervised model by adjusting model parameters.

However, while this sounds excellent so far, there is a flaw in the theory that has to be addressed. The fact that data labels don't exist for a semi-supervised solution means that the posterior distribution (that CPLE would use to calculate loss) is inaccessible. CPLE's solution to this is to be pessimistic. The CPLE algorithm takes the **Cartesian product** of all label/prediction combinations and then selects the posterior distribution that minimizes the gain in likelihood.

In real-world machine learning contexts, this is a very safe approach. It delivers the classification accuracy of a supervised approach with semi-supervised performance improvement derived via conservative assumptions. In real applications, these conservative assumptions enable high performance under testing. Even better, CPLE can deliver particular performance improvements on some of the most challenging unsupervised learning cases, where the labeled data is a poor representation of the unlabeled data (by virtue of poor sampling from one or more classes or just because of a shortage of unlabeled cases).

In order to understand how much more effective CPLE can be than semi-supervised or supervised approaches, let's apply the technique to a practical problem. We'll once again work with the semisup-learn library, a specialist Python library, focused on semi-supervised learning, which extends scikit-learn to provide CPLE across any scikit-learn-provided classifier. We begin with a CPLE class:

```
class CPLELearningModel(BaseEstimator):

    def __init__(self, basemodel, pessimistic=True, predict_from_
probabilities = False, use_sample_weighting = True, max_iter=3000,
verbose = 1):
        self.model = basemodel
        self.pessimistic = pessimistic
        self.predict_from_probabilities = predict_from_probabilities
        self.use_sample_weighting = use_sample_weighting
        self.max_iter = max_iter
        self.verbose = verbose
```

We're already familiar with the concept of `basemodel`. Earlier in this chapter, we employed S3VMs and semi-supervised LDE's. In this situation, we'll again use an LDE; the goal of this first assay will be to try and exceed the results obtained by the semi-supervised LDE from earlier in this chapter. In fact, we're going to blow those results out of the water!

Before we do so, however, let's review the other parameter options. The `pessimistic` argument gives us an opportunity to use a non-pessimistic (optimistic) model. Instead of following the `pessimistic` method of minimizing the loss between unlabeled and labeled discriminative likelihood, an optimistic model aims to maximize likelihood. This can yield better results (mostly during training), but is significantly more risky. Here, we'll be working with pessimistic models.

The `predict_from_probabilities` parameter enables optimization by allowing a prediction to be generated from the probabilities of multiple data points at once. If we set this as true, our CPLE will set the prediction as 1 if the probability we're using for prediction is greater than the mean, or 0 otherwise. The alternative is to use the base model probabilities, which is generally preferable for performance reasons, unless we'll be calling `predict` across a number of cases.

We also have the option to `use_sample_weighting`, otherwise known as **soft labels** (but most familiar to us as posterior probabilities). We would normally take this opportunity, as soft labels enable greater flexibility than hard labels and are generally preferred (unless the model only supports hard class labels).

The first few parameters provide a means of stopping CPLE training, either at maximum iterations or after log-likelihood stops improving (typically because of convergence). The `bestdl` provides the best discriminative likelihood value and corresponding soft labels; these values are updated on each training iteration:

```
self.it = 0
self.noimprovementsince = 0
self.maxnoimprovementsince = 3

self.buffersize = 200
self.lastdls = [0]*self.buffersize

self.bestdl = numpy.infty
self.bestlbls = []



self.id = str(unichr(numpy.random.randint(26)+97))+str(unichr(
numpy.random.randint(26)+97))
```

The `discriminative_likelihood` function calculates the likelihood (for discriminative models—that is, models that aim to maximize the probability of a target—$y = 1$, conditional on the input, X) of an input.

In this case, it's worth drawing your attention to the distinction between generative and discriminative models. While this isn't a basic concept, it can be fundamental in understanding why many classifiers have the goals that they do.

A classification model takes input data and attempts to classify cases, assigning each case a label. There is more than one way to do this.

One approach is to take the cases and attempt to draw a decision boundary between them. Then we can take each new case as it appears and identify which side of the boundary it falls on. This is a **discriminative** learning approach.

Another approach is to attempt to model the distribution of each class individually. Once a model has been generated, the algorithm can use Bayes' rule to calculate the posterior distribution on the labels given input data. This approach is **generative** and is a very powerful approach with significant weaknesses (most of which tie into the question of how well we can model our classes). Generative approaches include Gaussian discriminant models (yes, that is a slightly confusing name) and a broad range of Bayesian models. More information, including some excellent recommended reading, is provided in the *Further reading* section of this chapter.

In this case, the function will be used on each iteration to calculate the likelihood of the predicted labels:

```
def discriminative_likelihood(self, model, labeledData, labeledy =
None, unlabeledData = None, unlabeledWeights = None, unlabeledlambda =
1, gradient=[], alpha = 0.01):
    unlabeledy = (unlabeledWeights[:, 0]<0.5)*1
    uweights = numpy.copy(unlabeledWeights[:, 0])

    uweights[unlabeledy==1] = 1-uweights[unlabeledy==1]

    weights = numpy.hstack((numpy.ones(len(labeledy)), uweights))
    labels = numpy.hstack((labeledy, unlabeledy))
```

Having defined this much of our CPLE, we also need to define the fitting process for our supervised model. This uses familiar components, namely, `model.fit` and `model.predict_proba`, for probability prediction:

```
if self.use_sample_weighting:
        model.fit(numpy.vstack((labeledData, unlabeledData)),
labels, sample_weight=weights)
        else:
```

```
        model.fit(numpy.vstack((labeledData, unlabeledData)),
  labels)


        P = model.predict_proba(labeledData)
```

In order to perform pessimistic CPLE, we need to derive both the labeled and unlabeled discriminative log likelihood. In order, we then perform `predict_proba` on both the labeled and unlabeled data:

```
    try:

        labeledDL = -sklearn.metrics.log_loss(labeledy, P)
    except Exception, e:
        print e
        P = model.predict_proba(labeledData)


    unlabeledP = model.predict_proba(unlabeledData)



    try:
        eps = 1e-15
        unlabeledP = numpy.clip(unlabeledP, eps, 1 - eps)
        unlabeledDL = numpy.average((unlabeledWeights*numpy.
  vstack((1-unlabeledy, unlabeledy)).T*numpy.log(unlabeledP)).
  sum(axis=1))
        except Exception, e:
            print e
            unlabeledP = model.predict_proba(unlabeledData)
```

Once we're able to calculate the discriminative log likelihood for both the labeled and unlabeled classification attempts, we can set an objective via the `discriminative_ likelihood_objective` function. The goal here is to use the pessimistic (or optimistic, by choice) methodology to calculate `dl` on each iteration until the model converges or the maximum iteration count is hit.

On each iteration, a t-test is performed to determine whether the likelihoods have changed. Likelihoods should continue to change on each iteration preconvergence. Sharp-eyed readers may have noticed earlier in the chapter that three consecutive t-tests showing no change will cause the iteration to stop (this is configurable via the `maxnoimprovementsince` parameter):

```
    if self.pessimistic:
        dl = unlabeledlambda * unlabeledDL - labeledDL
    else:
        dl = - unlabeledlambda * unlabeledDL - labeledDL

    return dl


    def discriminative_likelihood_objective(self, model, labeledData,
labeledy = None, unlabeledData = None, unlabeledWeights = None,
unlabeledlambda = 1, gradient=[], alpha = 0.01):
        if self.it == 0:
            self.lastdls = [0]*self.buffersize

        dl = self.discriminative_likelihood(model, labeledData,
labeledy, unlabeledData, unlabeledWeights, unlabeledlambda, gradient,
alpha)

        self.it += 1
        self.lastdls[numpy.mod(self.it, len(self.lastdls))] = dl

        if numpy.mod(self.it, self.buffersize) == 0: # or True:
            improvement = numpy.mean((self.lastdls[(len(self.
lastdls)/2):])) - numpy.mean((self.lastdls[:(len(self.lastdls)/2)]))

            _, prob = scipy.stats.ttest_ind(self.lastdls[(len(self.
lastdls)/2):], self.lastdls[:(len(self.lastdls)/2)])

            noimprovement = prob > 0.1 and numpy.mean(self.
lastdls[(len(self.lastdls)/2):]) < numpy.mean(self.lastdls[:(len(self.
lastdls)/2)])
            if noimprovement:
                self.noimprovementsince += 1
                if self.noimprovementsince >= self.
maxnoimprovementsince:

                    self.noimprovementsince = 0
                    raise Exception(" converged.")
            else:
                self.noimprovementsince = 0
```

On each iteration, the algorithm saves the best discriminative likelihood and the best weight set for use in the next iteration:

```
if dl < self.bestdl:
    self.bestdl = dl
    self.bestlbls = numpy.copy(unlabeledWeights[:, 0])


return dl
```

One more element worth discussing is how the soft labels are created. We've discussed these earlier in the chapter. This is how they look in code:

```
f = lambda softlabels, grad=[]: self.discriminative_
likelihood_objective(self.model, labeledX, labeledy=labeledy,
unlabeledData=unlabeledX, unlabeledWeights=numpy.vstack((softlabels,
1-softlabels)).T, gradient=grad)

lblinit = numpy.random.random(len(unlabeledy))
```

In a nutshell, `softlabels` provide a probabilistic version of the discriminative likelihood calculation. In other words, they act as weights rather than hard, binary class labels. Soft labels are calculable using the `optimize` method:

```
try:
    self.it = 0
    opt = nlopt.opt(nlopt.GN_DIRECT_L_RAND, M)
    opt.set_lower_bounds(numpy.zeros(M))
    opt.set_upper_bounds(numpy.ones(M))
    opt.set_min_objective(f)
    opt.set_maxeval(self.max_iter)
    self.bestsoftlbl = opt.optimize(lblinit)
    print " max_iter exceeded."
except Exception, e:
    print e
    self.bestsoftlbl = self.bestlbls

if numpy.any(self.bestsoftlbl != self.bestlbls):
    self.bestsoftlbl = self.bestlbls
ll = f(self.bestsoftlbl)

unlabeledy = (self.bestsoftlbl<0.5)*1
uweights = numpy.copy(self.bestsoftlbl)

uweights[unlabeledy==1] = 1-uweights[unlabeledy==1]

weights = numpy.hstack((numpy.ones(len(labeledy)), uweights))
labels = numpy.hstack((labeledy, unlabeledy))
```

For interested readers, optimize uses the **Newton conjugate gradient** method of calculating gradient descent to find optimal weight values. A reference to Newton conjugate gradient is provided in the Further reading section at the end of this chapter.

Once we understand how this works, the rest of the calculation is a straightforward comparison of the best supervised labels and soft labels, setting the `bestsoftlabel` parameter as the best label set. Following this, the discriminative likelihood is computed against the best label set and a `fit` function is calculated:

```
if self.use_sample_weighting:
        self.model.fit(numpy.vstack((labeledX, unlabeledX)),
labels, sample_weight=weights)
        else:
        self.model.fit(numpy.vstack((labeledX, unlabeledX)),
labels)


if self.verbose > 1:
        print "number of non-one soft labels: ", numpy.sum(self.
bestsoftlbl != 1), ", balance:", numpy.sum(self.bestsoftlbl<0.5), " /
", len(self.bestsoftlbl)
        print "current likelihood: ", ll
```

Now that we've had a chance to understand the implementation of CPLE, let's get hands-on with an interesting dataset of our own! This time, we'll change things up by working with the University of Columbia's Million Song Dataset.

The central feature of this algorithm is feature analysis and metadata for one million songs. The data is preprepared and made up of natural and derived features. Available features include things such as the artist's name and ID, duration, loudness, time signature, and tempo of each song, as well as other measures including a crowd-rated danceability score and tags associated with the audio.

This dataset is generally labeled (via tags), but our objective in this case will be to generate genre labels for different songs based on the data provided. As the full million song dataset is a rather forbidding 300 GB, let's work with a 1% (1.8 GB) subset of 10,000 records. Furthermore, we don't particularly need this data as it currently exists; it's in an unhelpful format and a lot of the fields are going to be of little use to us.

The `10000_songs` dataset residing in the *Chapter 6, Text Feature Engineering* folder of our *Mastering Python Machine Learning* repository is a cleaned, prepared (and also rather large) subset of music data from multiple genres. In this analysis, we'll be attempting to predict genre from the genre tags provided as targets. We'll take a subset of tags as the labeled data used to kick-start our learning and will attempt to generate tags for unlabelled data.

In this iteration, we're going to raise our game as follows:

- Using more labeled data. This time, we'll use 1% of the total dataset size (100 songs), taken at random, as labeled data.

- Using an SVM with a linear kernel as our classifier, rather than the simple linear discriminant analysis we used with our naïve self-training implementation earlier in this chapter.

So, let's get started:

```python
import sklearn.svm
import numpy as np
import random

from frameworks.CPLELearning import CPLELearningModel
from methods import scikitTSVM
from examples.plotutils import evaluate_and_plot

kernel = "linear"

songs = fetch_mldata("10000_songs")
X = songs.data
ytrue = np.copy(songs.target)
ytrue[ytrue==-1]=0

labeled_N = 20
ys = np.array([-1]*len(ytrue))
random_labeled_points = random.sample(np.where(ytrue == 0)[0],
labeled_N/2)+\
                        random.sample(np.where(ytrue == 1)[0],
labeled_N/2)
ys[random_labeled_points] = ytrue[random_labeled_points]
```

For comparison, we'll run a supervised SVM alongside our CPLE implementation. We'll also run the naïve self-supervised implementation, which we saw earlier in this chapter, for comparison:

```
basemodel = SGDClassifier(loss='log', penalty='l1') # scikit logistic
regression
basemodel.fit(X[random_labeled_points, :], ys[random_labeled_points])
print "supervised log.reg. score", basemodel.score(X, ytrue)


ssmodel = SelfLearningModel(basemodel)
ssmodel.fit(X, ys)
print "self-learning log.reg. score", ssmodel.score(X, ytrue)


ssmodel = CPLELearningModel(basemodel)
ssmodel.fit(X, ys)
print "CPLE semi-supervised log.reg. score", ssmodel.score(X, ytrue)
```

The results that we obtain on this iteration are very strong:

```
# supervised log.reg. score 0.698
# self-learning log.reg. score 0.825
# CPLE semi-supervised log.reg. score 0.833
```

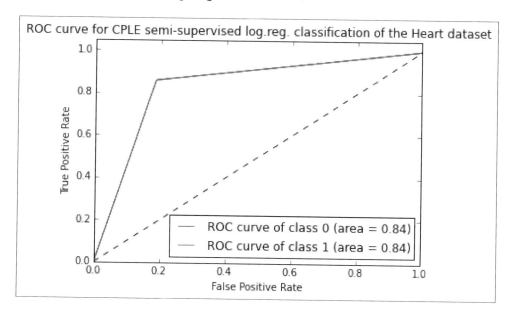

The CPLE semi-supervised model succeeds in classifying with 84% accuracy, a score comparable to human estimation and over 10% higher than the naïve semi-supervised implementation. Notably, it also outperforms the supervised SVM.

Further reading

A solid place to start understanding Semi-supervised learning methods is Xiaojin Zhu's very thorough literature survey, available at `http://pages.cs.wisc.edu/~jerryzhu/pub/ssl_survey.pdf`.

I also recommend a tutorial by the same author, available in the slide format at `http://pages.cs.wisc.edu/~jerryzhu/pub/sslicml07.pdf`.

The key paper on Contastive Pessimistic Likelihood Estimation is Loog's 2015 paper `http://arxiv.org/abs/1503.00269`.

This chapter made a reference to the distinction between generative and discriminative models. A couple of relatively clear explanations of the distinction between generative and discriminative algorithms are provided by Andrew Ng (`http://cs229.stanford.edu/notes/cs229-notes2.pdf`) and Michael Jordan (`http://www.ics.uci.edu/~smyth/courses/cs274/readings/jordan_logistic.pdf`).

For readers interested in Bayesian statistics, Allen Downey's book, *Think Bayes*, is a marvelous introduction (and one of my all-time favorite statistics books): `https://www.google.co.uk/#q=think+bayes`.

For readers interested in learning more about gradient descent, I recommend Sebastian Ruder's blog at `http://sebastianruder.com/optimizing-gradient-descent/`.

For readers interested in going a little deeper into the internals of conjugate descent, Jonathan Shewchuk's introduction provides clear and enjoyable definitions for a number of key concepts at `https://www.cs.cmu.edu/~quake-papers/painless-conjugate-gradient.pdf`.

Summary

In this chapter, we tapped into a very powerful but lesser known paradigm in machine learning—semi-supervised learning. We began by exploring the underlying concepts of transductive learning and self-training, and improved our understanding of the latter class of techniques by working with a naïve self-training implementation.

We quickly began to see weaknesses in self-training and looked for an effective solution, which we found in the form of CPLE. CPLE is a very elegant and highly applicable framework for semi-supervised learning that makes no assumptions beyond those of the classifier that it uses as a base model. In return, we found CPLE to consistently offer performance in excess of naïve semi-supervised and supervised implementations, at minimal risk. We've gained a significant amount of understanding regarding one of the most useful recent developments in machine learning.

In the next chapter, we'll begin discussing data preparation skills that significantly increase the effectiveness of all of the models that we've previously discussed.

6
Text Feature Engineering

Introduction

In preceding chapters, we've spent time assessing powerful techniques that enable the analysis of complex or challenging data. However, for the most difficult problems, the right technique will only get you so far.

The persistent challenge that deep learning and supervised learning try to solve for is that finding solutions often requires multiple big investments from the team in question. Under the old paradigm, one often has to perform specific preparation tasks, requiring time, specialist skills, and knowledge. Often, even the techniques used were domain-specific and/or data type-specific. This process, via which features are derived, is referred to as feature engineering.

Most of the deep learning algorithms which we've studied so far are intended to help find ways around needing to perform extensive feature engineering. However, at the same time, feature engineering continues to be seen as a hugely important skill for top-level ML practitioners. The following quotes come from leading Kaggle competitors, via David Kofoed Wind's contribution to the Kaggle blog:

> *"The features you use influence more than everything else the result. No algorithm alone, to my knowledge, can supplement the information gain given by correct feature engineering."*

> – *(Luca Massaron)*

"Feature engineering is certainly one of the most important aspects in Kaggle competitions and it is the part where one should spend the most time on. There are often some hidden features in the data which can improve your performance by a lot and if you want to get a good place on the leaderboard you have to find them. If you screw up here you mostly can't win anymore; there is always one guy who finds all the secrets. However, there are also other important parts, like how you formulate the problem. Will you use a regression model or classification model or even combine both or is some kind of ranking needed. This, and feature engineering, are crucial to achieve a good result in those competitions. There are also some competitions where (manual) feature engineering is not needed anymore; like in image processing competitions. Current state of the art deep learning algorithms can do that for you."

– (Josef Feigl)

There are a few key themes here; feature engineering is powerful and even a very small amount of feature engineering can have a big impact on one's classifiers. It is also frequently necessary to employ feature engineering techniques if one wishes to deliver the best possible results. Maximising the effectiveness of your machine learning algorithms requires a certain amount of both domain-specific and data type-specific knowledge (secrets).

One more quote:

"For most Kaggle competitions the most important part is feature engineering, which is pretty easy to learn how to do."

– (Tim Salimans)

Tim's not wrong; most of what you'll learn in this chapter is intuitive, effective tricks, and transformations. This chapter will introduce you to a few of the most effective and commonly-used preparation techniques applied to text and time series data, drawing from NLP and financial time series applications. We'll walk through how the techniques work, what one should expect to see, and how one can diagnose whether they're working as desired.

Text feature engineering

In preceding sections, we've discussed some of the methods by which we might take a dataset and extract a subset of valuable features. These methods have broad applicability but are less helpful when dealing with non-numerical/non-categorical data, or data that cannot be easily translated into numerical or categorical data. In particular, we need to apply different techniques when working with text data.

The techniques that we'll study in this section fall into two main categories—cleaning techniques and feature preparation techniques. These are typically implemented in roughly that order and we'll study them accordingly.

Cleaning text data

When we work with natural text data, a different set of approaches apply. This is because in real-world contexts, the idea of a naturally clean text dataset is pretty unsafe; text data is rife with misspellings, non-dictionary constructs like emoticons, and in some cases, HTML tagging. As such, we need to be very thorough with our cleaning.

In this section, we'll work with a number of effective text-cleaning techniques, using a pretty gnarly real-world dataset. Specifically, we'll be using the Impermium dataset from a 2012 Kaggle competition, where the competition's goal was to create a model which accurately detects insults in social commentary.

Yes, I do mean Internet troll detection.

Let's get started!

Text cleaning with BeautifulSoup

Our first step should be manually checking the input data. This is pretty critical; with text data, one needs to try and understand what issues exist in the data initially so as to identify the cleaning needed.

It's kind of painful to read through a dataset full of hateful Internet commentary, so here's an example entry:

ID	Date	Comment
132	20120531031917Z	`"""\xa0@Flip\xa0how are you not ded"""`

We have an ID field and date field which don't seem to need much work. The text fields, however, are quite challenging. From this one case, we can already see misspelling and HTML inclusion. Furthermore, many entries in the dataset contain attempts to bypass swear filtering, usually by including a space or punctuation element mid-word. Other data quality issues include multiple vowels (to extend a word), non-ascii characters, hyperlinks... the list goes on.

One option for cleaning this dataset is to use regular expressions, which run over the input data to scrub out data quality issues. However, the quantity and variety of problem formats make it impractical to use a regex-based approach, at least to begin with. We're likely both to miss a lot of cases and also to misjudge the amount of preparation needed, leading us to clean too aggressively, or not aggressively enough; in specific terms we risk cutting into real text content or leaving parts of tags in place. What we need is a solution that will wash out the majority of common data quality problems to begin with so that we can focus on the remaining issues with a script-based approach.

Enter `BeautifulSoup`. `BeautifulSoup` is a very powerful text cleaning library which can, among other things, remove HTML markup. Let's take a look at this library in action on our troll data:

```
from bs4 import BeautifulSoup
import csv

trolls = []
with open('trolls.csv', 'rt') as f:
    reader = csv.DictReader(f)
    for line in reader:
        trolls.append(BeautifulSoup(str(line["Comment"]), "html.
parser"))

print(trolls[0])

eg = BeautifulSoup(str(trolls), "html.parser")

print(eg.get_text())
```

ID	Date	Comments
132	20120531031917Z	@Flip how are you not ded

As we can see, we've already made headway on improving the quality of our text data. Yet, it's also clear from these examples that there's a lot of work left to do! As discussed, let's move on to using regular expressions to help further clean and tokenize our data.

Managing punctuation and tokenizing

Tokenisation is the process of creating a set of tokens from a stream of text. Many tokens are words, while others might be character sets (such as smilies or other punctuation strings, for example, ????????).

Now that we've removed a lot of the HTML ugliness from our initial dataset, we can take steps to further improve the cleanliness of our text data. To do this, we'll leverage the `re` module, which allows us to use operations over regular expressions, such as substring replacement. We'll perform a series of operations over our input text on this pass, which mostly focus on replacing variable or problematic text elements with tokens. Let's begin with a simple example, replacing e-mail addresses with an _EM token:

```
text = re.sub(r'[\w\-][\w\-\.]+@[\w\-][\w\-\.]+[a-zA-Z]{1,4}', '_EM',
text)
```

Similarly, we can remove URLs, replacing them with the _U token:

```
text = re.sub(r'\w+:\/\/\S+', r'_U', text)
```

We can automatically remove extra or problematic whitespace and newline characters, hyphens, and underscores. In addition, we'll begin managing the problem of multiple characters, often used for emphasis in informal conversation. Extended series of punctuation characters are encoded here using codes such as _BQ and BX; these longer tags are used as a means of differentiating from the more straightforward _Q and _X tags (which refer to the use of a question mark and exclamation mark, respectively).

We can also use regular expressions to manage extra letters; by cutting down such strings to two characters at most, we're able to reduce the number of combinations to a manageable amount and tokenize that reduced group using the _EL token:

```
# Format whitespaces
text = text.replace('"', ' ')
text = text.replace('\'', ' ')
text = text.replace('_', ' ')
text = text.replace('-', ' ')
text = text.replace('\n', ' ')
text = text.replace('\\n', ' ')
text = text.replace('\'', ' ')
text = re.sub(' +',' ', text)
text = text.replace('\'', ' ')


#manage punctuation
text = re.sub(r'([^!\?])(\?{2,})(\Z|[^!\?])', r'\1 _BQ\n\3', text)
text = re.sub(r'([^\.])(\.{2,})', r'\1 _SS\n', text)
text = re.sub(r'([^!\?])(\?|!){2,}(\Z|[^!\?])', r'\1 _BX\n\3', text)
text = re.sub(r'([^!\?])\?(\Z|[^!\?])', r'\1 _Q\n\2', text)
text = re.sub(r'([^!\?])!(\Z|[^!\?])', r'\1 _X\n\2', text)
```

```
text = re.sub(r'([a-zA-Z])\1\1+(\w*)', r'\1\1\2 _EL', text)
text = re.sub(r'([a-zA-Z])\1\1+(\w*)', r'\1\1\2 _EL', text)
text = re.sub(r'(\w+)\.(\w+)', r'\1\2', text)
text = re.sub(r'[^a-zA-Z]','', text)
```

Next, we want to begin creating other tokens of interest. One of the more helpful indicators available is the _SW token for swearing. We'll also use regular expressions to help identify and tokenize smileys into one of four buckets; big and happy smileys (_BS), small and happy ones (_S), big and sad ones (_BF), and small and sad ones (_F):

```
text = re.sub(r'([#%&\*\$]{2,})(\w*)', r'\1\2 _SW', text)
```

```
text = re.sub(r' [8x;:=]-?(?:\)|\}|\]|>){2,}', r' _BS', text)
text = re.sub(r' (?:[;:=]-?[\)\}\]d>])|(?:<3)', r' _S', text)
text = re.sub(r' [x:=]-?(?:\(|\[|\||\\|/|\{|<){2,}', r' _BF', text)
text = re.sub(r' [x:=]-?[\(\[\|\\/\{<]', r' _F', text)
```

Smileys are complicated by the fact that their uses change frequently; while this series of characters is reasonably current, it's by no means complete; for example, see emojis for a range of non-ascii representations. For several reasons, we'll be removing non-ascii text from this example (a similar approach is to use a dictionary to force compliance), but both approaches have the obvious drawback that they remove cases from the dataset, meaning that any solution will be imperfect. In some cases, this approach may lead to the removal of a substantial amount of data. In general, then, it's prudent to be aware of the general challenge around character-based images in text content.

Following this, we want to begin splitting text into phrases. This is a simple application of str.split, which enables the input to be treated as a vector of words (words) rather than as long strings (re):

```
phrases = re.split(r'[;:\.()\n]', text)
phrases = [re.findall(r'[\w%\*&#]+', ph) for ph in phrases]
phrases = [ph for ph in phrases if ph]

words = []

for ph in phrases:
        words.extend(ph)
```

This gives us the following:

ID	Date	Comments
132	20120531031917Z	[['Flip', 'how', 'are', 'you', 'not', 'ded']]

Next, we perform a search for single-letter sequences. Sometimes, for emphasis, Internet communication involves the use of spaced single-letter chains. This may be attempted as a method of avoiding curse word detection:

```
tmp = words
words = []
new_word = ''
for word in tmp:
    if len(word) == 1:
        new_word = new_word + word
    else:
        if new_word:
            words.append(new_word)
            new_word = ''
        words.append(word)
```

So far, then, we've gone a long way toward cleaning and improving the quality of our input data. There are still outstanding issues, however. Let's reconsider the example we began with, which now looks like the following:

ID	Date	Words
132	20120531031917Z	['_F', 'how', 'are', 'you', 'not', 'ded']

Much of our early cleaning has passed this example by, but we can see the effect of vectorising the sentence content as well as the now-cleaned HTML tags. We can also see that the emote used has been captured via the _F tag. When we look at a more complex test case, we see even more substantial change results:

Raw	Cleaned and split
GALLUP DAILY\nMay 24-26, 2012 \ u2013 Updates daily at 1 p.m. ET; reflects one-day change\ nNo updates Monday, May 28; next update will be Tuesday, May 29.\nObama Approval48%-\nObama Disapproval45%-1\nPRESIDENTIAL ELECTION\nObama47%-\nRomney45%-\ n7-day rolling average\n\n It seems the bump Romney got is over and the president is on his game.	['GALLUP', 'DAILY', 'May', 'u', 'Updates', 'daily', 'pm', 'ET', 'reflects', 'one', 'day', 'change', 'No', 'updates', 'Monday', 'May', 'next', 'update', 'Tuesday', 'May', 'Obama', 'Approval', 'Obama', 'Disapproval', 'PRESIDENTIAL', 'ELECTION', 'Obama', 'Romney', 'day', 'rolling', 'average', 'It', 'seems', 'bump', 'Romney', 'got', 'president', 'game']

However, there are two significant problems still obvious in both examples. In the first case, we have a misspelled word; we need to find a way to eliminate this. Secondly, a lot of the words in both examples (for example. are, pm) aren't terribly informative in and of themselves. The problem we find, particularly for shorter text samples, is that what's left after cleaning may contain only one or two meaningful terms. If these terms are not terribly common in the corpus as a whole, it can prove to be very difficult to train a classifier to recognise these terms' significance.

Tagging and categorising words

I expect that we all know that English language words come in several types—nouns, verbs, adverbs, and so on. These are commonly referred to as **parts of speech**. If we know that a certain word is an adjective, as opposed to a verb or stop word (such as a, the, or of), we can treat it differently or more importantly, our algorithm can!

If we can perform part of speech tagging by identifying and encoding word classes as categorical variables, we're able to improve the quality of our data by retaining only the valuable content. The full range of text tagging options and techniques is too broad to be effectively covered in one section of this chapter, so we'll look at a subset of the applicable tagging techniques. Specifically, we'll focus on n-gram tagging and backoff taggers, a pair of complimentary techniques that allow us to create powerful recursive tagging algorithms.

We'll be using a Python library called the **Natural Language Toolkit (NLTK)**. NLTK offers a wide array of functionality and we'll be relying on it at several points in this chapter. For now, we'll be using NLTK to perform tagging and removal of certain word types. Specifically, we'll be filtering out stop words.

To answer the obvious first question (why eliminate stop words?), it tends to be true that stop words add little to nothing to most text analysis and can be responsible for a degree of noise and training variance. Fortunately, filtering stop words is pretty straightforward. We'll simply import NLTK, download and import the dictionaries, then perform a scan over all words in our pre-existing word vector, removing any stop words found:

```
import nltk
nltk.download()
from nltk.corpus import stopwords

words = [w for w in words if not w in stopwords.words("english")]
```

I'm sure you'll agree that this was pretty straightforward! Let's move on to discuss more NLTK functionality, specifically, tagging.

Tagging with NLTK

Tagging is the process of identifying parts of speech, as we described previously, and applying tags to each term.

In its simplest form, tagging can be as straightforward as applying a dictionary over our input data, just as we did previously with stopwords:

```
tagged = ntlk.word_tokenize(words)
```

However, even brief consideration will make it obvious that our use of language is a lot more complicated than this allows. We may use a word (such as ferry) as one of several parts of speech and it may not be straightforward to decide how to treat each word in every utterance. A lot of the time, the correct tag can only be understood contextually given the other words and their positioning within the phrase.

Thankfully, we have a number of useful techniques available to help us solve linguistic challenges.

Sequential tagging

A sequential tagging algorithm is one that works by running through the input dataset, left-to-right and token-by-token (hence sequential!), tagging each token in succession. The decision over which token to assign is made based on that token, the tokens that preceded it, and the predicted tags for those preceding tokens.

In this section, we'll be using an **n-gram tagger**. An n-gram tagger is a type of sequential tagger, which is pretrained to identify appropriate tags. The n-gram tagger takes *(n-1)-many* preceding POS tags and the current token into consideration in producing a tag.

> For clarity, an n-gram is the term used for a contiguous sequence of n-many elements from a given set of elements. This may be a contiguous sequence of letters, words, numerical codes (for example, for state changes), or other elements. N-grams are widely used as a means of capturing the conjunct meaning of sets of elements—be those phrases or encoded state transitions—using n-many elements.

The simplest form of n-gram tagger is one where $n = 1$, referred to as a **unigram tagger**. A unigram tagger operates quite simply, by maintaining a conditional frequency distribution for each token. This conditional frequency distribution is built up from a training corpus of terms; we can implement training using a helpful train method belonging to the `NgramTagger` class in NLTK. The tagger assumes that the tag which occurs most frequently for a given token in a given sequence is likely to be the correct tag for that token. If the term **carp** is in the training corpus as a noun four times and as a verb twice, a unigram tagger will assign the noun tag to any token whose type is carp.

This might suffice for a first-pass tagging attempt but clearly, a solution that only ever serves up one tag for each set of homonyms isn't always going to be ideal. The solution we can tap into is using n-grams with a larger value of *n*. With $n = 3$ (a **trigram tagger**), for instance, we can see how the tagger might more easily distinguish the input *He tends to carp on a lot* from *He caught a magnificent carp*!

However, once again there is a trade-off here between accuracy of tagging and ability to tag. As we increase *n*, we're creating increasingly long n-grams which become increasingly rare. In a very short time, we end up in a situation where our n-grams are not occurring in the training data, causing our tagger to be unable to find any appropriate tag for the current token!

In practice, we find that what we need is a set of taggers. We want our most reliably accurate tagger to have the first shot at trying to tag a given dataset and, for any case that fails, we're comfortable with having a more reliable but potentially less accurate tagger have a try.

Happily, what we want already exists in the form of backoff tagging. Let's find out more!

Backoff tagging

Sometimes, a given tagger may not perform reliably. This is particularly common when the tagger has high accuracy demands and limited training data. At such times, we usually want to build an ensemble structure that lets us use several taggers simultaneously.

To do this, we create a distinction between two types of taggers: **subtaggers** and **backoff taggers**. Subtaggers are taggers like the ones we saw previously, **sequential** and **Brill taggers**. Tagging structures may contain one or multiple of each kind of tagger.

If a subtagger is unable to determine a tag for a given token, then a backoff tagger may be referred to instead. A backoff tagger is specifically used to combine the results of an ensemble of (one or more) subtaggers, as shown in the following example diagram:

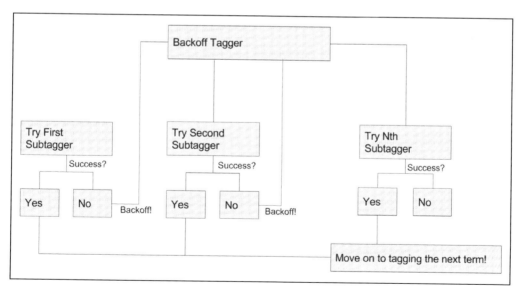

In simple implementations, the backoff tagger will simply poll the subtaggers in order, accepting the first none-null tag provided. If all subtaggers return null for a given token, the backoff tagger will assign a none tag to that token. The order can be determined.

Backoffs are typically used with multiple subtaggers of different types; this enables a data scientist to harness the benefits of multiple types of tagger simultaneously. Backoffs may refer to other backoffs as needed, potentially creating highly redundant or sophisticated tagging structures:

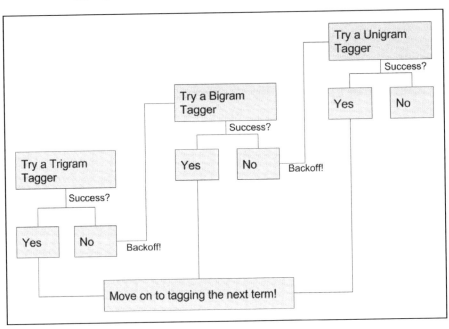

In general terms, backoff taggers provide redundancy and enable you to use multiple taggers in a composite solution. To solve our immediate problem, let's implement a nested series of n-gram taggers. We'll start with a trigram tagger, which will use a bigram tagger as its backoff tagger. If neither of these taggers has a solution, we'll have a unigram tagger as an additional backoff. This can be done very simply, as follows:

```
brown_a = nltk.corpus.brown.tagged_sents(categories= 'a')

tagger = None
for n in range(1,4):
    tagger = NgramTagger(n, brown_a, backoff = tagger)

words   = tagger.tag(words)
```

Creating features from text data

Once we've engaged in well-thought-out text cleaning practices, we need to take additional steps to ensure that our text becomes useful features. In order to do this, we'll look at another set of staple techniques in NLP:

- Stemming
- Lemmatising
- Bagging using random forests

Stemming

Another challenge when working with linguistic datasets is that multiple word forms exist for many word stems. For example, the root dance is the stem of multiple other words—dancing, dancer, dances, and so on. By finding a way to reduce this plurality of forms into stems, we find ourselves able to improve our n-gram tagging and apply new techniques such as lemmatisation.

The techniques that enable us to reduce words to their stems are called stemmers. Stemmers work by parsing words as consonant/vowel strings and applying a series of rules. The most popular stemmer is the **porter stemmer**, which works by performing the following steps;

1. Simplifying the range of suffixes by reducing (for example, *ies* becomes *i*) to a smaller set.
2. Removing suffixes in several passes, with each pass removing a set of suffix types (for example, past particple or plural suffixes such as ousness or alism).
3. Once all suffixes are removed, cleaning up word endings by adding 'e's where needed (for example, ceas becomes cease).
4. Removing double 'l's.

The porter stemmer works very effectively. In order to understand exactly how well it works, let's see it in action!

```
from nltk.stem import PorterStemmer

stemmer = PorterStemmer()

stemmer.stem(words)
```

The output of this `stemmer`, as demonstrated on our pre-existing example, is the root form of the word. This may be a real word, or it may not; dancing, for instance, becomes danci. This is okay, but it's not really ideal. We can do better than this!

To consistently reach a real word form, let's apply a slightly different technique, lemmatisation. Lemmatisation is a more complex process to determine word stems; unlike porter stemming, it uses a different normalisation process for different parts of speech. Unlike Porter Stemming it also seeks to find actual roots for words. Where a stem does not have to be a real word, a lemma does. Lemmatization also takes on the challenge of reducing synonyms down to their roots. For example, where a stemmer might turn the term books into the term book, it isn't equipped to handle the term tome. A lemmatizer can process both books and tome, reducing both terms to book.

As a necessary prerequisite, we need the POS for each input token. Thankfully, we've already applied a POS tagger and can work straight from the results of that process!

```
from nltk.stem import PorterStemmer, WordNetLemmatizer

lemmatizer = WordNetLemmatizer()

words = lemmatizer.lemmatize(words, pos = 'pos')
```

The output is now what we'd expect to see:

Source Text	Post-lemmatisation
The laughs you two heard were triggered by memories of his own high-flying exits off moving beasts	['The', 'laugh', 'two', 'hear', 'trigger', 'memory', 'high', 'fly', 'exit', 'move', 'beast']

We've now successfully stemmed our input text data, massively improving the effectiveness of lookup algorithms (such as many dictionary-based approaches) in handling this data. We've removed stop words and tokenized a range of other noise elements with regex methods. We've also removed any HTML tagging. Our text data has reached a reasonably processed state. There's one more linchpin technique that we need to learn, which will let us generate features from our text data. Specifically, we can use bagging to help quantify the use of terms.

Let's find out more!

Bagging and random forests

Bagging is part of a family of techniques that may collectively be referred to as subspace methods. There are several forms of method, with each having a separate name. If we draw random subsets from the sample cases, then we're performing pasting. If we're sampling from cases with replacement, it's referred to as bagging. If instead of drawing from cases, we work with a subset of features, then we're performing attribute bagging. Finally, if we choose to draw from both sample cases and features, we're employing what's known as a **random patches** technique.

The feature-based techniques, attribute bagging, and Random Patch methods are very valuable in certain contexts, particularly very high-dimensional ones. Medical and genetics contexts both tend to see a lot of extremely high-dimensional data, so feature-based methods are highly effective within those contexts.

In NLP contexts, it's common to work with bagging specifically. In the context of linguistic data, what we'll be dealing with is properly called a bag of words. A bag of words is an approach to text data preparation that works by identifying all of the distinct words (or tokens) in a dataset and then counting their occurrence in each sample. Let's begin with a demonstration, performed over a couple of example cases from our dataset:

ID	Date	Words
132	20120531031917Z	['_F', 'how', 'are', 'you', 'not', 'ded']
69	20120531173030Z	['you', 'are', 'living', 'proof', 'that', 'bath', 'salts', 'effect', 'thinking']

This gives us the following 12-part list of terms:

```
[

   "_F"

   "how"

   "are"

   "you"

   "not"

   "ded"

   "living"

   "proof"

   "that"

   "bath"
```

```
    "salts"

    "effect"

    "thinking"

]
```

Using the indices of this list, we can create a 12-part vector for each of the preceding sentences. This vector's values are filled by traversing the preceding list and counting the number of times each term occurs for each sentence in the dataset. Given our pre-existing example sentences and the list we created from them, we end up creating the following bags:

ID	Date	Comment	Bag of words
132	20120531031917Z	_F how are you not ded	[1, 1, 1, 1, 1, 1, 0, 0, 0, 0, 0, 0, 0]
69	20120531173030Z	you are living proof that bath salts effect thinking	[0, 0, 1, 1, 0, 0, 1, 1, 1, 1, 1, 1, 1]

This is the core of a bag of words implementation. Naturally, once we've translated the linguistic content of text into numerical vectors, we're able to start using techniques that add sophistication to how we use this text in classification.

One option is to use weighted terms. We can use a term weighting scheme to modify the values within each vector so that terms that are indicative or helpful for classification are emphasized. Weighting schemes may be straightforward masks, such as a binary mask that indicates presence versus absence.

Binary masking can be useful if certain terms are used much more frequently than normal; in such cases, specific scaling (for example, log-scaling) may be needed if a binary mask is not used. At the same time, though, frequency of term use can be informative (it may indicate emphasis, for instance) and the decision over whether to apply a binary mask is not always made simply.

Another weighting option is term frequency-inverse document frequency, or tf-idf. This scheme compares frequency of usage within a specific sentence and the dataset as a whole and uses values that increase if a term is used more frequently within a given sample than within the whole corpus.

Variations on tf-idf are frequently used in text mining contexts, including search engines. Scikit-learn provides a tf-idf implementation, TfidfVectoriser, which we'll shortly use to employ tf-idf for ourselves.

Now that we have an understanding of the theory behind bag of words and can see the range of technical options available to us once we develop vectors of word use, we should discuss how a bag of words implementation can be undertaken. Bag of words can be easily applied as a wrapper to a familiar model. While in general, subspace methods may use any of a range of base models (SVMs and linear regression models are common), it is very common to use random forests in a bag of words implementation, wrapping up preparation and learning into a concise script. In this case, we'll employ bag of words independently for now, saving classification via a random forest implementation for the next section!

While we'll discuss random forests in greater detail in *Chapter 8, Ensemble Methods*, (which describes the various types of ensemble that we can create), it is helpful for now to note that a random forest is a set of decision trees. They are powerful ensemble models that are created either to run in parallel (yielding a vote or other net outcome) or boost one another (by iteratively adding a new tree to model the parts of the solution that the pre-existing set of trees couldn't model well).

Due to the power and ease of use of random forests, they are commonly used as benchmarking algorithms.

The process of implementing bag of words is, again, fairly straightforward. We initialize our bagging tool (matter-of-factly referred to as a vectorizer). Note that for this example, we're putting a limit on the size of the feature vector. This is largely to save ourselves some time; each document must be compared against each item in the feature list, so when we get to running our classifier this could take a little while!

```
from sklearn.feature_extraction.text import TfidfVectorizer

vectorizer = TfidfVectorizer(analyzer = "word",     \
                            tokenizer = None,       \
                            preprocessor = None,  \
                            stop_words = None,      \
                            max_features = 5000)
```

Our next step is to fit the vectorizer on our word data via `fit_transform`; as part of the fitting process, our data is transformed into feature vectors:

```
train_data_features = vectorizer.fit_transform(words)

train_data_features = train_data_features.toarray()
```

This completes the pre-processing of our text data. We've taken this dataset through a full battery of text mining techniques, walking through the theory and reasoning behind each technique as well as employing some powerful Python scripts to process our test dataset.We're in a good position now to take a crack at Kaggle's insult detection challenge!

Testing our prepared data

So, now that we've done some initial preparation of the dataset, let's give the real problem a shot and see how we do. To help set the scene, let's consider Impermium's guidance and data description:

This is a single-class classification problem. The label is either 0 meaning a neutral comment, or 1 meaning an insulting comment (neutral can be considered as not belonging to the insult class. Your predictions must be a real number in the range [0,1] where 1 indicates 100% confident prediction that comment is an insult.

- *We are looking for comments that are intended to be insulting to a person who is a part of the larger blog/forum conversation.*

- *We are NOT looking for insults directed to non-participants (such as celebrities, public figures etc.).*

- *Insults could contain profanity, racial slurs, or other offensive language. But often times, they do not.*

- *Comments which contain profanity or racial slurs, but are not necessarily insulting to another person are considered not insulting.*

- *The insulting nature of the comment should be obvious, and not subtle.*

- *There may be a small amount of noise in the labels as they have not been meticulously cleaned. However, contestants can be confident the error in the training and testing data is < 1%.*

Contestants should also be warned that this problem tends to strongly overfit. The provided data is generally representative of the full test set, but not exhaustive by any measure. Impermium will be conducting final evaluations based on an unpublished set of data drawn from a wide sample.

This is pretty nice guidance, in that it raises two particular points of caution. The desired score is the **area under the curve** (**AUC**), which is a measure that is very sensitive both to false positives and to incorrect negative results (specificity and sensitivity).

The guidance clearly states that continuous predictions are desired rather than binary *0/1* outputs. This becomes critically important when using AUC; even a small amount of incorrect predictions given will radically decrease one's score if you only use categorical values. This suggests that rather than using the `RandomForestClassifier` algorithm, we'll want to use the `RandomForestRegressor`, a regression-focused alternative, and then rescale the results between zero and one.

Real Kaggle contests are run in a much more challenging and realistic environment — one where the correct solution is not available. In *Chapter 8, Ensemble Methods*, we'll explore how top data scientists react and thrive in such environments. For now, we'll take advantage of having the ability to confirm whether we're doing well on the test dataset. Note that this advantage also presents a risk; if the problem overfits strongly, we'll need to be disciplined to ensure that we're not overtraining on the test data!

In addition, we also have the benefit of being able to see how well real contestants did. While we'll save the real discussion for *Chapter 8, Ensemble Methods*, it's reasonable to expect each highly-ranking contestant to have submitted quite a large number of failed attempts; having a benchmark will help us tell whether we're heading in the right direction.

Specifically, the top 14 participants on the private (test) leaderboard managed to reach an AUC score of over *0.8*. The top scorer managed a pretty impressive *0.84*, while over half of the 50 teams who entered scored above *0.77*.

As we discussed earlier, let's begin with a random forest regression model.

A random forest is an ensemble of decision trees.

While a single decision tree is likely to suffer from variance- or bias-related issues, random forests are able to use a weighted average over multiple parallel trials to balance the results of modeling.

Random forests are very straightforward to apply and are a good first-pass technique for a new data challenge; applying a random forest classifier to the data early on enables you to develop a good understanding as to what initial, baseline classification accuracy will look like as well as giving valuable insight into how the classification boundaries were formed; during the initial stages of working with a dataset, this kind of insight is invaluable.

Scikit-learn provides `RandomForestClassifier` to enable the easy application of a random forest algorithm.

For this first pass, we'll use 100 trees; increasing the number of trees can improve classification accuracy but will take additional time. Generally speaking, it's sensible to attempt fast iteration in the early stages of model creation; the faster you can repeatedly run your model, the faster you can learn what your results are looking like and how to improve them!

We begin by initializing and training our model:

```
trollspotter = RandomForestRegressor(n_estimators = 100, max_depth =
10, max_features = 1000)

y = trolls["y"]

trollspotted = trollspotter.fit(train_data_features, y)
```

We then grab the test data and apply our model to predict a score for each test case. We rescale these scores using a simple stretching technique:

```
moretrolls = pd.read_csv('moretrolls.csv', header=True, names=['y',
'date', 'Comment', 'Usage'])
moretrolls["Words"] = moretrolls["Comment"].apply(cleaner)

y = moretrolls["y"]

test_data_features = vectorizer.fit_transform(moretrolls["Words"])
test_data_features = test_data_features.toarray()

pred = pred.predict(test_data_features)
pred = (pred - pred.min())/(pred.max() - pred.min())
```

Finally, we apply the `roc_auc` function to calculate an AUC score for the model:

```
fpr, tpr, _ = roc_curve(y, pred)
roc_auc = auc(fpr, tpr)
print("Random Forest benchmark AUC score, 100 estimators")
print(roc_auc)
```

As we can see, the results are definitely not at the level that we want them to be at:

```
Random Forest benchmark AUC score, 100 estimators

0.537894912105
```

Thankfully, we have a number of options that we can try to configure here:

- Our approach to how we work with the input (preprocessing steps and normalisation)
- The number of estimators in our random forest
- The classifier we choose to employ
- The properties of our bag of words implementation (particularly the maximum number of terms)
- The structure of our n-gram tagger

On our next pass, let's adjust the size of our bag of words implementation, increasing the term cap from a slightly arbitrary 5,000 to anywhere up to 8,000 terms; rather than picking just one value, we'll run over a range and see what we can learn. We'll also increase the number of trees to a more reasonable number (in this case, we stepped up to `1000`):

```
Random Forest benchmark AUC score, 1000 estimators
0.546439310772
```

These results are slightly better than the previous set, but not dramatically so. They're definitely a fair distance from where we want to be! Let's go further and set up a different classifier. Let's try a fairly familiar option—the SVM. We'll set up our own SVM object to work with:

```
class SVM(object):

    def __init__(self, texts, classes, nlpdict=None):

        self.svm = svm.LinearSVC(C=1000, class_weight='auto')
        if nlpdict:
            self.dictionary = nlpdict
        else:
            self.dictionary = NLPDict(texts=texts)
        self._train(texts, classes)

    def _train(self, texts, classes):
        vectors = self.dictionary.feature_vectors(texts)
        self.svm.fit(vectors, classes)

    def classify(self, texts):
        vectors = self.dictionary.feature_vectors(texts)
```

```
predictions = self.svm.decision_function(vectors)
predictions = p.transpose(predictions)[0:len(predictions)]
predictions = predictions / 2 + 0.5
predictions[predictions > 1] = 1
predictions[predictions < 0] = 0
return predictions
```

While the workings of SVM are almost impenetrable to human assessment, as an algorithm it operates effectively, iteratively translating the dataset into multiple additional dimensions in order to create complex hyperplanes at optimal class boundaries. It isn't a huge surprise, then, to see that the quality of our classification has increased:

SVM AUC score

0.625245653817

Perhaps we're not getting enough visibility into what's happening with our results. Let's try shaking things up with a different take on performance measurement. Specifically, let's look at the difference between the model's label predictions and actual targets to see whether the model is failing more frequently with certain types of input.

So we've taken our prediction quite far. While we still have a number of options on the table, it's worth considering the use of a more sophisticated ensemble of models as being a solid option. In this case, leveraging multiple models instead of just one can enable us to obtain the relative advantages of each. To try out an ensemble against this example, run the `score_trolls_blendedensemble.py` script.

 This ensemble is a blended/stacked ensemble. We'll be spending more time discussing how this ensemble works in *Chapter 8, Ensemble Methods*!

Plotting our results, we can see that performance has improved, but by significantly less than we'd hoped:

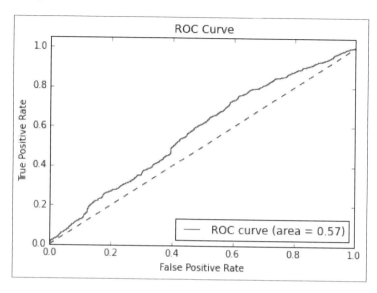

We're clearly having some issues with building a model against this data, but at this point, there isn't a lot of value in throwing a more developed model at the problem. We need to go back to our features and aim to extend the feature set.

At this point, it's worth taking some pointers from one of the most successful entrants of this particular Kaggle contest. In general, top-scoring entries tend to be developed by finding all of the tricks around the input data. The second-place contestant in the official Kaggle contest that this dataset was drawn from was a user named tuzzeg. This contestant provided a usable code repository at `https://github.com/tuzzeg/detect_insults`.

Tuzzeg's implementation differs from ours by virtue of much greater thoroughness. In addition to the basic features that we built using POS tagging, he employed POS-based bigrams and trigrams as well as subsequences (created from sliding windows of N-many terms). He worked with n-grams up to 7-grams and created character n-grams of lengths 2, 3, and 4.

Furthermore, tuzzeg took the time to create two types of composite model, both of which were incorporated into his solution—sentence level and ranking models. Ranking took our rationalization around the nature of the problem a step further by turning the cases in our data into ranked continuous values.

Meanwhile, the innovative sentence-level model that he developed was trained specifically on single-sentence cases in the training data. For prediction on test data, he split the cases into sentences, evaluated each separately, and took only the highest score for sentences within the case. This was to accommodate the expectation that in natural language, speakers will frequently confine insulting comments to a single part of their speech.

Tuzzeg's model created over 100 feature groups (where a stem-based bigram is an example feature group—a group in the sense that the bigram process creates a vector of features), with the most important ones (ranked by impact) being the following:

```
stem subsequence based            0.66
stem based (unigrams, bigrams)  0.18
char ngrams based (sentence)      0.07
char ngrams based                 0.04
all syntax                        0.006
all language models               0.004
all mixed                         0.002
```

This is interesting, in that it suggests that a set of feature translations that we aren't currently using is important in generating a usable solution. Particularly, the subsequence-based features are only a short step from our initial feature set, making it straightforward to add the extra feature:

```
def subseq2(n, xs):
    l = len(xs)
    return ['%s %s' % (xs[i], xs[j]) for i in xrange(l-1) for j in
xrange(i+1, i+n+1) if j < l]

def getSubseq2(seqF, n):
    def f(row):
        seq = seqF(row)
        return set(seq + subseq2(n, seq))
    return f

Subseq2test = getSubseq2(line, 2)
```

This approach yields excellent results. While I'd encourage you to export Tuzzeg's own solution and apply it, you can also look at the `score_trolls_withsubseq.py` script provided in this project's repository to get a feeling for how powerful additional features can be incorporated.

With these additional features added, we see a dramatic improvement in our AUC score:

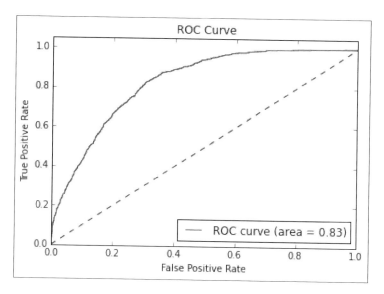

Running this code provides a very healthy `0.834` AUC score. This simply goes to show the power of thoughtful and innovative feature engineering; while the specific features generated in this chapter will serve you well in other contexts, specific hypotheses (such as hostile comments being isolated to specific sentences within a multi-sentence comment) can lead to very effective features.

As we've had the luxury of checking our reasoning against test data throughout this chapter, we can't reasonably say that we've worked under life-like conditions. We didn't take advantage of having access to the test data by reviewing it ourselves, but it's fair to say that knowing what the private leaderboard scored for this challenge made it easier for us to target the right fixes. In *Chapter 8, Ensemble Methods*, we'll be working on another tricky Kaggle problem in a more rigorous and realistic way. We'll also be discussing ensembles in depth!

Further reading

The quotes at the start of this chapter were sourced from the highly-readable Kaggle blog, No Free Hunch. Refer to `http://blog.kaggle.com/2014/08/01/learning-from-the-best/`.

There are many good resources for understanding NLP tasks. One fairly thorough, eight-part piece, is available online at `http://textminingonline.com/dive-into-nltk-part-i-getting-started-with-nltk`.

If you're keen to get started, one great option is to try Kaggle's for Knowledge NLP task, which is perfectly suited as a testbed for the techniques described in this chapter: `https://www.kaggle.com/c/word2vec-nlp-tutorial/details/part-1-for-beginners-bag-of-words`.

The Kaggle contest cited in this chapter is available at `https://www.kaggle.com/c/detecting-insults-in-social-commentary`.

For readers interested in further description of the ROC curve and the AUC measure, consider Tom Fawcett's excellent introduction, available at `https://ccrma.stanford.edu/workshops/mir2009/references/ROCintro.pdf`.

Summary

We've been introduced to a lot of useful and highly applicable skills in this chapter. In this chapter, we took a set of messy, complication-strewn text data and, through a series of rigorous steps, turned it into a large set of effective features. We began by picking up a set of data cleaning skills which stripped out a lot of the noise and problem elements, then we followed up by turning text into features using POS tagging and bag of words. In the process, you learned to apply a set of techniques that are widely applicable and very empowering, enabling us to solve difficult problems in many natural language processing contexts.

Through experimentation with multiple individual models and ensembles, we discovered that where a smarter algorithm might not yield a strong result, thorough and creative feature engineering can yield massive improvements in model performance.

7
Feature Engineering Part II

Introduction

We have recognized the importance of feature engineering. In the previous chapter, we discussed techniques that enable us to select from a range of features and work effectively to transform our original data into features, which can be effectively processed by the advanced ML algorithms that we have discussed thus far.

The adage *garbage in, garbage out* is relevant in this context. In earlier chapters, we have seen how image recognition and NLP tasks require carefully-prepared data. In this chapter, we will be looking at a more ubiquitous type of data: quantitative or categorical data that is collected from real-world applications.

Data of the type that we will be working with in this chapter is common to many contexts. We could be discussing telemetry data captured from sensors in a forest, game consoles, or financial transactions. We could be working with geological survey information or bioassay data collected through research. Regardless, the core principles and techniques remain the same.

In this chapter, you will be learning how to interrogate this data to weed out or mitigate quality issues, how to transform it into forms that are conducive to machine learning, and how to creatively enhance that data.

In general terms, the concepts that we'll be discussing in this chapter are as follows:

- The different approaches to feature set creation and the limits of feature engineering
- How to use a large set of techniques to enhance and improve an initial dataset
- How to tie in and use domain knowledge to understand valid options to transform and improve the clarity of existing data
- How we can test the value of individual features and feature combinations so that we only keep what we need

While we will begin with a detailed discussion of the underlying concepts, by the end of this chapter we will be working with multiple, iterative trials and using specialized tests to understand how helpful the features that we are creating will be to us.

Creating a feature set

The most important factor involved in successful machine learning is the quality of your input data. A good model with misleading, inappropriately normalized, or uninformative data will not see the same level of success anywhere near a model run over appropriately prepared data.

In some cases, you have the ability to specify data collection or have access to a useful, sizeable, and varied set of source data. With the right knowledge and skillset, you can use this data to create highly useful feature sets.

In general, having a strong knowledge as to how to construct good feature sets is very helpful as it enables you to audit and assess any new dataset for missed opportunities. In this chapter, we will introduce a design process and technique set that make it easier to create effective feature sets.

As such, we'll begin by discussing some techniques that we can use to extend or reinterpret existing features, potentially creating a large number of useful parameters to include in our models.

However, as we will see, there are limitations on the effective use of feature engineering techniques and we need to be mindful of the risks around engineered datasets.

Engineering features for ML applications

We have discussed what you can do about patching up data quality issues in your data and we have talked about how you can creatively use dimensions in what you have to join to external data.

Once you have a reasonably well-understood and quality-checked set of data in front of you, there is usually still a significant amount of work needed before you can produce effective models from that data.

Using rescaling techniques to improve the learnability of features

The main challenge with directly feeding unprepared data to many machine learning models is that the algorithm is sensitive to the relative size of different variables. If your dataset has multiple parameters whose ranges differ, some algorithms will treat the variables whose variance is greater as indicative of more significant change than algorithms with smaller values and less variance.

The key to resolving this potential problem is rescaling, a process by which parameter values' relative size is adjusted while retaining the initial ordering of values within each parameter (a monotonic translation).

Gradient descent algorithms (which include most deep learning algorithms— http://sebastianruder.com/optimizing-gradient-descent/) are significantly more efficient if the input data is scaled prior to training. To understand why, we'll resort to drawing some pictures. A given series of training steps may appear as follows:

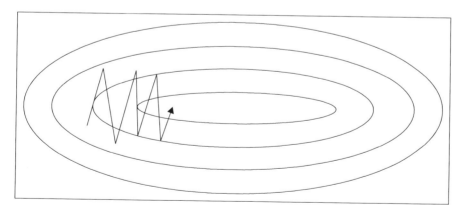

When applied to unscaled data, these training steps may not converge effectively (as per the left-hand example in the following diagram).

With each parameter having a differing scale, the parameter space in which models are attempting to train can be highly distorted and complex. The more complex this space, the harder it becomes to train a model within it. This is an involved subject that can be effectively described, in general terms, through a metaphor, but for readers looking for a fuller explanation there is an excellent reference in this chapter's *Further reading* section. For now, it is not unreasonable to think in terms of gradient descent models during training as behaving like marbles rolling down a slope. These marbles are prone to *getting stuck* in saddle points or other complex geometries on the slope (which, in this context, is the surface created by our model's objective function—the learning function whose output our models typically train to minimize). With scaled data, however, the surface becomes more regularly-shaped and training can become much more effective:

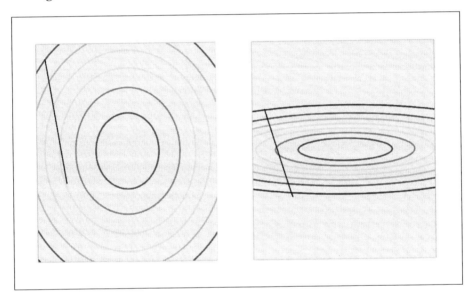

The classic example is a linear rescaling between *0* and *1*; with this method, the largest parameter value is rescaled to *1*, the smallest to *0*, with intermediate values falling in the *0-1* interval, proportionate to their original size relative to the largest and smallest values. Under such a transformation, the vector *[0,10,25,20,18]*, for instance, would become *[0,0.4, 1, 0.8, 0.72]*.

The particular value of this transformation is that, for multiple data points that may vary in magnitude in its raw form, the rescaled features will sit within the same range, enabling your machine learning algorithm to train on meaningful information content.

This is the most straightforward rescaling option, but there are some nonlinear scaling alternatives that can be much more helpful in the right circumstances; these include square scaling, square root scaling, and perhaps most commonly, log-scaling.

Log-scaling of parameter values is very common in physics and in contexts where the underlying data is frequently affected by a power law (for example, an exponential growth in y given a linear increase in x).

Unlike linear rescaling, log-scaling adjusts the relative spacing between data cases. This can be a double-edged sword. On the one hand, log-scaling handles outlying cases very well. Let's take an example dataset describing individual net wealth for members of a fictional population, described by the following summary statistics:

Statistic	Wealth
Min	1
First Quartile	42.5
Mean	3205433.343
Median	600
Third Quartile	1358
Max	10000000000

Prior to rescaling, this population is hugely skewed toward that single individual with absurd net worth. The distribution of cases per decile is as follows:

Range	Count of Cases
0 > 0.1	3060
0.1 > 0.2	0
0.2 > 0.3	0
0.3 > 0.4	0
0.4 > 0.5	0
0.5 > 0.6	0
0.6 > 0.7	0
0.7 > 0.8	0
0.8 > 0.9	0
0.9 > 1	1

After log-scaling, this distribution is far friendlier:

Range	Count of Cases
0 > 0.1	740
0.1 > 0.2	1633
0.2 > 0.3	544
0.3 > 0.4	141
0.4 > 0.5	0
0.5 > 0.6	1
0.6 > 0.7	0
0.7 > 0.8	1
0.8 > 0.9	0
0.9 > 1	1

We could've chosen to take scaling further and drawn out the first half of this distribution more by doing that. In this case, log-10 normalization significantly reduces the impact of these outlying values, enabling us to retain outliers in the dataset without losing detail at the lower end.

With this said, it's important to note that in some contexts, that same enhancement of clustered cases can enhance noise in variant parameter values and create the false impression of greater spacing between values. This tends not to negatively affect how log-scaling handles outliers; the impact is usually seen for groups of smaller-valued cases whose original values are very similar.

The challenges created by introducing nonlinearities through log-scaling are significant and in general, nonlinear scaling is only recommended for variables that you understand and have a nonlinear relationship or trend underlying them.

Creating effective derived variables

Rescaling is a standard part of preprocessing in many machine learning applications (for instance, almost all neural networks). In addition to rescaling, there are other preparatory techniques, which can improve model performance by strategically reducing the number of parameters input to the model. The most common example is of a derived measure that takes multiple existing data points and represents them within a single measure.

These are extremely prevalent; examples include acceleration (as a function of velocity values from two points in time), body mass index (as a function of height, weight, and age), and **price-earnings (P/E)** ratio for stock scoring. Essentially, any derived score, ratio, or complex measure that you ever encounter is a combination score formed from multiple components.

For datasets in familiar contexts, many of these pre-existing measures will be well-known. Even in relatively well-known areas, however, looking for new supporting measures or transformations using a mix of domain knowledge and existing data can be very effective. When thinking through derived measure options, some useful concepts are as follows:

- **Two variable combinations**: Multiplication, division, or normalization of the n parameter as a function of the m parameter.

- **Measures of change over time**: A classic example here is acceleration or 7D change in a measure. In more complex contexts, the slope of an underlying time series function can be a helpful parameter to work with instead of working directly with the current and past values.

- **Subtraction of a baseline**: Using a base expectation (a flat expectation such as the *baseline churn rate*) to recast a parameter in terms of that baseline can be a more immediately informative way of looking at the same variable. For the churn example, we could generate a parameter that describes churn in terms of deviation from an expectation. Similarly, in stock trading cases, we might look at closing price in terms of the opening price.

- **Normalization**: Following on from the previous case, normalization of parameter values based on the values of another parameter or baseline that is dynamically calculated given properties of other variables. One example here is *failed transaction rate*; in addition to looking at this value as a raw (or rescaled) count, it often makes sense to normalize this in terms of attempted transactions.

Creative recombination of these different elements lets us build very effective scores. Sometimes, for instance, a parameter that tells us the slope of customer engagement (declining or increasing) over time needs to be conditioned on whether that customer was previously highly engaged or hardly engaged, as a slight decline in engagement might mean very different things in each context. It is the data scientist's job to effectively and creatively feature sets that capture these subtleties for a given domain.

So far, this discussion has focused on numerical data. Often, however, useful data is locked up inside non-numeric parameters such as codes or categorical data. Accordingly, we will next discuss a set of effective techniques to turn non-numeric features into usable parameters.

Reinterpreting non-numeric features

A common challenge, which can be problematic and problem-specific, is how non-numeric features are treated. Frequently, valuable information is encoded within non-numerical shorthand values. In the case of stock trades, for instance, the identity of the stock itself (for example, AAPL) as well as that of the buyer and seller is interesting information that we expect to relate meaningfully to our problem. Taking this example further, we might also expect some stocks to trade differently from others even within the industry, and organizational differences within companies, which may occur at some or all points of time, also provide important context.

One simple option that works in some cases is building an aggregation or series of aggregations. The most obvious example is a count of occurrences with the possibility of creating extended measures (changes in count between two time windows) as described in the preceding section.

Building summary statistics and reducing the number of rows in the dataset introduces the risk of reducing the amount of information that your model has available to learn from (increasing the risk of model fragility and overfitting). As such, it's generally a bad idea to extensively aggregate and reduce input data. This is doubly true with deep learning techniques, such as the algorithms discussed and used in Chapters 2-4.

Rather than extensively using aggregation-based approaches, let's look at an alternative way of translating string-encoded values into numerical data. Another very popular class of techniques is encoding, with the most common encoding tactic being one-hot encoding. One-hot encoding is the process of turning a series of categorical responses (for example, age groups) into a set of binary variables, with each response option (for example, 18-30) represented by its own binary variable. This is a little more intuitive when presented visually:

Case	Age	Gender
1	22	M
2	25	M
3	34	F
4	23	M
5	25	F
6	41	F

After encoding, this dataset of categorical and continuous variables becomes a tensor of binary variables:

Case	Age_22	Age_23	Age_25	Age_34	Age_41	Gender_F	Gender_M
1	1	0	0	0	0	0	1
2	0	0	1	0	0	0	1
3	0	0	0	1	0	1	0
4	0	1	0	0	0	0	1
5	0	0	0	0	0	1	0
6	0	0	0	0	1	1	0

The advantage that this presents is significant; it enables us to tap into the very valuable tag information contained within a lot of datasets without aggregation or risk of reducing the information content of the data. Furthermore, one-hot allows us to separate specific response codes for encoded variables into separate features, meaning that we can identify more or less meaningful codes for a specific variable and only retain the important values.

Another very effective technique, used primarily for text codes, is known as the **hash trick**. A hash, in simple terms, is a function that translates data into a numeric representation. Hashes will be a familiar concept to many, as they're frequently used to encode sensitive parameters and summarize otherwise bulky data. In order to get the most out of the hash trick, however, it's important to understand how the trick works and what can be done with it.

We can use hashing to turn a text phrase into a numeric value that we can use as an identifier for that phrase. While there are many applications of different hashing algorithms, in this context even a simple hash makes it straightforward to turn string keys and codes into numerical parameters that we can model effectively.

A very simple hash might turn each alphabet character into a corresponding number. *a* would become *1*, *b* would be *2*, and so on. Hashes could be generated for words and phrases by summing those values. The phrase *cat gifs* would translate under this scheme as follows:

```
Cat: 3 + 1 + 20
Gifs: 7 + 9 + 6 + 19
Total: 65
```

This is a terrible hash for two reasons (quite disregarding the fact that the input contains junk words!). Firstly, there's no real limit on how many outputs it can present. When one remembers that the whole point of the hash trick is to provide dimensionality reduction, it stands to reason that the number of possible outputs from a hash must be bounded! Most hashes limit the range of numbers that they output, so part of the decision in terms of selecting a hash is related to the number of features you'd prefer your model to have.

 One common behavior is to choose a power of two as the hash range; this tends to speed things up by allowing bitwise operations during the hashing process.

The other reason that this hash kind of sucks is that changes to the word have a small impact rather than a large one. If *cat* became *bat*, we'd want our hash output to change substantially. Instead, it changes by one (becoming *64*). In general, a good hash function is one where a small change in the input text will cause a large change in the output. This is partly because language structures tend to be very uniform (thus scoring similarly), but slightly different sets of nouns and verbs within a given structure tend to confer very different meanings to one another (*the cat sat on the mat* versus *the car sat on the cat*).

So we've described hashing. The hash trick takes things a little further. Hypothetically, turning every word into a hashed numerical code is going to lead to a large number of *hash collisions*—cases where two words have the same hash value. Naturally, these are rather bad.

Handily, there's a distribution underlying how frequently different terms are used that work in our favor. Called the **Zipf distribution**, it entails that the probability of encountering the nth most common term is approximated by $P(n) = 0.1/n$ up to around 1,000 (Zipf's law). This entails that each term is much less likely to be encountered than the preceding term. After $n = 1000$, terms tend to be sufficiently obscure that it's unlikely to encounter two that have the same hash in one dataset.

At the same time, a good hashing function has a limited range and is significantly affected by small changes in input. These properties make the hash collision chance largely independent of term usage frequency.

These two concepts—Zipf's law and a good hash's independence of hash collision chance and term usage frequency—mean that there is very little chance of a hash collision, and where one occurs it is overwhelmingly likely to be between two infrequently-used words.

This gives the hash trick a peculiar property. Namely, it is possible to reduce the dimensionality of a set of text input data massively (from tens of thousands of naturally occurring words to a few hundred or fewer) without reducing the performance of a model trained on hashed data, compared to training on unhashed bag-of-words features.

Proper use of the hash trick enables a lot of possibilities, including augmentations to the techniques that we discussed (specifically, bag-of-words). References to different hashing implementations are included in the *Further reading* section at the end of this chapter.

Using feature selection techniques

Now that we have a good selection of options for feature creation, as well as an understanding of the creative feature engineering possibilities, we can begin building our existing features into more effective variants. Given this new-found feature engineering skillset, we run the risk of creating extensive and hard-to-manage datasets.

Adding features without limit increases the risk of model fragility and overfitting for certain types of models. This is tied to the complexity of the trends that you're attempting to model. In the simplest case, if you're attempting to identify a significant distinction between two large groups, your model is likely to support a large number of features. However, as the model you need to fit to make this distinction becomes more complex and as the group sizes that you have to work with become smaller, adding more and more features can harm the model's ability to classify consistently and effectively.

This challenge is compounded by the fact that it isn't always obvious which parameter or variation is best-suited for the task. Suitability can vary by the underlying model; decision forests, for instance, don't perform any better with monotonic transformations (that is, transformations that retain the initial ordering of data cases; one example is log-scaling) than with the unscaled base data; however, for other algorithms, the choice to rescale and the rescaling method used are both very impactful choices.

Traditionally, the quantity of features and limits on the parameter amount were tied to the desire to develop a mathematical function that relates key inputs to the desired outcome scores. In this context, additional parameters needed to be incorporated as moving or nuisance variables.

Each new parameter introduces another dimension that makes the modeled relationship more complex and the resultant model more likely to be overfitting the data that exists. A trivial example is if you introduce a parameter that is just a unique label for each case; at this point, your algorithm will just learn those labels, making it very likely that your model fails entirely when introduced to a new dataset.

Less trivial examples are no less problematic; the proportion of cases to features becomes very important when your features are separating cases down to very small groups. In short, increasing the complexity of the modeled function causes your model to be more liable to overfit and adding features can exacerbate this effect. According to this principle, we should be beginning with very small datasets and adding parameters only after justifying that they improve the model.

However, in recent times, an opposing methodology — now generally seen as being part of a common way of *doing data science* — has gained ground. This methodology suggests that it's a good idea to add very large feature sets to incorporate every potentially valuable feature and *work down* to a smaller feature set that does the job.

This methodology is supported by techniques that enable decisions to be made over huge feature sets (potentially hundreds or thousands of features) and that tend to operate in a *brute force* manner. These techniques will exhaustively test feature combinations, running models in series or in parallel until the most effective parameter subsets are identified.

These techniques work, which is why this methodology has become popular. It is definitely worth knowing about these techniques, if not using them, so you'll be learning how to apply them later in this chapter.

The main disadvantage around using brute force techniques for feature selection is that it becomes very easy to trust the outcomes of the algorithm, irrespective of what the features it selects actually mean. It is sensible to balance the use of highly effective, black-box algorithms against domain knowledge and an understanding of what's being undertaken. Therefore, this chapter will enable you to use techniques from both paradigms (*build up* and *build down*) so that you can adapt to different contexts. We'll begin by learning how to narrow down the feature set that you have to work with, from many features to the most valuable subset.

Performing feature selection

Having built a large dataset, often the next challenge one faces is how to narrow down the options to retain only the most effective data. In this section, we'll discuss a variety of techniques that support feature selection, working by themselves or as wrappers to familiar algorithms.

These techniques include correlation analysis, regularization techniques, and **Recursive Feature Elimination** (**RFE**). When we're done, you'll be able to confidently use these techniques to support your selection of feature sets, potentially saving yourself a significant amount of work every time you work with a new dataset!

Correlation

We'll begin our discussion of feature selection by looking for a simple source of major problems for regression models: multicollinearity. Multicollinearity is the fancy name for moderate or high degrees of correlation between features in a dataset. An obvious example is how pizza slice count is collinear with pizza price.

There are two types of multicollinearity: structural and data-based. Structural multicollinearity occurs when the creation of new features, such as feature *f1* from feature *f*, creates multiple features that may be highly correlated with one another. Data-based multicollinearity tends to occur when two variables are affected by the same causative factor.

Both kinds of multicollinearity can cause some unfortunate effects. In particular, our models' performance tends to become affected by which feature combinations are used; when collinear features are used, the performance of our model will tend to degrade.

In either case, our approach is simple: we can test for multicollinearity and remove underperforming features. Naturally, underperforming features are ones that add very little to model performance. They might be underperforming because they replicate information available in other features, or they may simply not provide data that is meaningful to the problem at hand. There are multiple ways to test for weak features as many feature selection techniques will sift out multicollinear feature combinations and recommend their removal if they're underperformant.

In addition, there is a specific multicollinearity test that's worth considering; namely, inspecting the eigenvalues of our data's correlation matrix. Eigenvectors and eigenvalues are fundamental concepts in the matrix theory with many prominent applications. More details are given at the end of this chapter. For now, suffice it to say that eigenvalues in the correlation matrix generated by our dataset provide us with a quantified measure of multicollinearity. Consider a set of eigenvalues as indicative of how much "new information content" our features bring to the dataset; a low eigenvalue suggests that the data may be correlated with other features. For an example of this at work, consider the following code, which creates a feature set and then adds collinearity to features *0*, *2*, and *4*:

```
import numpy as np


x = np.random.randn(100, 5)
noise = np.random.randn(100)
x[:,4] = 2 * x[:,0] + 3 * x[:,2] + .5 * noise
```

When we generate the correlation matrix and compute eigenvalues, we find the following:

```
corr = np.corrcoef(x, rowvar=0)
w, v = np.linalg.eig(corr)

print('eigenvalues of features in the dataset x')
print(w)

eigenvalues of features in the dataset x
 [ 0.00716428  1.94474029  1.30385565  0.74699492  0.99724486]
```

Clearly, our *0th* feature is suspect! We can then inspect the eigenvalues of this feature via calling v:

```
print('eigenvalues of eigenvector 0')
print(v[:,0])

eigenvalues of eigenvector 0
[-0.35663659 -0.00853105 -0.62463305  0.00959048  0.69460718]
```

From the small values of features in position one and three, we can tell that features *2* and *4* are highly multicollinear with feature *0*. We ought to remove two of these three features before proceeding!

LASSO

Regularized methods are among the most helpful feature selection techniques as they provide sparse solutions: ones where weaker features return zero, leaving only a subset of features with real coefficient values.

The two most used regularization models are L1 and L2 regularization, referred to as LASSO and ridge regression respectively in linear regression contexts.

Regularized methods function by adding a penalty to the loss function. Instead of minimizing a loss function $E(X,Y)$, the penalty leads to $E(X,Y) + a||w||$. The hyperparameter a relates to the amount of regularization (enabling us to tune the strength of our regularization and thus the proportion of the original feature set that is selected).

In LASSO regularization, the specific penalty function used is $a\sum ni=1|wi|$. Each non-zero coefficient adds to the size of the penalty term, forcing weaker features to return coefficients of 0. Selecting an appropriate penalty term can be achieved using scikit-learn's parameter optimization support for hyperparameters. In this case, we'll be using `estimator.get_params()` to perform a grid search for appropriate hyperparameter values. For more information on how grid searches operate, see the *Further reading* section at the end of this chapter.

In scikit-learn, logistic regression is provided with an L1 penalty for classification. Meanwhile, the LASSO module is provided for linear regression. For now, let's begin by applying LASSO to an example dataset. In this case, we'll use the Boston housing dataset:

```
fromsklearn.linear_model import Lasso
fromsklearn.preprocessing import StandardScaler
fromsklearn.datasets import load_boston

boston = load_boston()
scaler = StandardScaler()
X = scaler.fit_transform(boston["data"])
Y = boston["target"]
names = boston["feature_names"]

lasso = Lasso(alpha=.3)
lasso.fit(X, Y)

print "Lasso model: ", pretty_print_linear(lasso.coef_, names, sort =
True)

Lasso model: -3.707 * LSTAT + 2.992 * RM + -1.757 * PTRATIO + -1.081
* DIS + -0.7 * NOX + 0.631 * B + 0.54 * CHAS + -0.236 * CRIM + 0.081 *
ZN + -0.0 * INDUS + -0.0 * AGE + 0.0 * RAD + -0.0 * TAX
```

Several of the features in the original set returned a correlation of `0.0`. Increasing the correlation makes the solution increasingly sparse. For instance, we see the following results when `alpha = 0.4`:

```
Lasso model: -3.707 * LSTAT + 2.992 * RM + -1.757 * PTRATIO + -1.081
* DIS + -0.7 * NOX + 0.631 * B + 0.54 * CHAS + -0.236 * CRIM + 0.081 *
ZN + -0.0 * INDUS + -0.0 * AGE + 0.0 * RAD + -0.0 * TAX
```

We can immediately see the value of L1 regularization as a feature selection technique. However, it is important to note that L1 regularized regression is unstable. Coefficients can vary significantly, even with small data changes, when features in the data are correlated.

This problem is effectively addressed with L2 regularization, or ridge regression, which develops a feature coefficient with different applications. L2 normalization adds an additional penalty, the L2 norm penalty, to the loss function. This penalty takes the form $(a\sum ni=1w2i)$. A sharp-eyed reader will notice that, unlike the L1 penalty $(a\sum ni=1|wi|)$, the L2 penalty uses squared coefficients. This causes the coefficient values to be spread out more evenly and has the added effect that correlated features tend to receive similar coefficient values. This significantly improves stability as the coefficients no longer fluctuate on small data changes.

However, L2 normalization isn't as directly useful for feature selection as L1. Rather, as interesting features (with predictive power) tend to have non-zero coefficients, L2 is more useful as an exploratory tool allowing inference about the quality of features in the classification. It has the added merit of being more stable and reliable than L1 regularization.

Recursive Feature Elimination

RFE is a greedy, iterative process that functions as a wrapper over another model, such as an SVM (SVM-RFE), which it repeatedly runs over different subsets of the input data.

As with LASSO and ridge regression, our goal is to find the best-performing feature subset. As the name suggests, on each iteration a feature is set aside allowing the process to be repeated with the rest of the feature set until all features in the dataset have been eliminated. The ordering with which features are eliminated becomes their rank. After multiple iterations with incrementally smaller subsets, each feature is accurately scored and relevant subsets can be selected for use.

To get a better understanding of how this works, let's look at a simple example. We'll use the (by now familiar) digits dataset to understand how this approach works in practice:

```
print(__doc__)

from sklearn.svm import SVC
fromsklearn.datasets import load_digits
fromsklearn.feature_selection import RFE
importmatplotlib.pyplot as plt

digits = load_digits()
X = digits.images.reshape((len(digits.images), -1))
y = digits.target
```

We'll use an SVM as our base estimator via the SVC operator for **Support Vector Classification (SVC)**. We then apply the RFE wrapper over this model. RFE takes several arguments, with the first being a reference to the estimator of choice. The second argument is n_features_to_select, which is fairly self-explanatory. In cases where the feature set contains many interrelated features whose subsets possess multivariate distributions that are highly effective classification features, it's possible to opt for feature combinations of two or more.

Stepping enables the removal of multiple features on each iteration. When given a value between *0.0* and *1.0*, each step enables the removal of a percentage of the feature set, corresponding to the proportion given in the step argument:

```
svc = SVC(kernel="linear", C=1)
rfe = RFE(estimator=svc, n_features_to_select=1, step=1)
rfe.fit(X, y)
ranking = rfe.ranking_.reshape(digits.images[0].shape)

plt.matshow(ranking)
plt.colorbar()
plt.title("Ranking of pixels with RFE")
plt.show()
```

Given that we're familiar with the digits dataset, we know that each instance is an 8 x 8 image of a handwritten digit, as shown in the following image. Each image is located in the center of the 8 x 8 grid:

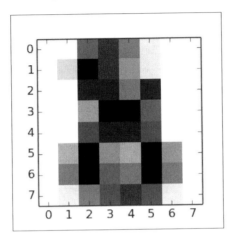

When we apply RFE over the digits dataset, we can see that it broadly captures this information in applying a ranking:

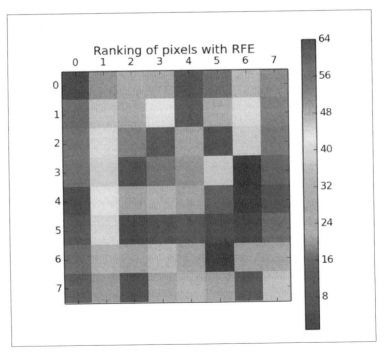

The first pixels to be cut were in and around the (typically empty) vertical edges of the image. Next, the algorithm began culling normally whitespace areas around the vertical edges or near the top of the image. The pixels that were retained longest were those that enabled the most differentiation between the different characters— pixels that would be present for some numbers and not for others.

This example gives us great visual confirmation that RFE works. What it doesn't give us is evidence for how consistently the technique works. The stability of RFE is dependent on the stability of the base model and, in some cases, ridge regression will provide a more stable solution. (For more information on which cases and the conditions involved, consult the *Further reading* section at the end of this chapter.)

Genetic models

Earlier in this chapter, we discussed the existence of algorithms that enable feature selection with very large parameter sets. Some of the most prominent techniques of this type are genetic algorithms, which emulate natural selection to generate increasingly effective models.

A genetic solution for feature selection works roughly as follows:

- An initial set of variables (predictors is the term typically used in this context) are combined into multiple subsets (candidates) and a performance measure is calculated for each candidate

- The predictors from candidates with the best performance are randomly recombined into a new iteration (generation) of models

- During this recombination step, for each subset there is the probability of a mutation, whereby a predictor may be added or removed from a subset

This algorithm typically iterates for multiple generations. The appropriate iteration amount is dependent on the complexity of the dataset and the model required. As with gradient descent techniques, the typical relationship between the performance and iteration count is present for genetic algorithms, where performance improvement declines nonlinearly as the count of iterations increases, eventually hitting a minimum before the overfitting risk increases.

To find an effective iteration count, we can perform testing using training data; by running the model for a large number of iterations and plotting the **Root Mean Squared Error** (**RMSE**), we're able to find an appropriate amount of iterations given our input data and model configuration.

Let's talk in a little more detail about what happens within each generation. Specifically, let's talk about how candidates are created, how performance is scored, and how recombination is performed.

The candidates are initially configured to use a random sample of the available predictors. There is no hard and fast rule concerning how many predictors to use in the first generation; it depends on how many features are available, but it's common to see first generation candidates using 50% to 80% of the available features (with a smaller percentage used in cases with more features).

The fitness measure can be difficult to define, but a common practice is to use two forms of cross-validation. Internal cross-validation (testing each model solely in the context of its own parameters without comparing models) is typically used to track performance at a given iteration; the fitness measures from internal cross-validation are used to select models to recombine in the next generation. External cross-validation (testing against a dataset that was not used in validation at any iteration) is also needed in order to confirm that the search process produced a model that has not overfitted to the internal training data.

Recombination is controlled by three key parameters: mutation, cross-over probabilities, and elitism. The latter is an optional parameter that one may use to reserve n-many of the top-performing models from the current generation; by doing so, one may preserve particularly effective candidates from being lost entirely during recombination. This can be done while also using that candidate in mutated variants and/or using them as parents to next-generation candidates.

The mutation probability defines the chance of a next-generation model being randomly readjusted (via some predictors, typically one, being added or removed). Mutation tends to help the genetic algorithm maintain a broad coverage of the candidate variables, reducing the risk of falling into a parameter-local solution.

Cross-over probability defines the likelihood that a pair of candidates will be selected for recombination into a next-generation model. There are several cross-over algorithms: parts of each parent's feature set might be spliced (for example, first half/second half) into the child or a random selection of each parent's features might be used. Common features to both parents might also be used by default. Random sampling from the set of both parent's unique predictors is a common default approach.

These are the main parts of a general genetic algorithm, which can be used as a wrapper to existing models (logistic regression, SVM, and others). The technique described here can be varied in many different ways and is related to feature selection techniques used slightly differently across multiple quantitative fields. Let's take the theory that we've covered thus far and start applying it to a practical example.

Feature engineering in practice

Depending on the modeling technique that you're using, some of this work may be more valuable than other parts. Deep learning algorithms tend to perform better on less-engineered data than shallower models and it might be that less work is needed to improve results.

The key to understanding what is needed is to iterate quickly through the whole process from dataset acquisition to modeling. On a first pass with a clear target for model accuracy, find the acceptable minimum amount of processing and perform that. Learn whatever you can about the results and make a plan for the next iteration.

To show how this looks in practice, we'll work with an unfamiliar, high-dimensional dataset, using an iterative process to generate increasingly effective modeling.

I was recently living in Vancouver. While it has many positive qualities, one of the worst things about living in the city was the somewhat unpredictable commute. Whether I was traveling by car or taking Translink's Skytrain system (a monorail-meets-rollercoaster high-speed line), I found myself subject to hard-to-predict delays and congestion issues.

In the spirit of putting our new feature engineering skillset into practice, let's take a look at whether we can improve this experience by taking the following steps:

- Writing code to harvest data from multiple APIs, including text and climate streams

- Using our feature engineering techniques to derive variables from this initial data

- Testing our feature set by generating commute delay risk scores

Unusually, in this example, we'll focus less on building and scoring a highly performant model. Instead, our focus is on creating a self-sufficient solution that you can adjust and apply for your own local area. While it suits the goals of the current chapter to take this approach, there are two additional and important motivations.

Firstly, there are some challenges around sharing and making use of Twitter data. Part of the terms of use of Twitter's API is an obligation on the developer to ensure that any adjustments to the state of a timeline or dataset (including, for instance, the deletion of a tweet) are reproduced in datasets that are extracted from Twitter and publicly shared. This makes the inclusion of real Twitter data in this chapter's GitHub repository impractical. Ultimately, this makes it difficult to provide reproducible results from any downstream model based on streamed data because users will need to build their own stream and accumulate data points and because variations in context (such as seasonal variations) are likely to affect model performance.

The second element here is simple enough: not everybody lives in Vancouver! In order to generate something of value to an end user, we should think in terms of an adjustable, general solution rather than a geographically-specific one.

The code presented in the next section is therefore intended to be something to build from and develop. It offers potential as the basis of a successful commercial app or simply a useful, data-driven life hack. With this in mind, review this chapter's content (and leverage the code in the associated code directory) with an eye to finding and creating new applications that fit your own situation, locally available data, and personal needs.

Acquiring data via RESTful APIs

In order to begin, we're going to need to collect some data! We're going to need to look for rich, timestamped data that is captured at sufficient frequency (preferably at least one record per commute period) to enable model training.

A natural place to begin with is the Twitter API, which allows us to harvest recent tweet data. We can put this API to two uses.

Firstly, we can harvest tweets from official transit authorities (specifically, bus and train companies). These companies provide transit service information on delays and service disruptions that, helpfully for us, takes a consistent format conducive to tagging efforts.

Secondly, we can tap into commuter sentiment by listening for tweets from the geographical area of interest, using a customized dictionary to listen for terms related to cases of disruption or the causes thereof.

In addition to mining the Twitter API for data to support our model, we can leverage other APIs to extract a wealth of information. One particularly valuable source of data is the **Bing Traffic API**. This API can be easily called to provide traffic congestion or disruption incidents across a user-specified geographical area.

In addition, we can leverage weather data from the **Yahoo Weather API**. This API provides the current weather for a given location, taking zip codes or location input. It provides a wealth of local climate information including, but not limited to, temperature, wind speed, humidity, atmospheric pressure, and visibility. Additionally, it provides a text string description of current conditions as well as forecast information.

While there are other data sources that we can consider tying into our analysis, we'll begin with this data and see how we do.

Testing the performance of our model

In order to meaningfully assess our commute disruption prediction attempt, we should try to define test criteria and an appropriate performance score.

What we're attempting to do is identify the risk of commute disruption on the current day, each day. Preferably, we'd like to know the commute risk with sufficient advance notice that we can take action to mitigate it (for example, by leaving home earlier).

In order to do this, we're going to need three things:

- An understanding of what our model is going to output
- A measure we can use to quantify model performance
- Some target data we can use to score model performance according to our measure

We can have an interesting discussion about why this matters. It can be argued, effectively, that some models are information in purpose. Our commute risk score, it might be said, is useful insofar as it generates information that we didn't previously have.

The reality of the situation, however, is that there is inalienably going to be a performance criterion. In this case, it might simply be my satisfaction with the results output by my model, but it's important to be aware that there is always some performance criterion at play. Quantifying performance is therefore valuable, even in contexts where a model appears to be informational (or even better, unsupervised). This makes it prudent to resist the temptation to waive performance testing; at least this way, you have a quantified performance measure to iteratively improve on.

A sensible starting point is to assert that our model is intended to output a numerical score in a *0-1* range for outbound (home to work) commutes on a given day. We have a few options with regard to how we present this score; perhaps the most obvious option would be to apply a log rescaling to the data. There are good reasons to log-scale and in this situation it might not be a bad idea. (It's not unlikely that the distribution of commute delay time obeys a power law.) For now, we won't reshape this set of scores. Instead, we'll wait to review the output of our model.

In terms of delivering practical guidance, a *0-1* score isn't necessarily very helpful. We might find ourselves wanting to use a bucketed system (such as high risk, mid risk, or low risk) with bucket boundaries at specific boundaries in the *0-1* range. In short, we would transition to treating the problem as a multiclass classification problem with categorical output (class labels), rather than as a regression problem with a continuous output.

This might improve model performance. (More specifically, because it'll increase the margin of free error to the full breadth of the relevant bucket, which is a very generous performance measure.) Equally though, it probably isn't a great idea to introduce this change on the first iteration. Until we've reviewed the distribution of real commute delays, we won't know where to draw the boundaries between classes!

Next, we need to consider how we measure the performance of our model. The selection of an appropriate scoring measure generally depends on the characteristics of the problem. We're presented with a lot of options around classifier performance scoring. (For more information around performance measures for machine learning algorithms, see the *Further reading* section at the end of this chapter.)

One way of deciding which performance measure is suitable for the task at hand is to consider the confusion matrix. A confusion matrix is a table of contingencies; in the context of statistical modeling, they typically describe the label prediction versus actual labels. It is common to output a confusion matrix (particularly for multiclass problems with more classes) for a trained model as it can yield valuable information about classification failures by failure type and class.

In this context, the reference to a confusion matrix is more illustrative. We can consider the following simplified matrix to assess whether there is any contingency that we don't care about:

		Actual Result	
		TRUE	FALSE
Prediction	TRUE	**True Positive**	**False Positive**
	FALSE	**False Negative**	**True Negative**

In this case, we care about all four contingency types. False negatives will cause us to be caught in unexpected delays, while false positives will cause us to leave for our commute earlier than necessary. This implies that we want a performance measure that values both high sensitivity (true positive rate) and high specificity (false positive rate). The ideal measure, given this, is **area under the curve (AUC)**.

The second challenge is how to measure this score; we need some target against which to predict. Thankfully, this is quite easy to obtain. I do, after all, have a daily commute to do! I simply began self-recording my commute time using a stopwatch, a consistent start time, and a consistent route.

It's important to recognize the limitations of this approach. As a data source, I am subject to my own internal trends. I am, for instance, somewhat sluggish before my morning coffee. Similarly, my own consistent commute route may possess local trends that other routes do not. It would be far better to collect commute data from a number of people and a number of routes.

However, in some ways, I was happy with the use of this target data. Not least because I am attempting to classify disruption to my own commute route and would not want natural variance in my commute time to be misinterpreted through training, say, against targets set by some other group of commuters or routes. In addition, given the anticipated slight natural variability from day-to-day, should be disregarded by a functional model.

It's rather hard to tell what's good enough in terms of model performance. More precisely, it's not easy to know when this model is outperforming my own expectations. Unfortunately, not only do I not have any very reliable with regard to the accuracy of my own commute delay predictions, it also seems unlikely that one person's predictions are generalizable to other commutes in other locations. It seems ill-advised to train a model to exceed a fairly subjective target.

Let's instead attempt to outperform a fairly simple threshold—a model that naively suggests that every single day will not contain commute delays. This target has the rather pleasing property of mirroring our actual behavior (in that we tend to get up each day and act as though there will not be transit disruption).

Of the 85 target data cases, 14 commute delays were observed. Based on this target data and the score measure we created, our target to beat is therefore *0.5*.

Twitter

Given that we're focusing this example analysis on the city of Vancouver, we have an opportunity to tap into a second Twitter data source. Specifically, we can use service announcements from Vancouver's public transit authority, Translink.

Translink Twitter

As noted, this data is already well-structured and conducive both to text mining and subsequent analysis; by processing this data using the techniques we reviewed in the last two chapters, we can clean the text and then encode it into useful features.

We're going to apply the Twitter API to harvest Translink's tweets over an extended period. The Twitter API is a pretty friendly piece of kit that is easy enough to work with from Python. (For extended guidance around how to work with the Twitter API, see the *Further reading* section at the end of this chapter!) In this case, we want to extract the date and body text from the tweet. The body text contains almost everything we need to know, including the following:

- The nature of the tweet (delay or non-delay)
- The station affected
- Some information as to the nature of the delay

One element that adds a little complexity is that the same Translink account tweets service disruption information for Skytrain lines and bus routes. Fortunately, the account is generally very uniform in the terms that it uses to describe service issues for each service type and subject. In particular, the Twitter account uses specific hashtags (**#RiderAlert** for bus route information, **#SkyTrain** for train-related information, and **#TransitAlert** for general alerts across both services, such as statutory holidays) to differentiate the subjects of service disruption.

Similarly, we can expect a delay to always be described using the word delay, a detour by the term detour, and a diversion, using the word diversion. This means that we can filter out unwanted tweets using specific key terms. Nice job, Translink!

The data used in this chapter is provided within the GitHub solution accompanying this chapter in the `translink_tweet_data.json` file. The scraper script is also provided within the chapter code; in order to leverage it, you'll need to set up a developer account with Twitter. This is easy to achieve; the process is documented here and you can sign up here.

Once we've obtained our tweet data, we know what to do next—we need to clean and regularize the body text! As per *Chapter 6, Text Feature Engineering*, let's run BeautifulSoup and NLTK over the input data:

```
from bs4 import BeautifulSoup

tweets = BeautifulSoup(train["TranslinkTweets.text"])

tweettext = tweets.get_text()

brown_a = nltk.corpus.brown.tagged_sents(categories= 'a')

tagger = None
for n in range(1,4):
    tagger = NgramTagger(n, brown_a, backoff = tagger)

taggedtweettext = tagger.tag(tweettext)
```

We probably will not need to be as intensive in our cleaning as we were with the troll dataset in the previous chapter. Translink's tweets are highly formulaic and do not include non-ascii characters or emoticons, so the specific "deep cleaning" regex script that we needed to use in *Chapter 6, Text Feature Engineering*, won't be needed here.

This gives us a dataset with lower-case, regularized, and dictionary-checked terms. We are ready to start thinking seriously about what features we ought to build out of this data.

We know that the base method of detecting a service disruption issue within our data is the use of a delay term in a tweet. Delays happen in the following ways:

- At a given location
- At a given time
- For a given reason
- For a given duration

Each of the first three factors is consistently tracked within Translink tweets, but there are some data quality concerns that are worth recognizing.

Location is given in terms of an affected street or station *at 22nd Street*. This isn't a perfect description for our purpose as we're unlikely to be able to turn a street name and route start/end points into a general *affected area* without doing substantial additional work (as no convenient reference exists that allows us to draw a bounding box based on this information).

Time is imperfectly given by the tweet datetime. While we don't have visibility on whether tweets are made within a consistent time from service disruption, it's likely that Translink has targets around service notification. For now, it's sensible to proceed under the assumption that the tweet times are likely to be sufficiently accurate.

The exception is likely to be for long-running issues or problems that change severity (delays that are expected to be minor but which become significant). In these cases, tweets may be delayed until the Translink team recognizes that the issue has become tweet-worthy. The other possible cause of data quality issues is inconsistency in Translink's internal communications; it's possible that engineering or platform teams don't always inform the customer service notifications team at the same speed.

We're going to have to take a certain amount on faith though, as there isn't a huge amount we can do to measure these delay effects without a dataset of real-time, accurate Translink service delays. (If we had that, we'd be using it instead!)

Reasons for Skytrain service delays are consistently described by Translink and can fall into one of the following categories:

- Rail
- Train
- Switch
- Control
- Unknown
- Intrusion
- Medical
- Police
- Power

With each category described within the tweet body using the specific proper term given in the preceding list. Obviously, some of these categories (Police, Power, Medical) are less likely to be relevant as they wouldn't tell us anything useful about road conditions. The rate of train, track, and switch failure may be correlated with detour likelihood; this suggests that we may want to keep those cases for classification purposes.

Meanwhile, bus route service delays contain a similar set of codes, many of which are very relevant to our purposes. These codes are as follows:

- **Motor Vehicle Accident (MVA)**
- Construction
- Fire
- Watermain
- Traffic

Encoding these incident types is likely to prove useful! In particular, it's possible that certain service delay types are more impactful than others, increasing the risk of a longer service delay. We'll want to encode service delay types and use them as parameters in our subsequent modeling.

To do this, let's apply a variant of one-hot encoding, which does the following:

- It creates a conditional variable for each of the service risk types and sets all values to zero
- It checks tweet content for each of the service risk type terms
- It sets the relevant conditional variable to 1 for each tweet that contains a specific risk term

This effectively performs one-hot encoding without taking the bothersome intermediary step of creating the factorial variable that we'd normally be processing:

```
from sklearn import preprocessing

enc = preprocessing.OneHotEncoder(categorical_features='all', dtype=
'float', handle_unknown='error', n_values='auto', sparse=True)

tweets.delayencode = enc.transform(tweets.delaytype).toarray()
```

Beyond what we have available to use as a feature on a per-incident basis, we can definitely look at the relationship between service disruption risk and disruption frequency. If we see two disruptions in a week, is a third more likely or less likely?

While these questions are interesting and potentially fruitful, it's usually more prudent to work up a limited feature set and simple model on a first pass than to overengineer a sprawling feature set. As such, we'll run with the initial incidence rate features and see where we end up.

Consumer comments

A major cultural development in 2010 was the widespread use of public online domains for self-expression. One of the happier products of this is the availability of a wide array of self-reported information on any number of subjects, provided we know how to tap into this.

Commute disruptions are frequently occurring events that inspire a personal response, which means that they tend to be quite broadly reported on social media. If we write an appropriate dictionary for key-term search, we can begin using Twitter particularly as a source of timestamped information on traffic and transit issues around the city.

In order to collect this data, we'll make use of a dictionary-based search approach. We're not interested in the majority of tweets from the period in question (and as we're using the RESTful API, there are return limits to consider). Instead, we're interested in identifying tweet data containing key terms related to congestion or delay.

Unfortunately, tweets harvested from a broad range of users tend not to conform to consistent styles that aid analysis. We're going to have to apply some of the techniques we developed in the preceding chapter to break down this data into a more easily analyzed format.

In addition to using a dictionary-based search, we could do some work to narrow the search area down. The most authoritative way to achieve this is to use a bounding box of coordinates as an argument to the Twitter API, such that any related query exclusively returns results gathered from within this area.

As always, on our first pass, we'll keep things simple. In this case, we'll count up the number of traffic disruption tweets in the current period. There is some additional work that we could benefit from doing with this data on subsequent iterations. Just as the Translink data contained clearly-defined delay cause categories, we could try to use specialized dictionaries to isolate delay types based on key terms (for example, a dictionary of construction-related terms and synonyms).

We could also look at defining a more nuanced quantification of disruption tweet rate than a simple count of recent. We could, for instance, look at creating a weighted count feature that increases the impact of multiple simultaneous tweets (potentially indicative of severe disruption) via a nonlinear weighting.

The Bing Traffic API

The next API we're going to tap into is the Bing Traffic API. This API has the advantage of being easily accessed; it's freely available (whereas some competitor APIs sit behind paywalls), returns data, and provides a good level of detail. Among other things, the API returns an incident location code, a general description of the incident, together with congestion information, an incident type code, and start/end timestamps.

Helpfully, the incident type codes provided by this API describe a broad set of incident types, as follows:

1. `Accident`.
2. `Congestion`.
3. `DisabledVehicle`.
4. `MassTransit`.
5. `Miscellaneous`.
6. `OtherNews`.
7. `PlannedEvent`.
8. `RoadHazard`.
9. `Construction`.
10. `Alert`.
11. `Weather`.

Additionally, a severity code is provided with the severity values translated as follows:

1. `LowImpact`.
2. `Minor`.
3. `Moderate`.
4. `Serious`.

One downside, however, is that this API doesn't receive consistent information between regions. Querying in France, for instance, returns codes from multiple other incident types, (I observed 1, 3, 5, 8 for a town in northern France over a period of one month.) but doesn't seem to show every code. In other locations, even less data is available. Sadly, Vancouver tends to show data for codes 9 or 5 exclusively, but even the miscellaneous-coded incidents appear to be construction-related:

```
Closed between Victoria Dr and Commercial Dr - Closed. Construction
work. 5
```

This is a somewhat bothersome limitation. Unfortunately, it's not something that we can easily fix; Bing's API is simply not sourcing all of the data that we want! Unless we pay for a more complete dataset (or an API with fuller data capture is available in your area!), we're going to need to keep working with what we have.

An example of querying this API is as follows:

```
importurllib.request, urllib.error, urllib.parse
import json

latN = str(49.310911)
latS = str(49.201444)
lonW = str(-123.225544)
lonE = str(-122.903931)

url = 'http://dev.virtualearth.net/REST/v1/Traffic/Incidents/'
+latS+','+lonW+','+latN+','+lonE+'?
key='GETYOUROWNKEYPLEASE'

response = urllib.request.urlopen(url).read()
data = json.loads(response.decode('utf8'))
resources = data['resourceSets'][0]['resources']

print('-------------------------------------------------')
print('PRETTIFIED RESULTS')
print('-------------------------------------------------')
for resourceItem in resources:
    description = resourceItem['description']
typeof = resourceItem['type']
    start = resourceItem['start']
    end = resourceItem['end']
print('description:', description);
print('type:', typeof);
print('starttime:', start);
print('endtime:', end);
print('-------------------------------------------------')



This example yields the following data;


-------------------------------------------------

PRETTIFIED RESULTS
-------------------------------------------------
description: Closed between Boundary Rd and PierviewCres - Closed due
to roadwork.
```

```
type: 9
severity 4
starttime: /Date(1458331200000)/
endtime: /Date(1466283600000)/
-----------------------------------------------------
description: Closed between Commercial Dr and Victoria Dr - Closed due
to roadwork.
type: 9
severity 4
starttime: /Date(1458327600000)/
endtime: /Date(1483218000000)/
-----------------------------------------------------
description: Closed between Victoria Dr and Commercial Dr - Closed.
Construction work.
type: 5
severity 4
starttime: /Date(1461780543000)/
endtime: /Date(1481875140000)/
-----------------------------------------------------
description: At Thurlow St - Roadwork.
type: 9
severity 3
starttime: /Date(1461780537000)/
endtime: /Date(1504112400000)/
-----------------------------------------------------
```

Even after recognizing the shortcomings of uneven code availability across different geographical areas, the data from this API should provide us with some value. Having a partial picture of traffic disruption incidents still gives us data for a reasonable period of dates. The ability to localize traffic incidents within an area of our own definition and returning data relevant to the current date is likely to help the performance of our model.

Deriving and selecting variables using feature engineering techniques

On our first pass over the input data, we repeatedly made the choice to keep our initial feature set small. Though we saw lots of opportunities in the data, we prioritized viewing an initial result above following up on those opportunities.

It is likely, however, that our first dataset won't help us solve the problem very effectively or hit our targets. In this event, we'll need to iterate over our feature set, both by creating new features and winnowing our feature set to reduce down to the valuable outputs of that feature creation process.

One helpful example involves one-hot encoding and RFE. In this chapter, we'll use one-hot to turn weather data and tweet dictionaries into tensors of m*n size. Having produced m-many new columns of data, we'll want to reduce the liability of our model to be misled by some of these new features (for instance, in cases where multiple features reinforce the same signal or where misleading but commonly-used terms are not cleaned out by the data cleaning processes we described in *Chapter 6, Text Feature Engineering*). This can be done very effectively by RFE, the technique for feature selection that we discussed earlier in this chapter.

In general, it can be helpful to work using a methodology that applies the techniques seen in the last two chapters using an expand-contract process. First, use techniques that can generate potentially valuable new features, such as transformations and encodings, to expand the feature set. Then, use techniques that can identify the most performant subset of those features to remove the features that do not perform well. Throughout this process, test different target feature counts to identify the best available feature set at different numbers of features.

Some data scientists interpret how this is done differently from others. Some will build all of their features using repeated iterations over the feature creation techniques we've discussed, then reduce that feature set — the motivation being that this workflow minimizes the risk of losing data. Others will perform the full process iteratively. How you choose to do this is entirely up to you!

On our initial pass over the input data, then, we have a feature set that looks as follows:

```
{
  'DisruptionInformation': {
    'Date': '15-05-2015',
    'TranslinkTwitter': [{
      'Service': '0',
      'DisruptionIncidentCount': '4'
    }, {
      'Service': '1',
      'DisruptionIncidentCount': '0'
    }]
  },
  'BingTrafficAPI': {
    'NewIncidentCount': '1',
    'SevereIncidentCount': '1',
    'IncidentCount': '3'
  },
  'ConsumerTwitter': {
    'DisruptionTweetCount': '4'
  }
}
```

It's unlikely that this dataset is going to perform well. All the same, let's run it through a basic initial algorithm and get a general idea as to how near our target we are; this way, we can learn quickly with minimal overhead!

In the interest of expedience, let's begin by running a first pass using a very simple regression algorithm. The simpler the technique, the faster we can run it (and often, the more transparent it is to us what went wrong and why). For this reason (and because we're dealing with a regression problem with a continuous output rather than a classification problem), on a first pass we'll work with a simple linear regression model:

```
from sklearn import linear_model

tweets_X_train = tweets_X[:-20]
tweets_X_test = tweets_X[-20:]


tweets_y_train = tweets.target[:-20]
tweets_y_test = tweets.target[-20:]

regr = linear_model.LinearRegression()

regr.fit(tweets_X_train, tweets_y_train)

print('Coefficients: \n', regr.coef_)
print("Residual sum of squares: %.2f" % np.mean((regr.
predict(tweets_X_test) - tweets_y_test) ** 2))

print('Variance score: %.2f' % regr.score(tweets_X_test, tweets_y_
test))

plt.scatter(tweets_X_test, tweets_y_test,  color='black')
plt.plot(tweets_X_test, regr.predict(tweets_X_test),
color='blue',linewidth=3)

plt.xticks(())
plt.yticks(())
plt.show()
```

At this point, our AUC is pretty lousy; we're looking at a model with an AUC of 0.495. We're actually doing worse than our target! Let's print out a confusion matrix to see what this model's doing wrong:

		Prediction	
		TRUE	FALSE
Actual Result	TRUE	1	9
	FALSE	18	136

According to this matrix, it's doing everything not very well. In fact, it's claiming that almost all of the records show no incidents, to the extent of missing 90% of real disruptions!

This actually isn't too bad at all, given the early stage that we're at with our model and our features, as well as the uncertain utility of some of our input data. At the same time, we should expect an incidence rate of 6% (as our training data suggests that incidents have been seen to occur roughly once every 16 commutes). We'd still be doing a little better by guessing that every day will involve a disrupted commute (if we ignore the penalty to our lifestyle entailed by leaving home early each day).

Let's consider what changes we could make in a next pass.

1. First off, we could stand to improve our input data further. We identified a number of new features that we could create from existing sources using a range of transformation techniques.

2. Secondly, we could look at extending our dataset using additional information. In particular, a weather dataset describing both temperature and humidity may help us improve our model.

3. Finally, we could upgrade our algorithm to something with a little more grunt, random forests or SVM being obvious examples. There are good reasons not to do this just yet. The main reason is that we can continue to learn a lot from linear regression; we can compare against earlier results to understand how much value our changes are adding, while retaining a fast iteration loop and simple scoring methods. Once we begin to get minimal returns on our feature preparation, we should consider upgrading our model.

For now, we'll continue to upgrade our dataset. We have a number of options here. We can encode location into both traffic incident data from the Bing API's "description" field and into Translink's tweets. In the case of Translink, this is likely to be more usefully done for bus routes than Skytrain routes (given that we restricted the scope of this analysis to focus solely on traffic commutes).

We can achieve this goal in one of two ways;

- Using a corpus of street names/locations, we can parse the input data and build a one-hot matrix
- We can simply run one-hot encoding over the entire body of tweets and entire set of API data

Interestingly, if we intend to use dimensionality reduction techniques after performing one-hot encoding, we can encode the entire body of both pieces of text information without any significant problems. If features relating to the other words used in tweets and text are not relevant, they'll simply be scrubbed out during RFE.

This is a slightly laissez-faire approach, but there is a subtle advantage. Namely, if there is some other potentially useful content to either data source that we've so far overlooked as a potential feature, this process will yield the added benefit of creating features based on that information.

Let's encode locations in the same way we encoded delay types:

```
from sklearn import preprocessing

enc = preprocessing.OneHotEncoder(categorical_features='all', dtype=
'float', handle_unknown='error', n_values='auto', sparse=True)

tweets.delayencode = enc.transform(tweets.location).toarray()
```

Additionally, we should follow up on our intention to create recent count variables from Translink and Bing maps incident logging. The code for this aggregation is available in the GitHub repository accompanying this chapter!

Rerunning our model with this updated data produced results with a very slight improvement; the predicted variance score rose to 0.56. While not dramatic, this is definitely a step in the right direction.

Next, let's follow up on our second option—adding a new data source that provides weather data.

The weather API

We've previously grabbed data that will help us tell whether commute disruption is happening—reactive data sources that identify existing delays. We're going to change things up a little now, by trying to find data that relates to the causes of delays and congestion. Roadworks and construction information definitely falls into this category (along with some of the other Bing Traffic API codes).

One factor that is often (anecdotally!) tied to increased commute time is bad weather. Sometimes this is pretty obvious; heavy frost or high winds have a clear impact on commute time. In many other cases, though, it's not clear what the strength and nature of the relationship between climatic factors and disruption likelihood is for a given commute.

By extracting pertinent weather data from a source with sufficient granularity and geo coverage, we can hopefully use strong weather signals to help improve our correct prediction of disruption.

For our purposes, we'll use the Yahoo Weather API, which provides a range of temperature, atmospheric, pressure-related, and other climate data, both current and forecasted. We can query the Yahoo Weather API without needing a key or login process, as follows:

```
import urllib2, urllib, json

baseurl = https://query.yahooapis.com/v1/public/yql?

yql_query = "select item.condition from weather.forecast where woeid=9807"
yql_url = baseurl + urllib.urlencode({'q':yql_query}) + "&format=json"
result = urllib2.urlopen(yql_url).read()
data = json.loads(result)
print data['query']['results']
```

To get an understanding for what the API can provide, replace `item.condition` (in what is fundamentally an embedded SQL query) with *. This query outputs a lot of information, but digging through it reveals valuable information, including the current conditions:

```
{
    'channel': {
      'item': {
        'condition': {
            'date': 'Thu, 14 May 2015 03:00 AM PDT', 'text': 'Cloudy',
    'code': '26', 'temp': '46'
        }
      }
    }
}
```

7-day forecasts containing the following information:

```
{
    'item': {
      'forecast': {
        'code': '39', 'text': 'Scattered Showers', 'high': '60',
'low': '44', 'date': '16 May 2015', 'day': 'Sat'
      }
    }
}
```

And other current weather information:

```
'astronomy': {
    'sunset': '8:30 pm', 'sunrise': '5:36 am'

  'wind': {
    'direction':  '270', 'speed': '4', 'chill': '46'
```

For the purpose of building a training dataset, we extracted data on a daily basis via an automated script that ran from May 2015 to January 2016. The forecasts may not be terribly useful to us as it's likely that our model will rerun over current data on a daily basis rather than being dependent on forecasts. However, we will definitely make use of the `wind.direction`, `wind.speed`, and `wind.chill` variables, as well as the `condition.temperature` and `condition.text` variables.

In terms of how to further process this information, one option jumps to mind. One-hot encoding of weather tags would enable us to use weather condition information as categorical variables, just as we did in the preceding chapter. This seems like a necessary step to take. This significantly inflates our feature set, leaving us with the following data:

```
{
  'DisruptionInformation': {
    'Date': '15-05-2015',
    'TranslinkTwitter': [{
      'Service': '0',
      'DisruptionIncidentCount': '4'
    }, {
      'Service': '1',
      'DisruptionIncidentCount': '0'
    }]
  },
  'BingTrafficAPI': {
    'NewIncidentCount': '1',
    'SevereIncidentCount': '1',
```

```
      'IncidentCount': '3'
    },
    'ConsumerTwitter': {
      'DisruptionTweetCount': '4'
    },
    'YahooWeather':{
      'temp: '45'
      'tornado': '0',
      'tropical storm': '0',
      'hurricane': '0',
      'severe thunderstorms': '0',
      'thunderstorms': '0',
      'mixed rain and snow': '0',
      'mixed rain and sleet': '0',
      'mixed snow and sleet': '0',
  'freezing drizzle': '0',
  'drizzle': '0',
  'freezing rain': '0',
  'showers': '0',
  'snow flurries': '0',
  'light snow showers': '0',
  'blowing snow': '0',
  'snow': '0',
  'hail': '0',
  'sleet': '0',
  'dust': '0',
  'foggy': '0',
  'haze': '0',
  'smoky': '0',
  'blustery': '0',
  'windy': '0',
  'cold': '0',
  'cloudy': '1',
  'mostly cloudy (night)': '0',
  'mostly cloudy (day)': '0',
  'partly cloudy (night)': '0',
  'partly cloudy (day)': '0',
  'clear (night)': '0',
  'sunny': '0',
  'fair (night)': '0',
  'fair (day)': '0',
  'mixed rain and hail': '0',
  'hot': '0',
  'isolated thunderstorms': '0',
```

```
'scattered thunderstorms': '0',
'scattered showers': '0',
'heavy snow': '0',
'scattered snow showers': '0',
'partly cloudy': '0',
'thundershowers': '0',
'snow showers': '0',
'isolated thundershowers': '0',
'not available': '0',
}
```

It's very likely that a lot of time could be valuably sunk into further enriching the weather data provided by the Yahoo Weather API. For the first pass, as always, we'll remain focused on building a model that takes the features that we described previously.

It's definitely worth considering how we would do further work with this data. In this case, it's important to distinguish between cross-column data transformations and cross-row transformations.

A cross-column transformation is one where variables from different features in the same input case were transformed based on one another. For instance, we might take the start date and end date of a case and use it to calculate the duration. Interestingly, the majority of the techniques that we've studied in this book won't gain a lot from many such transformations. Most machine learning techniques capable of drawing nonlinear decision boundaries tend to encode relationships between variables in their modeling of a dataset. Deep learning techniques often take this capability a step further. This is part of the reason that some feature engineering techniques (particularly basic transformations) add less value for deep learning applications.

Meanwhile, a cross-row transformation is typically an aggregation. The central tendency of the last n-many duration values, for instance, is a feature that can be derived by an operation over multiple rows. Naturally, some features can be derived by a combination of column-wise and row-wise operations. The interesting thing about cross-row transformations is that it's usually quite unlikely that a model will train to recognize them, meaning that they tend to continue to add value in very particular contexts.

The reason that this information is relevant, of course, is that recent weather is a context in which features derived from cross-row operations might add new information to our model. Change in barometric pressure or temperature over the last n hours, for instance, might be a more useful variable than the current pressure or temperature. (Particularly, when that our model is intended to predict commutes to take place later in the same day!)

The next step is to rerun our model. This time, our AUC is a little higher; we're scoring *0.534*. Looking at our confusion matrix, we're also seeing improvements:

		Prediction	
		TRUE	FALSE
Actual Result	TRUE	3	7
	FALSE	22	132

If the issues are linked to weather factors, continuing to pull weather data is a good idea; setting this solution up to run over an extended period will gradually gather longitudinal inputs from each source, gradually giving us much more reliable predictions.

At this point, we're only a short distance away from our MVP target. We can continue to extend our input dataset, but the smart solution is to find another way to approach the problem. There are two actions that we can meaningfully take.

Being human, data scientists tend to think in terms of simplifying assumptions. One of these that crops up quite frequently is basically an application of the Pareto principle to cost/benefit analysis decisions. Fundamentally, the Pareto principle states that for many events, roughly 80% of the value or effect comes from roughly 20% of the input effort, or cause, obeying what's referred to as a Pareto distribution. This concept is very popular in software engineering contexts among others, as it can guide efficiency improvements.

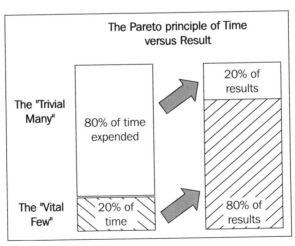

To apply this theory to the current case, we know that we could spend more time finessing our feature engineering. There are techniques that we haven't applied and other features that we could create. However, at the same time, we know that there are entire areas that we haven't touched: external data searches and model changes, particularly, which we could quickly try. It makes sense to explore these cheap but potentially impactful options on our next pass before digging into additional dataset preparation.

During our exploratory analysis, we noticed that some of our variables are quite sparse. It wasn't immediately clear how helpful they all were (particularly for stations where fewer incidents of a given type occurred).

Let's test out our variable set using some of the techniques that we worked with earlier in the chapter. In particular, let's apply `Lasso` to the problem of reducing our feature set to a performant subset:

```
fromsklearn.preprocessing import StandardScaler


scaler = StandardScaler()
X = scaler.fit_transform(DisruptionInformation["data"])
Y = DisruptionInformation["target"]
names = DisruptionInformation["feature_names"]

lasso = Lasso(alpha=.3)
lasso.fit(X, Y)

print "Lasso model: ", pretty_print_linear(lasso.coef_, names, sort =
True)
```

This output is immediately valuable. It's obvious that many of the weather features (either through not showing up sufficiently often or not telling us anything useful when they do) are adding nothing to our model and should be removed. In addition, we're not getting a lot of value from our traffic aggregates. While these can remain in for the moment (in the hope that gathering more data will improve their usefulness), for our next pass we'll rerun our model without the poorly-scoring features that our use of LASSO has revealed.

There is one fairly cheap additional change, which we ought to make: we should upgrade our model to one that can fit nonlinearly and thus can fit to approximate any function. This is worth doing because, as we observed, some of our features showed a range of skewed distributions indicative of a nonlinear underlying trend. Let's apply a random forest to this dataset:

```
fromsklearn.ensemble import RandomForestClassifier,
ExtraTreesClassifier
rf = RandomForestRegressor(n_jobs = 3, verbose = 3, n_estimators=20)
rf.fit(DisruptionInformation_train.targets,DisruptionInformation_
train.data)

r2 = r2_score(DisruptionInformation.data, rf.predict(DisruptionInforma
tion.targets))
mse = np.mean((DisruptionInformation.data - rf.predict(DisruptionInfor
mation.targets))**2)

pl.scatter(DisruptionInformation.data, rf.predict(DisruptionInformati
on.targets))
pl.plot(np.arange(8, 15), np.arange(8, 15), label="r^2=" + str(r2),
c="r")
pl.legend(loc="lower right")
pl.title("RandomForest Regression with scikit-learn")
pl.show()
```

Let's return again to our confusion matrix:

		Prediction	
		TRUE	FALSE
Actual Result	TRUE	4	6
	FALSE	15	134

At this point, we're doing fairly well. A simple upgrade to our model has yielded significant improvements, with our model correctly identifying almost 40% of commute delay incidents (enough to start to be useful to us!), while misclassifying a small amount of cases.

Frustratingly, this model would still be getting us out of bed early incorrectly more times than it would correctly. The gold standard, of course, would be if it were predicting more commute delays than it was causing false (early) starts! We could reasonably hope to achieve this target if we continue to gather feature data over a sustained period; the main weakness of this model is that it has very few cases to sample from, given the rarity of commute disruption events.

We have, however, succeeded in gathering and marshaling a range of data from different sources in order to create a model from freely-available data that yields a recognizable, real-world benefit (reducing the amount of late arrivals at work by 40%). This is definitely an achievement to be happy with!

Further reading

My suggested go-to introduction to feature selection is Ando Sabaas' four-part exploration of a broad range of feature selection techniques. It's full of Python code snippets and informed commentary. Get started at `http://blog.datadive.net/selecting-good-features-part-i-univariate-selection/`.

For a discussion on feature selection and engineering that ranges across materials in chapters 6 and 7, consider Alexandre Bourhard-Côté's slides at `http://people.eecs.berkeley.edu/~jordan/courses/294-fall09/lectures/feature/slides.pdf`. Also consider reviewing Jeff Howbert's slides at `http://courses.washington.edu/css490/2012.Winter/lecture_slides/05a_feature_creation_selection.pdf`.

There is a shortage of thorough discussion of feature creation, with a lot of available material discussing either dimensionality reduction techniques or very specific feature creation as required in specific domains. One way to get a more general understanding of the range of possible transformations is to read code documentation. A decent place to build on your existing knowledge is Spark ML's feature-transformation algorithm documentation at `https://spark.apache.org/docs/1.5.1/ml-features.html#feature-transformers`, which describes a broad set of possible transformations on numerical and text features. Remember, though, that feature creation is often problem-specific, domain-specific, and a highly creative process. Once you've learned a range of technical options, the trick is in figuring out how to apply these techniques to the problem at hand!

For readers with an interest in hyperparameter optimization, I recommend that you read Alice Zheng's posts on Turi's blog as a great place to start: `http://blog.turi.com/how-to-evaluate-machine-learning-models-part-4-hyperparameter-tuning`.

I also find the scikit-learn documentation to be a useful reference for grid search specifically: `http://scikit-learn.org/stable/modules/grid_search.html`.

Summary

In this chapter, you learned and applied a set of techniques that enable us to effectively build and finesse datasets for machine learning, starting from very little initial data. These powerful techniques enable a data scientist to turn seemingly shallow datasets into opportunities. We demonstrated this power using a set of customer service tweets to create a travel disruption predictor.

In order to take that solution into production, though, we'd need to add some functionality. Removing some locations in the penultimate step was a questionable decision; if this solution is intended to identify journey disruption risk, then removing locations seems like a non-starter! This is particularly true given that we do not have year-round data and so cannot identify the effect of seasonal or longitudinal trends (like extended maintenance works or a scheduled station closure). We were a little hasty in removing these elements and a better solution would be to retain them for a longer period.

Following on from these concerns, we should recognize the need to start building some dynamism into our solution. When spring rolls around and our dataset starts to contain new climate conditions, it is entirely likely that our model will fail to adapt as effectively. In the next chapter, we will be looking at building more sophisticated model ensembles and discuss methods of building robustness into your model solutions.

8
Ensemble Methods

As we progressed through the earlier chapters of this book, you learned how to apply a number of new techniques. We developed our use of several advanced machine learning algorithms and acquired a broad range of companion techniques used to enhance your use of learning techniques via more effective feature selection and preparation. This chapter seeks to enhance your existing technique set using ensemble methods: techniques that bind multiple different models together to solve a real-world problem.

Ensemble techniques have become a fundamental part of the data scientist's toolset. The use of ensembles has become common practice in competitive machine learning contexts, and ensembles are now considered an indispensable tool in many contexts. The techniques that we'll develop in this chapter give our models an edge in performance, while increasing their robustness to underlying data change.

We'll examine a series of ensembling options, discussing both the code and application of these techniques. We'll color this explanation with guidance and reference to real-world applications, including the models created by successful Kagglers.

The development of any of the models that we reviewed in this title allows us to solve a wide range of data problems, but applying our models to production contexts raises an additional set of problems. Our solutions are still vulnerable to changes in the underlying observations. Whether this is expressed in a different population of individuals, in temporal variations (for example, seasonal changes in the phenomenon being captured) or by other changes to the underlying conditions, the end result is often the same—the models that worked well in the conditions they were trained against are frequently unable to generalize and continue to perform well as time passes.

The final section of this chapter describes methodologies to transfer the techniques from this book to operational environments and the kinds of additional monitoring and support you should consider if your intended applications have to be resilient to change.

Introducing ensembles

> *"This is how you win ML competitions: you take other peoples' work and ensemble them together."*
>
> *– Vitaly Kuznetsov NIPS2014*

In the context of machine learning, an ensemble is a set of models that is used to solve a shared problem. An ensemble is made up of two components: a set of models and a set of decision rules that govern how the results of those models are combined into a single output.

Ensembles offer a data scientist the ability to construct multiple solutions for a given problem and then combine these into a single final result that draws from the best elements of each input solution. This provides robustness against noise, which is reflected in more effective training against an initial dataset (leading to lower levels of overfitting and reductions in training error) and against data change of the kinds discussed in the preceding section.

It is no exaggeration to say that ensembles are the most important recent development in machine learning.

In addition, ensembles enable greater flexibility in how one solves for a given problem, in that they enable the data scientist to test different parts of a solution and resolve issues specific to subsets of the input data or parts of the models in use, without completely retuning the whole model. As we'll see, this can make life easier!

Ensembles are typically considered as falling into one of several classes, based on the nature of the decision rules used. The key ensemble types are as follows:

- **Averaging methods**: They develop models in parallel and then use averaging or voting techniques to develop a combined estimator
- **Stacking (or Blending) methods**: They use the weighted output of multiple classifiers as inputs to a next-layer model
- **Boosting methods**: They involve building models in sequence where each added model aims to improve the score of the combined estimator

Given the importance and utility of both of these classes of the ensemble method, we'll treat each one in turn: discussing theory, algorithm options, and real-world examples.

Understanding averaging ensembles

Averaging ensembles have a long and rich history in the physical sciences and statistical modeling, seeing a common application in many contexts including molecular dynamics and audio signal processing. Such ensembles are typically seen as almost exactly replicated cases of a given system. The average (mean) values of and variance between cases in this system are key values for the system as a whole.

In a machine learning context, an averaging ensemble is a collection of models that train on the same dataset, whose results are aggregated in a range of ways. Depending on implementation goals, an averaging ensemble can bring several benefits.

Averaging ensembles can be used to reduce the variability of a model's performance. One common method involves creating multiple model configurations that take different parameter subsets as input. Techniques that take this approach are referred to collectively as bagging algorithms.

Using bagging algorithms

Different bagging implementations will operate differently but share the common property of taking random subsets of the feature space. There are four main types of the bagging approach. Pasting draws random subsets of the samples without replacement. When this is done with replacement, then the approach is simply called **bagging**. Pasting is typically computationally cheaper than bagging and can yield similar results in simpler applications.

When samples are taken feature-wise, the method is known as **random subspaces**. Random subspace methods provide a slightly different capability; they essentially reduce the need for extensive, highly optimized feature selection. Where such activities typically lead to a single model with optimized input, random subspaces allow the use of multiple configurations in parallel, with a flattening of the variance of any one solution.

While the use of an ensemble to reduce the variability in model performance may sound like a performance hit (the natural response might be but why not just pick the single best performing model in the ensemble?), there are big advantages to this approach.

Firstly, as discussed, averaging improves the ability of your model set to adapt to unfamiliar noise (that is, it reduces overfitting). Secondly, an ensemble can be used to target different elements of the input dataset to model effectively. This is a common approach in competitive machine learning contexts, where a data scientist will iteratively adjust the ensemble based on the results of classification and particular types of failure cases. In some cases, this is an exhaustive process involving the inspection of model results (commonly as part of a normal, iterative model development process) but many data scientists prefer techniques or a solution that they will implement first.

Random subspaces can be a very powerful approach, particularly if it's possible to use multiple subspace sizes and exhaustively check feature combinations. The cost of random subspace methods increases nonlinearly with the size of your dataset and, beyond a certain point, it will become costly to test every configuration of parameters for multiple subspace sizes.

Finally, an ensemble's estimators may be created from subsets drawn from both samples and features, in a method known as **random patches**. On a like-for-like case, the performance of random patches is usually around the same level as that of random subspace techniques with significantly reduced memory consumption.

As we've discussed the theory behind bagging ensembles, let's look at how we go about implementing one. The following code describes a random patches classifier implemented using sklearn's `BaggingClassifier` class:

```
from sklearn.cross_validation import cross_val_score
from sklearn.ensemble import BaggingClassifier
from sklearn.neighbors import KNeighborsClassifier
from sklearn.datasets import load_digits
from sklearn.preprocessing import scale

digits = load_digits()
data = scale(digits.data)
X = data
y = digits.target


bagging = BaggingClassifier(KNeighborsClassifier(), max_samples=0.5,
max_features=0.5)
scores = cross_val_score(bagging, X, y)
```

```
mean = scores.mean()
print(scores)
print(mean)
```

As with many sklearn classifiers, the core code needed is very straightforward; the classifier is initialized and used to score the dataset. Cross-validation (via `cross_val_score`) adds no meaningful complexity.

This bagging classifier used a **K-Nearest Neighbors** (**KNN**) classifier (`KNeighboursClassifier`) as a base, with feature-wise and case-wise sampling rates each set to 50%. This outputs very strong results against the digits dataset, correctly classifying a mean of 93% of cases after cross-validation:

```
[ 0.94019934  0.92320534  0.9295302 ]


0.930978293043
```

Using random forests

An alternative set of averaging ensemble techniques is referred to collectively as random forests. Perhaps the most successful ensemble technique used by competitive data scientists, random forests develop parallel sets of decision tree classifiers. By introducing two main sources of randomness to the classifier construction, the forest ends up containing diverse trees. The data that is used to build each tree is sampled with replacement from the training set, while the tree creation process no longer uses the best split from all features, instead choosing the best split from a random subset of the features.

Random forests can be easily called using the `RandomForestClassifier` class in `sklearn`. For a simple example, consider the following:

```
import numpy as np
from sklearn.ensemble import RandomForestClassifier
from sklearn.datasets import load_digits
from sklearn.preprocessing import scale

digits = load_digits()
data = scale(digits.data)

n_samples, n_features = data.shape
n_digits = len(np.unique(digits.target))
labels = digits.target

clf = RandomForestClassifier(n_estimators=10)
```

```
clf = clf.fit(data, labels)
scores = clf.score(data,labels)
print(scores)
```

The scores output by this ensemble, 0.999, are difficult to beat. Indeed, we haven't seen performance at this level from any of the individual models we employed in preceding chapters.

A variant of random forests, called **extremely randomized trees (ExtraTrees)**, uses the same random subset of features method in selecting the best split at each branch in the tree. However, it also randomizes the discrimination threshold; where a decision tree normally chooses the most effective split between classes, ExtraTrees split at a random value.

Due to the relatively efficient training of decision trees, a random forest algorithm can potentially support a large number of varied trees with the effectiveness of the classifier improving as the number of nodes increases. The randomness introduced provides a degree of robustness to noise or data change; like the bagging algorithms we reviewed earlier, however, this gain typically comes at the cost of a slight drop in performance. In the case of ExtraTrees, the robustness may increase further while the performance measure improves (typically a bias value reduces).

The following code describes how ExtraTrees work in practice. As with our random subspace implementation, the code is very straightforward. In this case, we'll develop a set of models to compare how ExtraTrees shape up against tree and random forest approaches:

```
from sklearn.cross_validation import cross_val_score
from sklearn.ensemble import RandomForestClassifier
from sklearn.ensemble import ExtraTreesClassifier
from sklearn.tree import DecisionTreeClassifier
from sklearn.datasets import load_digits
from sklearn.preprocessing import scale

digits = load_digits()
data = scale(digits.data)
X = data
y = digits.target

clf = DecisionTreeClassifier(max_depth=None, min_samples_split=1,
    random_state=0)
scores = cross_val_score(clf, X, y)
print(scores)

clf = RandomForestClassifier(n_estimators=10, max_depth=None,
```

```
      min_samples_split=1, random_state=0)
  scores = cross_val_score(clf, X, y)
  print(scores)


  clf = ExtraTreesClassifier(n_estimators=10, max_depth=None,
      min_samples_split=1, random_state=0)
  scores = cross_val_score(clf, X, y)
  print(scores)
```

The scores, respectively, are as follows:

```
[ 0.74252492   0.82136895   0.75671141]
[ 0.88372093   0.9015025    0.8909396 ]
[ 0.91694352   0.93489149   0.91778523]
```

Given that we're working with entirely tree-based methods here, the score is simply the proportion of correctly-labeled cases. We can see here that there isn't much in it between the two forest methods, which both perform strongly with mean scores of *0.9*. In this example, random forest actually wins out marginally (on the order of an *0.002* increase) over ExtraTrees, while both techniques substantially outperform the basic decision tree, whose mean score sits at *0.77*.

One drawback when working with random forests (especially as the size of the forest increases) is that it can be hard to review the effectiveness of, or tune, a given implementation. While individual trees are extremely easy to work with, the sheer number of trees in a developed ensemble and the obfuscation created by random splitting can make it challenging to refine a random forest implementation. One option is to begin looking at the decision boundaries that individual models draw. By contrasting the models within one's ensemble, it becomes easier to identify where one model performs better at dividing classes than others.

In this example, for instance, we can easily see how our models perform at a high level without digging into specific details:

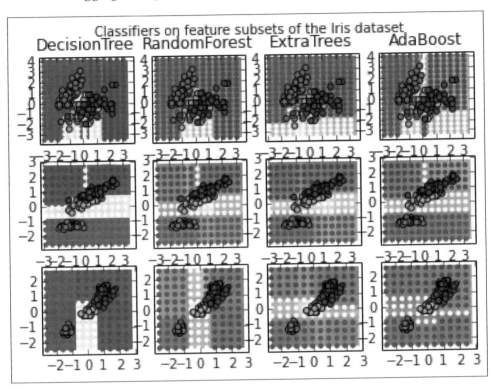

While it can be challenging to understand beyond a simple level (using high-level plots and summary scores) how a random forest implementation is performing, the hardship is worthwhile. Random forests perform very strongly with only a minimal cost in additional computation. They are very often a good technique to throw at a problem during the early stages, while one is still determining an angle of attack, because their ability to yield strong results fast can provide a useful benchmark. Once you know how a random forest implementation performs, you can begin to optimize and extend your ensemble.

To this end, we should continue exploring the different ensemble techniques so as to further build out our toolkit of ensembling options.

Applying boosting methods

Another approach to ensemble creation is to build boosting models. These models are characterized by their use of multiple models in sequence to iteratively "boost" or improve the performance of the ensemble.

Boosting models frequently use a series of weak learners, models that provide only marginal gain compared to random guessing. At each iteration, a new weak learner is trained on an adjusted dataset. Over multiple iterations, the ensemble is extended with one new tree (whichever tree optimized the ensemble performance score) at each iteration.

Perhaps the most well-known boosting method is **AdaBoost**, which adjusts the dataset at each iteration by performing the following actions:

- Selecting a decision stump (a shallow, often one-level decision tree, effectively the most significant decision boundary for the dataset in question)

- Increasing the weighting of cases that the decision stump labeled incorrectly, while reducing the weighting of correctly labeled cases

This iterative weight adjustment causes each new classifier in the ensemble to prioritize training the incorrectly labeled cases; the model adjusts by targeting highly-weighted data points. Eventually, the stumps are combined to form a final classifier.

AdaBoost can be used both in classification and regression contexts and achieves impressive results. The following example shows an AdaBoost implementation in action on the `heart` dataset:

```
import numpy as np

from sklearn.tree import DecisionTreeClassifier
from sklearn.ensemble import AdaBoostClassifier
from sklearn.datasets.mldata import fetch_mldata
from sklearn.cross_validation import cross_val_score

n_estimators = 400
# A learning rate of 1. may not be optimal for both SAMME and SAMME.R
learning_rate = 1.

heart = fetch_mldata("heart")
X = heart.data
y = np.copy(heart.target)
```

```
y[y==-1]=0

X_test, y_test = X[189:], y[189:]
X_train, y_train = X[:189], y[:189]

dt_stump = DecisionTreeClassifier(max_depth=1, min_samples_leaf=1)
dt_stump.fit(X_train, y_train)
dt_stump_err = 1.0 - dt_stump.score(X_test, y_test)

dt = DecisionTreeClassifier(max_depth=9, min_samples_leaf=1)
dt.fit(X_train, y_train)
dt_err = 1.0 - dt.score(X_test, y_test)

ada_discrete = AdaBoostClassifier(
    base_estimator=dt_stump,
    learning_rate=learning_rate,
    n_estimators=n_estimators,
    algorithm="SAMME")
ada_discrete.fit(X_train, y_train)

scores = cross_val_score(ada_discrete, X_test, y_test)
print(scores)
means = scores.mean()
print(means)
```

In this case, the `n_estimators` parameter dictates the number of weak learners used; in the case of averaging methods, adding estimators will always reduce the bias of your model, but will increase the probability that your model has overfit its training data. The `base_estimator` parameter can be used to define different weak learners; the default is decision trees (as training a weak tree is straightforward, one can use stumps, very shallow trees). When applied to the `heart` dataset, as in this example, AdaBoost achieved correct labeling in just over 79% of cases, a reasonably solid performance for a first pass:

```
[ 0.77777778  0.81481481  0.77777778]
```

```
0.79012345679
```

Boosting models provide a significant advantage over averaging models; they make it much easier to create an ensemble that identifies problem cases or types of problem cases and address them. A boosting model will usually target the easiest to predict cases first, with each added model fitting against a subset of the remaining incorrectly predicted cases.

One resulting risk is that a boosting model begins to overfit (in the most extreme case, you can imagine ensemble components that have fit to specific cases!) the training data. Managing the correct amount of ensemble components is a tricky problem but thankfully we can resort to a familiar technique to resolve it. In *Chapter 1, Unsupervised Machine Learning*, we discussed a visual heuristic called the **elbow method**. In that case, the plot was of K (the number of means), against a performance measure for the clustering implementation. In this case, we can employ an analogous process using the number of estimators (n) and the bias or error rate for the ensemble (which we'll call e). For a range of different boosting estimators, we can plot their outputs as follows:

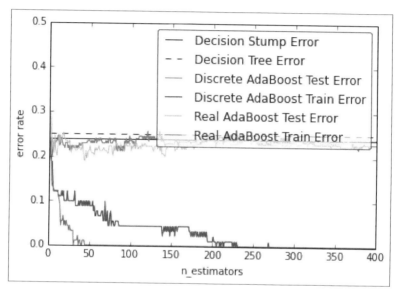

By identifying a point at which the curve has begun to level off, we can reduce the risk that our model has overfit, which becomes increasingly likely as the curve begins to level off. This is true for the simple reason that as the curve levels, it necessarily means that the added gains from each new estimator are the correct classification of fewer and fewer cases!

Part of the appeal of a visual aid of this kind is that it enables us to get a feel for how likely our solution is to be overfitting. We can (and should!) be applying validation techniques wherever we can, but in some cases (for example, when aiming to hit a particular MVP target for a model implementation, whether that be informed by use cases or the distribution of scores on the Kaggle public leaderboard), we may be tempted to press forward with a performant implementation. Understanding exactly how attenuated the gains we're receiving are as we add each new estimator is critical to understanding the risk of overfitting.

Using XGBoost

In mid-2015, a new algorithm to solve structured machine learning problems, XGboost, has taken the competitive data science world by storm. **Extreme Gradient Boosting (XGBoost)** is a well-written, performant library that provides a generalized boosting algorithm (Gradient Boosting).

XGBoost works much like AdaBoost with one key difference — the means by which the model is improved is different.

At each iteration, XGBoost is seeking to improve the performance of the existing model set by reducing the residuals (the differences between targets and label predictions) of that ensemble. Every iteration, the model added is selected based on whether it is most able to reduce the existing ensemble's residuals. This is analogous to gradient descent (where a function is iteratively minimized by moving against a loss gradient); hence, the name Gradient Boosting.

Gradient Boosting has proven to be highly successful in recent Kaggle contests, where it has supported the winners of the CrowdFlower Competition and Microsoft Malware Classification Challenge, along with many other structured data competitions in the final half of 2015.

To apply XGBoost, let's grab the XGBoost library. The best way to get this is via `pip`, with the `pip install xgboost` command on the command line. For Windows users, `pip` installation is currently (late 2015) disabled on Windows. For your benefit, a cold copy of XGBoost is available in the `Chapter 8` folder of this book's GitHub repository.

Applying XGBoost is fairly straightforward. In this case, we'll apply the library to a multiclass classification task, using the UCI Dermatology dataset. This dataset contains an age variable and a large number of categorical variables. An example row of data looks like this:

```
3,2,0,2,0,0,0,0,0,0,0,0,1,2,0,2,1,1,1,0,0,0,1,0,0,0,0,0,0,0,1,0,10,2
```

A small number of age values (penultimate feature) are missing, encoded by ?. The objective in working with this dataset is to correctly classify one of six different skin conditions, per the following class distribution:

```
Database:  Dermatology


Class code:    Class:              Number of instances:

1              psoriasis      112

2              seboreic dermatitis       61

3              lichen planus             72
```

4	pityriasis rosea	49
5	cronic dermatitis	52
6	pityriasis rubra pilaris	20

We'll begin applying XGBoost to this problem by loading up the data and dividing it into test and train cases via a 70/30 split:

```
import numpy as np
import xgboost as xgb

data = np.loadtxt('./dermatology.data', delimiter=',',converters={33:
lambda x:int(x == '?'), 34: lambda x:int(x)-1 } )
sz = data.shape

train = data[:int(sz[0] * 0.7), :]
test = data[int(sz[0] * 0.7):, :]


train_X = train[:,0:33]
train_Y = train[:, 34]


test_X = test[:,0:33]
test_Y = test[:, 34]
```

At this point, we initialize and parameterize our model. The `eta` parameter defines the step size shrinkage. In gradient descent algorithms, it's very common to use a shrinkage parameter to reduce the size of an update. Gradient descent algorithms have a tendency (especially close to convergence) to zigzag back and forth over the optimum; using a shrinkage parameter to downscale the size of a change makes the effect of gradient descent more precise. A common (and default) scaling value is `0.3`. In this example, `eta` has been set to `0.1` for even greater precision (at the possible cost of more iterations).

The `max_depth` parameter is intuitive; it defines the maximum depth of any tree in the example. Given six output classes, six is a reasonable value to begin with. The `num_round` parameter defines how many rounds of Gradient Boosting the algorithm will perform. Again, you typically require more rounds for a multiclass problem with more classes. The `nthread` parameter, meanwhile, defines how many CPU threads the code will run over.

The DMatrix structure used here is purely for the training speed and memory optimization. It's generally a good idea to use these while using XGBoost; they can be built from numpy.arrays. Using DMatrix enables the watchlist functionality, which unlocks some advanced features. In particular, watchlist allows us to monitor the evaluation results on all the data in the list provided:

```
xg_train = xgb.DMatrix( train_X, label=train_Y)
xg_test = xgb.DMatrix(test_X, label=test_Y)

param = {}

param['objective'] = 'multi:softmax'

param['eta'] = 0.1
param['max_depth'] = 6
param['nthread'] = 4
param['num_class'] = 6

watchlist = [ (xg_train,'train'), (xg_test, 'test') ]
num_round = 5
bst = xgb.train(param, xg_train, num_round, watchlist );
```

We train our model, bst, to generate an initial prediction. We then repeat the training process to generate a prediction with softmax enabled (via multi:softprob):

```
pred = bst.predict( xg_test );

print ('predicting, classification error=%f' % (sum( int(pred[i]) !=
test_Y[i] for i in range(len(test_Y))) / float(len(test_Y)) ))


param['objective'] = 'multi:softprob'
bst = xgb.train(param, xg_train, num_round, watchlist );

yprob = bst.predict( xg_test ).reshape( test_Y.shape[0], 6 )
ylabel = np.argmax(yprob, axis=1)

print ('predicting, classification error=%f' % (sum( int(ylabel[i]) !=
test_Y[i] for i in range(len(test_Y))) / float(len(test_Y)) ))
```

Using stacking ensembles

The traditional ensembles that we saw earlier in this chapter all shared a common design philosophy: they involve multiple classifiers trained to fit a set of target labels and involve the models themselves being applied to generate some meta-function through strategies including model voting and boosting.

There is an alternative design philosophy as regards ensemble creation, known as stacking or, alternatively, as blending. Stacking involves multiple layers of models in a configuration where the output of one layer of models is used as training data for a model at the next layer. It's possible to blend hundreds of different models successfully.

Stacking ensembles can also make up the blended set of features at a layer's output from multiple sub-blends (sometimes called **blend-of-blends**). To add to the fun, it's also possible to also extract particularly effective parameters from the models of a stacking ensemble and use them as meta-features, within blends or sub-blends at different levels.

All of this combines to make stacking ensembles a very powerful and extensible technique. The winners of the Kaggle Netflix prize (and associated $1 million award) used stacking ensembles over hundreds of features to great effect. They used several additional tricks to improve the effectiveness of their prediction:

- They trained and optimized their ensemble while holding out some data. They then retrained using the held-out data and again optimized before applying their model to the test dataset. This isn't an uncommon practice, but it yields good results and is worth keeping in mind.

- They trained using gradient descent and RMSE as the performance function. Crucially, they used the RMSE of the ensemble, rather than that of any of the models, as the relevant performance indicator (the measure of residuals). This should be considered a healthy practice whenever working with ensembles.

- They used model combinations that are known to improve on the residuals of other models. Neighborhood-based approaches, for instance, improve on the residuals of the RBM, which we examined earlier in this book. By getting to know the relative strengths and weaknesses of your machine learning algorithms, you can find ideal ensemble configurations.

- They calculated the residuals of their blend using k-fold cross-validation, another technique that we explored and applied earlier in this book. This helped overcome the fact that they'd trained their blend's constituent models using the same dataset as the resulting blend.

The main point to take away from the highly customized nature of the **Pragmatic Chaos** model used to win the Netflix prize is that a first-class model is usually the product of intensive iteration and some creative network configuration changes. The other key takeaway is that the basic architectural pattern of a stacking ensemble is as follows:

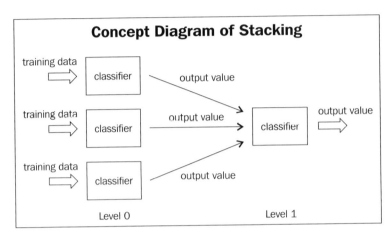

Now that you've learned the fundamentals of how the stacking ensemble work, let's try applying them to solve data problems. To get us started, we'll use the `blend.py` code provided in the GitHub repository accompanying `Chapter 8, `. Versions of this blending code have been used by highly-scoring Kagglers across multiple contests.

To begin with, we'll examine how stacking ensembles can be applied to attack a real data science problem: the Kaggle contest *Predicting a Biological Response* aimed to build as effective a model as possible in order to predict the biological response of molecules given their chemical properties. We'll be looking at one particularly successful entry in this competition to understand how stacking ensembles can work in practice.

In this dataset, each row represents a molecule, while each of the 1,776 features describe characteristics of the molecule in question. The goal was to predict a binary response from the molecule in question, given these properties.

The code that we'll be applying comes from a competitor in that tournament who used a stacking ensemble to combine five classifiers: two differently configured random forest classifiers, two extra trees classifiers, and a gradient boosting classifier, which helps to yield slightly differentiated predictions from the other four components.

The duplicated classifiers were provided with different split criteria. One used the **Gini Impurity** (gini), a measure of how often a random record would be incorrectly labeled if it were randomly labeled according to the distribution of labels in the potential branch in question. The other tree used information gain (entropy), a measure of information content. The information content of a potential branch can be measured by the number of bits that would be required to encode it. Using entropy as a measure to determine the appropriate split leads branches to become increasingly less diverse, but it's important to recognize that the entropy and `gini` criteria can yield quite different results:

```
if __name__ == '__main__':

    np.random.seed(0)

    n_folds = 10
    verbose = True
    shuffle = False

    X, y, X_submission = load_data.load()

    if shuffle:
        idx = np.random.permutation(y.size)
        X = X[idx]
        y = y[idx]

    skf = list(StratifiedKFold(y, n_folds))

    clfs = [RandomForestClassifier(n_estimators=100, n_jobs=-1,
criterion='gini'),
            RandomForestClassifier(n_estimators=100, n_jobs=-1,
criterion='entropy'),
            ExtraTreesClassifier(n_estimators=100, n_jobs=-1,
criterion='gini'),
            ExtraTreesClassifier(n_estimators=100, n_jobs=-1,
criterion='entropy'),
            GradientBoostingClassifier(learning_rate=0.05,
subsample=0.5, max_depth=6, n_estimators=50)]

    print "Creating train and test sets for blending."

    dataset_blend_train = np.zeros((X.shape[0], len(clfs)))
    dataset_blend_test = np.zeros((X_submission.shape[0], len(clfs)))

    for j, clf in enumerate(clfs):
```

```
        print j, clf
        dataset_blend_test_j = np.zeros((X_submission.shape[0],
len(skf)))
        for i, (train, test) in enumerate(skf):
            print "Fold", i
            X_train = X[train]
            y_train = y[train]
            X_test = X[test]
            y_test = y[test]
            clf.fit(X_train, y_train)
            y_submission = clf.predict_proba(X_test)[:,1]
            dataset_blend_train[test, j] = y_submission
            dataset_blend_test_j[:, i] =
clf.predict_proba(X_submission)[:,1]
        dataset_blend_test[:,j] = dataset_blend_test_j.mean(1)

    print
    print "Blending."
    clf = LogisticRegression()
    clf.fit(dataset_blend_train, y)
    y_submission = clf.predict_proba(dataset_blend_test)[:,1]

    print "Linear stretch of predictions to [0,1]"
    y_submission = (y_submission - y_submission.min()) /
(y_submission.max() - y_submission.min())

    print "Saving Results."
    np.savetxt(fname='test.csv', X=y_submission, fmt='%0.9f')
```

When we try running this submission on the private leaderboard, we find ourselves in a rather impressive 12th place (out of 699 competitors)! Naturally, we can't draw too many conclusions from a competition that we entered after completion, but, given the simplicity of the code, this is still a rather impressive result!

Applying ensembles in practice

One particularly important quality to be mindful of while applying ensemble methods is that your goal is to tune the performance of the ensemble rather than of the models that comprise it. Your approach should therefore be largely focused on building a strong ensemble performance score, rather than the strongest set of individual model performances.

The amount of attention that you pay to the models within your ensemble will vary. With an arrangement of differently configured or initialized models of a single type (for example, a random forest), it is sensible to focus almost entirely on the performance of the ensemble and metaparameters that shape it.

For more challenging problems, we frequently need to pay closer attention to the individual models within our ensemble. This is most obviously true when we're trying to create smaller ensembles for more challenging problems, but to build a truly excellent ensemble, it is often necessary to be considerate of the parameters and algorithms underlying the structure that you've built.

With this said, you'll always be looking at the performance of the ensemble as well as the performance of models within the set. You'll be inspecting the results of your models to try and work out *what each model did well*. You'll also be looking for the less obvious factors that affect ensemble performance, most notably the correlation of model predictions. It's generally recognized that a more effective ensemble will tend to contain performant but uncorrelated components.

To understand this claim, consider techniques such as correlation measures and PCA that we can use to measure the amount of information content present in dataset variables. In the same way, we can use Pearson's correlation coefficient against the predictions output by each of our models to understand the relationship between performance and correlation for each model.

Taking us back to stacking ensembles specifically, our ensemble's models are outputting metafeatures that are then used as inputs to a next-layer model. Just as we would vet the features used by a more conventional neural network, we want to ensure that the features output by our ensemble's components work well as a dataset. The calculation of the Pearson correlation coefficient across model outputs and use of the results in model selection is an excellent place to start in this regard.

When we deal with single-model problems, we almost always have to spend some time inspecting the problem and identifying an appropriate learning algorithm. If we're faced with a two-class classification problem with a moderate amount of features (*10's*) and labeled training cases, we might select a logistic regression, an SVM, or some other appropriate algorithm for the context. Different approaches will apply to different problems and through trial and error, parallel testing, and experience (both personal and posted online!), you will identify the appropriate approach for a specific objective given specific input data.

A similar logic applies to ensemble creation. Rather than identifying a single appropriate model, the challenge is to identify combinations of models that effectively describe different elements of an input dataset in such a way that the dataset as a whole is adequately described. By understanding the strengths and weaknesses of your component models as well as by exploring and visualizing your dataset, you'll be able to draw conclusions about how to develop your ensemble effectively through multiple iterations.

Ultimately, at this level, data science is a field with a great many techniques at hand. The best practitioners are able to apply their knowledge of their own algorithms and options to develop very effective solutions over many iterations.

These solutions involve the knowledge of algorithms and interaction of model combinations, model parameter adjustments, dataset translations, and ensemble manipulation. Just as importantly, they require an uninhibited and creative mindset.

One good example of this is the work of prominent Kaggle competitor, Alexander Guschin. Focusing on one specific example — the **Otto Product Classification** contest — can give us an idea as to the range of options available to a confident and creative data scientist.

Most model development processes begin with a period in which you throw different solutions at the problem, attempting to find the tricks underlying the data and figuring out what works. Settling on a stacking model, Alexander set about building metafeatures. While we looked at XGBoost as an ensemble in its own right, in this case it was used as a component to the stacking ensemble in order to generate some of the metafeatures to be used by the final model. Neural networks were used in addition to the gradient boosted trees as both algorithms tend to produce good results.

To add some contrast to the mixture, Alexander added a KNN implementation, specifically because the results (and therefore the metaparameters) generated by a KNN tend to differ significantly from the models already included. This approach of picking up components whose outputs tend to differ is crucial in creating an effective stacking ensemble (and to most ensemble types).

To further develop this model, Alexander added some custom elements to the second layer of his model. While combining the XGBoost and neural network predictions, he also added bagging at this layer. At this point, most of the techniques that we've discussed in this chapter have shown up in some part of this model. In addition to the model development, some feature engineering (in particular, the use of TF-IDF on half of the training and test data) and the use of plotting techniques to identify class differentiation were used throughout.

A truly mature model that can tackle the most significant data science challenges is one that combines the techniques we've seen throughout this book, created using a solid understanding of the underlying algorithms and the possibilities for how these techniques can interact with each other.

This book so far has taught many of the fundamentals—the base of practical knowledge—that a practitioner has to collect. It has used many examples and an increasing amount of real-world cases to demonstrate how a broad base of knowledge becomes increasingly powerful in letting you develop effective solutions to difficult problems.

What's required of you as a data scientist is to first apply this broad set of techniques to develop an experience of how they can perform and what they could do for you. Then it is up to you to develop that creativity and experimental mindset that distinguishes some of the best data scientists.

Using models in dynamic applications

We've spent this chapter discussing the use of techniques to manage model performance under conditions that might be seen as ideal; specifically, conditions in which all of the data is available ahead of time so that a model can be trained on all data. These assumptions are frequently valid in research contexts or when dealing with one-time problems, but in many contexts they are unsafe assumptions. The range of unsafe contexts goes beyond the cases where the data is simply unavailable, such as data science contests where a held-out dataset is used to establish the final leaderboard.

Returning to a subject from earlier in this chapter, you'll recall the Pragmatic Chaos algorithm, which won the Netflix prize? By the time Netflix came to assessing the algorithm for implementation, both the business context and requirements had shifted so dramatically that the minimal accuracy gains provided by that algorithm didn't justify implementation costs. The $1M algorithm was redundant and was never implemented in production! The point to take from this example is that in commercial contexts, it is critical for our models to have as much adaptability as we can provide.

The really challenging applications of machine learning algorithms, in which our existing run once methodologies become less valuable, are ones where real data changes occur across time (or other dimensions). In these contexts, one knows that a substantial data change will occur and that existing models cannot be easily trained to adapt to this data change. At that point, new techniques are needed as well as new information.

To adapt and gather this information, we need to become better able to predict the ways in which data change is liable to occur. With this information, our model building and the content of our ensembles can start to change in order to cover the most likely data change scenarios that we see ahead. This adaptation lets us pre-empt data change and reduce the adjustment time required. As we'll see later in this chapter, in real-world applications any reduction in the time it takes us to pivot based on data change is valuable.

In the next section, we'll be looking at tools that we can use to make our models more robust to changing data. We'll discuss the means by which we can maintain a broad set of model options, simultaneously accommodating one or multiple data change scenarios, without reducing the performance of our models.

Understanding model robustness

It's important to understand exactly what the problem is here and how and when it is presented. This involves defining two things; the first being robustness as it applies to machine learning algorithms. The second, of course, is data change. Some of the content in the first part of this section is at an introductory level, but experienced data scientists may still find value in reviewing the section!

In academic terms, the robustness of a machine learning algorithm is the property that characterizes how effective your algorithm is while being applied to a dataset other than the dataset on which it was trained.

Robustness testing is a core part of machine learning methodology in any context. The importance of validation techniques such as k-fold cross-validation and the use of tests when developing models for even the simplest contexts is a consequence of machine learning algorithm vulnerability to data change.

Most datasets contain both a signal and noise. Noise may be predictable (and thus more easily managed) or it may be stochastic and difficult to treat. A dataset may contain more or less noise. Typically, datasets with more or less predictable noise are harder to train and test against the same datasets with this noise removed (which can be easily tested).

When one has trained a model on a given dataset, it is almost inevitable that this model has learned based on both the signal and noise. The concept of overfitting is generally used to describe a model that has fit so well to a given dataset that it has learned to predict based on both the signal and noise, rendering it less powerful against other samples than a model with a less exact fit.

Part of the goal of training a model is to reduce the impact of any local noise on learning as much as possible. The purpose of validation techniques that hold out a set of data to test is to ensure that any learning of noise during training happens only on noise that is local to the training set. The difference between training and test error can be used to understand the degree of overfitting between model implementations.

We've applied cross-validation in *Chapter 1, Unsupervised Machine Learning*. Another useful means of testing models for the overfitting is to directly add random noise in the form of jitter to the training dataset. This technique was introduced via a Kaggle notebook in October 2015 by Alexander Minushkin and offers a very interesting test. The concept is simple; by adding jitter and looking at the accuracy of prediction on the training data, we can distinguish an overfitted model (whose training error will increase more quickly as we add jitter) from a well- or poorly-fitted model:

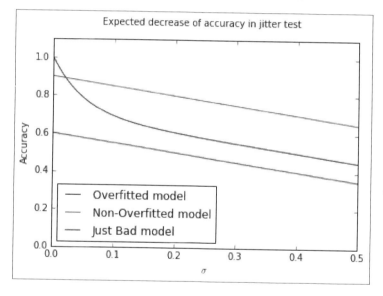

In this case, we're able to plot the results of a jitter test to easily identify whether a model has overfit. From a very strong initial position, an overfit model will typically rapidly decline in performance as small amounts of jitter are added. For better-fitting models, the loss in performance with added jitter is much reduced, with the degree of overfitting in a model being particularly obvious at low levels of added jitter (where a well-fit model will tend to outperform an overfit counterpart).

Let's look at how we implement a jitter test for overfitting. We use a familiar score, accuracy_score, defined as the proportion of class labels predicted correctly, as the basis for test scoring. Jitter is defined by simply adding random noise to the data (using np.random.normal) with the amount of noise defined by the configurable scale parameter:

```
from sklearn.metrics import accuracy_score

def jitter(X, scale):
    if scale > 0:
        return X + np.random.normal(0, scale, X.shape)
    return X

def jitter_test(classifier, X, y, metric_FUNC = accuracy_score, sigmas
= np.linspace(0, 0.5, 30), averaging_N = 5):
    out = []

    for s in sigmas:
        averageAccuracy = 0.0
        for x in range(averaging_N):
            averageAccuracy += metric_FUNC( y, classifier.
predict(jitter(X, s)))

        out.append( averageAccuracy/averaging_N)

    return (out, sigmas, np.trapz(out, sigmas))

allJT = {}
```

The jitter_test itself is defined as a wrapper to normal sklearn classification, given a classifier, training data, and a set of target labels. The classifier is then called to predict against a version of the data that first has the jitter operation called against it.

At this point, we'll begin creating a number of datasets to run our jitter test over. We'll use sklearn's make_moons dataset, commonly used as a dataset to visualize clustering and classification algorithm performance. This dataset is comprised of two classes whose data points create interleaving half-circles. By adding varying amounts of noise to make_moons and using differing amounts of samples, we can create a range of example cases to run our jitter test against:

```
import sklearn
import sklearn.datasets

import warnings
```

```
warnings.filterwarnings("ignore", category=DeprecationWarning)

Xs = []
ys = []

#low noise, plenty of samples, should be easy
X0, y0 = sklearn.datasets.make_moons(n_samples=1000, noise=.05)
Xs.append(X0)
ys.append(y0)

#more noise, plenty of samples
X1, y1 = sklearn.datasets.make_moons(n_samples=1000, noise=.3)
Xs.append(X1)
ys.append(y1)

#less noise, few samples
X2, y2 = sklearn.datasets.make_moons(n_samples=200, noise=.05)
Xs.append(X2)
ys.append(y2)

#more noise, less samples, should be hard
X3, y3 = sklearn.datasets.make_moons(n_samples=200, noise=.3)
Xs.append(X3)
ys.append(y3)
```

This done, we then create a `plotter` object that we'll use to show our models' performance directly against the input data:

```
def plotter(model, X, Y, ax, npts=5000):

    xs = []
    ys = []
    cs = []
    for _ in range(npts):
        x0spr = max(X[:,0])-min(X[:,0])
        x1spr = max(X[:,1])-min(X[:,1])
        x = np.random.rand()*x0spr + min(X[:,0])
        y = np.random.rand()*x1spr + min(X[:,1])
        xs.append(x)
        ys.append(y)
        cs.append(model.predict([x,y]))
    ax.scatter(xs,ys,c=list(map(lambda x:'lightgrey' if x==0 else
'black', cs)), alpha=.35)
    ax.hold(True)
```

```
        ax.scatter(X[:,0],X[:,1],
                      c=list(map(lambda x:'r' if x else 'lime',Y)),
                      linewidth=0,s=25,alpha=1)
        ax.set_xlim([min(X[:,0]), max(X[:,0])])
        ax.set_ylim([min(X[:,1]), max(X[:,1])])
        return
```

We'll use an SVM classifier as the base model for our jitter tests:

```
import sklearn.svm
classifier = sklearn.svm.SVC()


allJT[str(classifier)] = list()


fig, axes = plt.subplots(nrows=2, ncols=2, figsize=(11,13))
i=0
for X,y in zip(Xs,ys):
    classifier.fit(X,y)
    plotter(classifier,X,y,ax=axes[i//2,i%2])
    allJT[str(classifier)].append (jitter_test(classifier, X, y))
    i += 1
plt.show()
```

The jitter test provides an effective means of assessing model overfitting and performs comparably to cross-validation; indeed, Minushkin provides evidence that it can outperform cross-validation as a tool to measure model fit quality.

Both of these tools to mitigate the overfitting work well in contexts where your algorithm is either run over data on a one-off basis or where underlying trends don't vary substantially. This is true for the majority of single-dataset problems (such as most academic or web repository datasets) or data problems where the underlying trends change slowly.

However, there are many contexts where the data involved in modeling might change over time in one or several dimensions. This can occur because of change in the methods by which data is captured, usually because new instruments or techniques come into use. For instance, video data captured by commonly-available devices has improved substantially in resolution over the decade since 2005 and the quality (and size!) of such data has increased. Whether you're using the video frames themselves or instead the file size as a parameter, you'll observe noticeable shifts in the nature, quality, and distributions of features.

Alternatively, changes in dataset variables might be caused by differences in underlying trends. The classic data schema concept of measures and dimensions comes back into play here, as we can better understand how data change is affected by considering what dimensions influence our measurement.

The key example is time. Depending on context, many variables are subject to day-of-week, month-of-year, or seasonal variations. In many cases, a helpful option might be to parameterize these variables, (as we discussed in the preceding chapter, techniques such as one-hot encoding can help our algorithms learn to parse such trends) particularly if we're dealing with periodic trends that are easily predicted (for example, the impact of month-of-year on scarf sales in a given location) and easily modeled.

A more problematic type of time series trend is non-periodic change. As in the preceding video camera example, some types of time series trends change irrevocably and in ways that might not be trivial to predict. Telemetry from software tends to be influenced by the quality and functionality of the software build live at the time the telemetry was emitted. As builds change over time, the values sent in telemetry and the variables created from those values can change radically overnight in hard-to-predict ways.

Human behavior, a hugely important factor in many datasets, helpfully changes both periodically and non-periodically. People shop more around seasonal holidays, but also change their shopping habits permanently based on new societal or technological developments.

Some of the added complexity here comes not just from the fact that single variables and their distributions are affected by time series trends, but also from how relationships between relevant factors and their associated variables will change. The relationships between variables may change in quantifiable terms. One example is how, for humans, height and weight are two variables whose relationship varies between times and locations. The BMI feature, which we might use to track this relationship, shows differing distributions when sampled across periods of time or between locations.

Furthermore, variables can change in another serious way; namely, their importance to a performant modeling algorithm may vary over time! Some variables whose values are highly relevant in some periods of time will be less relevant in others. As an example, consider how climate and weather variables affect agriculture markets. For some crops and the companies dealing in them, these variables are fairly unimportant for much of the year. At the time of crop growth and harvest, however, they become fundamentally important. To make this more complex, the strength of these factors' importance is also tied to location (and local climate).

The challenge for modeling is clear. For models that are trained once and run again on new data, managing data change can present serious challenges. For models that are dynamically recomputed based on new input data, data change can still create problems as variable distributions and relationships change and available variables become more or less valuable in generating an effective solution.

Part of the key to successfully managing data change in your application of ML is to recognize the dimensions (and there are common culprits) where change is probable and liable to affect the distributions of your features, relationships, and feature importance, which a model will attempt to pick up on.

Once you have an understanding as to what the factors in your data are that are likely to influence overfitting, you're better positioned to develop a solution that manages these factors effectively.

This said, it will still seem hugely challenging to build a single model that can resolve any potential issues. The simple response to this is that if one faces serious data change issues, the solution probably isn't to try to solve for them with a single model! In the next section, we'll be looking at ensemble methods to provide a better answer.

Identifying modeling risk factors

While it is in many cases quite straightforward to identify which elements present a risk to your model over time, it can help to employ a structured process for identification. This section briefly describes some of the heuristics and techniques you can employ to screen your models for the risk of data change.

Most data scientists keep a data dictionary for datasets that are intended for general use or automated applications. This is especially likely to happen if the data or applications are complex, but keeping a data dictionary is generally good practice. Some of the most effective work you can do in identifying risk factors is to run through these features and tag them based on different risk types.

Some of the tags that I tend to use include the following:

- **Longitudinally variant**: Is this parameter liable to change over a long time due to longitudinal trends that many not be fully visible in the span of the training data that you have available? The most obvious example is the ecological seasons, which affect many areas of human behavior as well as the many things that depend on some more fundamental climatic variables. Other longitudinal trends include the financial year and the working month, but extend to include many other longitudinal trends relevant to your area of investigation. The life cycle of new iPhone models or the population flux of voles might be an important longitudinal factor depending on the nature of your work.

- **Slowly changing**: Is this categorical parameter likely to gain new values over time? This concept is borrowed from data warehousing best practices. A slowly changing dimension in the classical sense will gain new parameter codes (for example, as a new store opens or a new case is identified). These can throw your model entirely if not managed properly or if they appear in sufficient number. Another impact of slowly changing data, which can be more problematic to handle, is that it can begin to affect the distribution of your features. This can have a substantial impact on the effectiveness of your model.

- **Key parameter**: A combination of data value monitoring and recalculation of decision boundaries/regression equations will often handle a certain amount of slowly changing data and seasonal variance well, but consider taking action should you see an unexpectedly large amount of new cases or case types, especially when they affect variables depended on heavily by your model. For this reason, also make sure that you know which variables are most relied upon by your solution!

The process of tagging in this way is helpful (not least as an export of your own memory) mostly because it helps you to do the following:

- Organize your expectations and develop a kind of checklist for your development of monitoring readiness. If you aren't able to keep track of at least your longitudinally variant and slowly changing parameter change, you are effectively blind to any output from your model besides changes in the parameters that it favors when recomputed and its (likely slowly declining) performance measure.

- Investigate mitigation (for example, improved normalization or extra parameters that codify those dimensions in which your data is variant). In many ways, mitigation and the addition of parameters is the best solution you can tap to handle data change.

- Set up robustness testing using constructed datasets, where your risk features are deliberately varied to simulate data change. Stress-test your model under these conditions and find out exactly how much variance it'll tolerate. With this information, you can easily set yourself up to use your monitoring values as an early alert system; once data change exceeds a certain safe threshold, you know how much degradation to expect in the model performance.

Strategies to managing model robustness

We've discussed a number of effective ensemble techniques that allow us to balance the twin needs for performant and robust models. However, throughout our exposition and use of these techniques, we had to decide how and when we would reduce our model's performance to improve robustness.

Indeed, a common theme in this chapter has been how to balance the conflicting objectives of creating an effective, performant model, without making this model too inflexible to respond to data change. Many of the solutions that we've seen so far have required that we trade-off one outcome against the other, which is less than ideal.

At this point, it's worth our taking a slightly wider view of our options and drawing from complimentary techniques. The need for robust, performant statistical models within evolving business landscapes is neither new nor untreated; fields such as credit risk modeling have a long history of applied statistical modeling in changing domains and have developed effective decision management methodologies in order to succeed. Data scientists can turn some of these established techniques to our own benefit via using them to help organize our own models.

One effective methodology is **Champion/Challenger**, a test-centric approach that involves running multiple, parallel model configurations. In addition to the model whose outputs are applied (to direct business activities or inform reporting), champion/challenger approaches training one or more alternative model configurations.

By maintaining and monitoring multiple models, one can arrange to substitute the current model as and when an alternative outperforms it. This is usually done by maintaining a performance scoring process for all models and observing the results so that a manual decision call can be made about whether and when to switch to a challenger.

While the simplest implementation may involve switching to a challenger as soon as it outperforms the main model, this is rarely done as there are risks around specific challenger models being exposed to local minima (for example, the day-of-week or month-of-year local trends). It is normal to spend a significant period assessing a challenger model, particularly ahead of sensitive applications. In complex real cases, one may even want to do additional testing by providing a sample of treatment cases to a promising challenger to determine whether it generates significant lift over the champion.

There is scope for some creativity beyond simple, "replace the challenger" succession rules. Voting-based approaches are quite common, where a top subset of the trained ensembles provides scores on a case-by-case basis and those scores treated as (weighted or unweighted) votes. Another approach involves using a **Borda count**, a voting system where each voter ranks the candidate solutions in order of preference. In the context of ensembling, one would typically assign each individual model's prediction a point value equal to its inverse rank (keeping each model separate!). Then one can combine these votes (usually experimenting with a range of different weightings) to generate a result.

Voting can perform fairly well with a larger number of models but is dependent on the specific modeling context and factors like the similarity of the different voters. As we discussed earlier in this chapter, it's critical to use tests such as Pearson's correlation coefficient to ensure that your model set is both performant and uncorrelated.

One may find that particular classes of input data (users, say, with specific segmentation tags) are more effectively treated by a given challenger and may implement a case routing system where multiple champions deal with different user subgroups. This approach overlaps somewhat with the benefits of boosting ensembles, but can help in production circumstances by separating concerns. However, maintaining multiple champions will increase the monitoring and oversight burden for your data team, so this option is best avoided if not entirely necessary.

A major concern to address is how we go about scoring our models, not least because there are immediate practical challenges. In particular, it is hard to compare multiple models in real contexts, given that class labels (to guide correctness) typically aren't available. In predictive contexts, this problem is compounded by the fact that the champion model's predictions are typically used to take actions that alter predicted events. This activity makes it very difficult to make assertions about how a challenger model's predictions would've performed; by taking action based on our champion's predictions, we're unable to confirm the results of our models!

The most common implementation process is to provide each challenger model with a statistically viable sample of the input data and then compare the lift from each approach. This approach inherently limits the number of challengers that one can support for some modeling problems. Another option is to leave just one statistically viable sample out of any treatment activity and use it to create a single regression test. This test is applied to the entire set of champion and challenger models, providing a meaningful basis for comparison.

The downside to this approach is that the change to a more effective model will always trail the data change by however long it takes to generate correct class labels for the test cases. While in many cases this isn't crippling (the champion model remains in place for the period it takes to generate accurate models), it can present problems in contexts where underlying conditions change rapidly compared to the training time for models.

It's worth making one brief comment on the relationship between model training time and data change frequency. It isn't always clearly stated as such, but the typical goal in applied machine learning contexts is to reduce the factor of training time to data change frequency to the smallest value possible. To take the worst case, if the length of time it takes to train a model is longer than the length of time that model will be accurate for (and the ratio is equal to or greater than one), your model will never generate current results that can directly drive current actions. In general, a high ratio should prompt review and adjustment activities (either an investigation into whether faster score delivery at lower confidence delivers more value or adjustment to the rate at which controllable environment variables change).

The smaller this ratio becomes, the more leeway your team has to apply your model's outputs to drive actions and generate value. Depending on how variant and quantifiable this ratio is for your modeling context, it can be a useful concept to promote within your organization as a health measure for your automated modeling solution.

These alternative models may simply be the next best-performing ensemble configurations; they may be older models, kept around for observation. In sophisticated operations, some challengers are configured to handle different *what-if* scenarios (for example, *what if the temperature in this region is 2 C below expectations* or *what if sales are significantly below expectations*). These models may have been trained on the same data as the main model or on deliberately skewed or prepared data that simulates the what-if scenario.

More challengers tend to be better (providing improved robustness and performance), provided that the challengers are not all minute variations on the same theme. Challenger models also provide a safe venue for innovation and testing, while observing effective challengers can provide useful insights into how robust your champion ensemble is likely to be to a range of possible environmental changes.

The techniques that you've learned to apply in this section have provided us with the tools to apply our existing toolkit of models to real applications in evolving environments. This chapter also discussed complications that can arise when applying ML models to production; data change, between samples or across dimensions, will cause our models to become increasingly ineffective. By thoroughly unpacking the concept of data change, we became better able to characterize this risk and recognize where and how it might present itself.

The remainder of the chapter was dedicated to techniques that provide improved model robustness. We discussed how to identify model degradation risk by looking at the underlying data and discussed some helpful heuristics to this end. We drew from existing decision management methods to learn about and use Champion/Challenger, a well-regarded process with a long history in contexts including applied machine learning. Champion/Challenger helps us organize and test multiple models in healthy competition. In conjunction with effective performance monitoring, a proactive tactical plan for model substitution will give you faster and more controllable management of the model life cycle and quality, all the while providing a wealth of valuable operational insights.

Further reading

Perhaps the most wide-ranging and informative tour of Ensembles and ensemble types is provided by the Kaggle competitor, Triskelion, at `http://mlwave.com/kaggle-ensembling-guide/`.

For discussion of the Netflix Prize-winning model, Pragmatic Chaos, refer to `http://www.stat.osu.edu/~dmsl/GrandPrize2009_BPC_BellKor.pdf`. For an explanation by Netflix on how changing business contexts rendered that $1M-model redundant, refer to the Netflix Tech blog at `http://techblog.netflix.com/2012/04/netflix-recommendations-beyond-5-stars.html`.

For a walkthrough on applying random forest ensembles to commercial contexts, with plenty of space given to all-important diagnostic charts and reasoning, consider Arshavir Blackwell's blog at `https://citizennet.com/blog/2012/11/10/random-forests-ensembles-and-performance-metrics/`.

For further information on random forests specifically, I find the scikit-learn documentation helpful: `http://scikit-learn.org/stable/modules/generated/sklearn.ensemble.RandomForestClassifier.html`.

A great introduction to gradient-boosted trees is provided within the XGBoost documentation at `http://xgboost.readthedocs.io/en/latest/model.html`.

For a write-up of Alexander Guschin's entry to the Otto Product Classification challenge, refer to the No Free Hunch blog: `http://blog.kaggle.com/2015/06/09/otto-product-classification-winners-interview-2nd-place-alexander-guschin/`.

Alexander Minushkin's Jitter test for overfitting is described at `https://www.kaggle.com/miniushkin/introducing-kaggle-scripts/jitter-test-for-overfitting-notebook`.

Summary

In this chapter, we covered a lot of ground. We began by introducing ensembles, some of the most powerful and popular techniques in competitive machine learning contexts. We covered both the theory and code needed to apply ensembles to our machine learning projects, using a combination of expert knowledge and practical examples.

In addition, this chapter also dedicates a section to discussing the unique considerations that arise when you run models for weeks and months at a time. We discussed what data change can mean, how to identify it, and how to think about guarding against it. We gave specific consideration to the question of how to create sets of models running in parallel, which you can switch between based on seasonal change or performance drift in your model set.

During our review of these techniques, we spent significant time with real-world examples with the specific aim of learning more about the creative mindset and broad range of knowledge required of the best data scientists.

The techniques throughout this book have led up to a point that, armed with technical knowledge, code to reapply, and an understanding of the possibilities, you are truly able to take on any data modeling challenge.

9
Additional Python Machine Learning Tools

Over the course of the eight preceding chapters, we have examined and applied a range of techniques that help us enrich and model data for many applications.

We approached the content in these chapters using a combination of Python libraries, particularly NumPy and Theano, while the other libraries were drawn upon as and when we needed to access specific algorithms. We did not spend a great deal of time discussing what other options existed in terms of tools, what the unique differentiators of these tools were, or why we might be interested.

The primary goal of this final chapter is to highlight some other key libraries and frameworks that are available to you to use. These tools streamline and simplify the process of creating and applying models. This chapter presents these tools, demonstrates their application, and provides extensive advice regarding *Further reading*.

A major contributor to succeed in solving data science challenges and being successful as a data scientist is having a good understanding of the latest developments in algorithms and libraries. As professionals, data scientists tend to be highly dependent on the quality of the data they use, but it is also very important to have the best tools available.

In this chapter, we will review some of the best in the recent tools available to data scientists, identifying the benefits they offer, and discussing how to apply them alongside tools and techniques discussed earlier in this book within a consistent working process.

Alternative development tools

Over the last couple of years, a number of new machine learning frameworks have emerged that offer advantages in terms of workflow. Usually these frameworks are highly focused on a specific use case or objective. This makes them very useful, perhaps even must-have tools, but it also means that you may need to use multiple workflow improvement libraries.

With an ever-growing set of new Python ML projects being lit up to address specific workflow challenges, it's worth discussing two libraries that add to our existing workflow and which accelerate or improve the work we've done in the preceding chapters. In this chapter, we'll be introducing **Lasagne** and **TensorFlow**, discussing the code and capabilities of each library and identifying why each framework is worth considering as a part of your toolset.

Introduction to Lasagne

Let's face it; sometimes creating models in Python takes longer than we'd like. However, they can be efficient for models that are more complex and offer big benefits (such as GPU acceleration and configurability) libraries similar to Theano can be relatively complex to use when working on simple cases. This is unfortunate because we often want to work with simple models, for instance, when we're setting up benchmarks.

Lasagne is a library developed by a team of deep learning and music data mining researchers to work as an interface to Theano. It is designed specifically to nail a particular goal—to allow for fast and efficient prototyping of new models.

This focus dictated how Lasagne was created, to call Theano functions and return Theano expressions or numpy data types, in a much less complex and more easily understood manner than the same operations written in native Theano code.

In this section, we'll take a look at the conceptual model underlying Lasagne, apply some Lasagne code, and understand what the library adds to our existing practices.

Getting to know Lasagne

Lasagne operates using the concept of layers, a familiar concept in machine learning. A layer is a set of neurons and operating rules that will take an input and generate a score, label, or other transformations. Neural networks generally function as a set of layers that feed input data in at one end and push output values out at the other (though the ways in which this gets done vary broadly).

It has become very popular in deep learning contexts to start treating individual layers as first class citizens. Traditionally, in machine learning work, a network would be established from layers using only a few parameter specifications (such as node count, bias, and weight values).

In recent years, data scientists seeking that extra edge have begun to take increasing interest in the configuration of individual layers. Nowadays it is not unusual in advanced machine learning environments to see layers that contain sub-models and transformed inputs. Even features, nowadays, might skip layers as needed and new features may be added to layers partway through a model. As an example of some of this refinement, consider the convolutional neural network architectures employed by Google to solve image recognition challenges. These networks are extensively refined at a layer level to generate performance improvements.

It therefore makes sense that Lasagne treats layers as its basic model component. What Lasagne adds to the model creation process is the ability to stack different layers into a model quickly and intuitively. One may simply call a class within lasagne.layers to stack a class onto your model. The code for this is highly efficient and looks as follows:

```
l0 = lasagne.layers.InputLayer(shape=X.shape)

l1 = lasagne.layers.DenseLayer(
l0, num_units=10, nonlinearity=lasagne.nonlinearities.tanh)

l2 = lasagne.layers.DenseLayer(l1, num_units=N_CLASSES,
nonlinearity=lasagne.nonlinearities.softmax)
```

In three simple statements, we have created the basic structure of a network using simple and configurable functions.

This code creates a model using three layers. The layer l0 calls the InputLayer class, acting as an input layer for our model. This layer translates our input dataset into a Theano tensor, based on the expected shape of the input (defined using the shape parameter).

The next layers, l1 and l2 are each fully connected (dense) layers. Layer l2 is defined as an output layer, with a number of units equal to the number of classes, while l1 uses the same DenseLayer class to create a hidden layer of 10 units.

In addition to configuration of the standard parameters (weights, biases, unit count and nonlinearity type) available to the `DenseLayer` class, it is possible to employ entirely different network types using different classes. Lasagne provides classes for a broad set of familiar layers, including dense, convolutional and pooling layers, recurrent layers, normalisation and noise layers, amongst others. There is, furthermore, a special-purpose layer class, which provides a range of additional functionality.

If something more bespoke than what these classes provide is needed, of course, the user can resort to defining their own layer type easily and use it in conjunction with other Lasagne classes. However, for a majority of prototyping and fast, iterative development contexts, this is a great amount of pre-prepared capability.

Lasagne provides a similarly succinct interface to define the loss calculation for a network:

```
true_output = T.ivector('true_output')
objective = lasagne.objectives.Objective(l2, loss_function=lasagne.
objectives.categorical_crossentropy)

loss = objective.get_loss(target=true_output)
```

The `loss` function defined here is one of the many available functions, including squared error, hinge loss for binary and multi-class cases, and `crossentropy` functions. An accuracy scoring function for validation is also provided.

With these two components, a `loss` function and a network architecture, we again have everything we need to train a network. To do this, we need to write a little more code:

```
all_params = lasagne.layers.get_all_params(l2)
updates = lasagne.updates.sgd(loss, all_params, learning_rate=1)
train = theano.function([l0.input_var, true_output], loss,
updates=updates)

get_output = theano.function([l0.input_var], net_output)

for n in xrange(100):
  train(X, y)
```

This code leverages the `theano` functionality to train our example network, using our `loss` function, to iteratively train to classify a given set of input data.

Introduction to TensorFlow

When we reviewed Google's take on the **convolutional neural network (CNN)** in *Chapter 4, Convolutional Neural Networks,* we found a convoluted, many-layered beast. The question of how to create and monitor such networks only became more important as the network scales in layer count and complexity to attack challenges that are more complex.

To address this challenge, the Machine Intelligence research organisation at Google developed and distributed a library named TensorFlow, which exists to enable easier refinement and modeling of very involved machine learning models.

TensorFlow does this by providing two main benefits; a clear and simple programming interface (in this case, a Python API) onto familiar structures (such as NumPy objects), and powerful diagnostic and graph visualisation tools, such as **TensorBoard**, to enable informed tuning of a data architecture.

Getting to know TensorFlow

TensorFlow enables a data scientist to design data transformation operations as a flow across a computation graph. This graph can be extended and modified, while individual nodes can be tuned extensively, enabling detailed refinements of individual layers or model components. The TensorFlow workflow typically involves two phases. The first of these is referred to as the construction phase, during which a graph is assembled.

During the construction phase, we can write code using the Python API for Tensorflow. Like Lasagne, TensorFlow offers a relatively simple interface to writing network layers, requiring simply that we specify weights and bias before creating our layers. The following example shows initial setting of weight and bias variables, before creating (using one line of code each) a convolutional layer and a simple max-pooling layer. Additionally, we use `tf.placeholder` to generate placeholder variables for our input data.

```
x = tf.placeholder(tf.float32, shape=[None, 784])
y_ = tf.placeholder(tf.float32, shape=[None, 10])

W = tf.Variable(tf.zeros([5, 5, 1, 32]))
b = tf.Variable(tf.zeros([32]))


h_conv = tf.nn.relu(conv2d(x_image, W) + b)
h_pool = max_pool_2x2(h_conv)
```

This structure can be extended to include a `softmax` output layer, just as we did with Lasagne.

```
W_out = tf.Variable(tf.zeros([1024,10]))
B_out = tf.Variable(tf.zeros([10]))


y = tf.nn.softmax(tf.matmul(h_conv, W_out) + b_out)
```

Again, we can see significant improvements in the iteration time over writing directly in Theano and Python libraries. Being written in C++, TensorFlow also provides performance gains over Python, providing advantages in execution time.

Next up, we need to train and evaluate our model. Here, we'll need to write a little code to define our `loss` function for training (cross entropy, in this case), an `accuracy` function for validation and an optimisation method (in this case, steepest gradient descent).

```
cross_entropy = tf.reduce_mean(-tf.reduce_sum(y_ * tf.log(y),
reduction_indices=[1]))

train_step = tf.train.GradientDescentOptimizer(0.5).minimize(cross_
entropy)

correct_prediction = tf.equal(tf.argmax(y_,1), tf.argmax(y_,1))

accuracy = tf.reduce_mean(tf.cast(correct_prediction, tf.float32))
```

Following this, we can simply begin running our model iteratively. This is all succinct and very straightforward:

```
sess.run(tf.initialize_all_variables())
for i in range(20000):
  batch = mnist.train.next_batch(50)
  if i%100 == 0:
    train_accuracy = accuracy.eval(feed_dict={
        x:batch[0], y_: batch[1], keep_prob: 1.0})
    print("step %d, training accuracy %g"%(i, train_accuracy))
    train_step.run(feed_dict={x: batch[0], y_: batch[1], keep_prob:
0.5})

print("test accuracy %g"%accuracy.eval(feed_dict={
    x: mnist.test.images, y_: mnist.test.labels, keep_prob: 1.0}))
```

Using TensorFlow to iteratively improve our models

Even from the single example in the preceding section, we should be able to recognise what TensorFlow brings to the table. It offers a simple interface for the task of developing complex architectures and training methods, giving us easier access to the algorithms we've learnt about earlier in this book.

As we know, however, developing an initial model is only a small part of the model development process. We usually need to test and dissect our models repeatedly to improve their performance. However, this tends to be an area where our tools are less unified in a single library or technique, and the tests and monitoring solutions less consistent across models.

TensorFlow looks to solve the problem of how to get good insight into our models during iteration, in what it calls the execution phase of model development. During the execution phase, we can make use of tools provided by the TensorFlow team to explore and improve our models.

Perhaps the most important of these tools is TensorBoard, which provides an explorable, visual representation of the model we've built. TensorBoard provides several capabilities, including dashboards that show both basic model information (including performance measurements during each iteration for test and/or training).

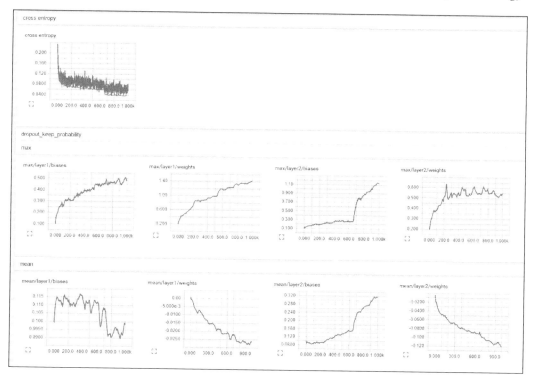

In addition, TensorBoard dashboards provide lower-level information including plots of the range of values for weights, biases and activation values at every model layer; tremendously useful diagnostic information during iteration. The process of accessing this data is hassle-free and it is immediately useful.

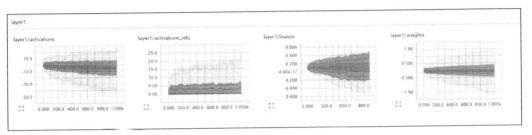

Further to this, TensorBoard provides a detailed graph of the tensor flow for a given model. The tensor is an n-dimensional array of data (in this case, of n-many features); it's what we tend to think of when we use the term *the input dataset*. The series of operations that is applied to a tensor is described as the tensor flow and in TensorFlow it's a fundamental concept, for a simple and compelling reason. When refining and debugging a machine learning model, what matters is having information about the model and its operations at even a low level.

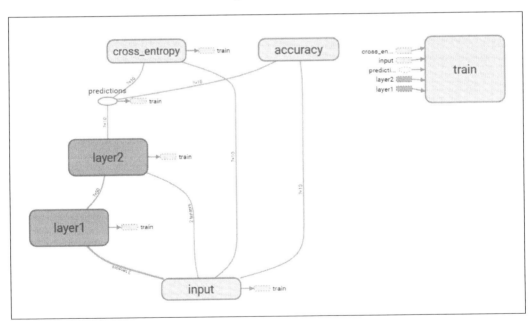

TensorBoard graphs show the structure of a model in variable detail. From this initial view, it is possible to dig into each component of the model and into successive sub-elements. In this case, we are able to view the specific operations that take place within the dropout function of our second network layer. We can see what happens and identify what to tweak for our next iteration.

This level of transparency is unusual and can be very helpful when we want to tweak model components, especially when a model element or layer is underperforming (as we might see, for instance, from TensorBoard graphs showing layer metaparameter values or from network performance as a whole).

TensorBoards can be created from event logs and generated when TensorFlow is run. This makes the benefits of TensorBoards easily obtained during the course of everyday development using TensorFlow.

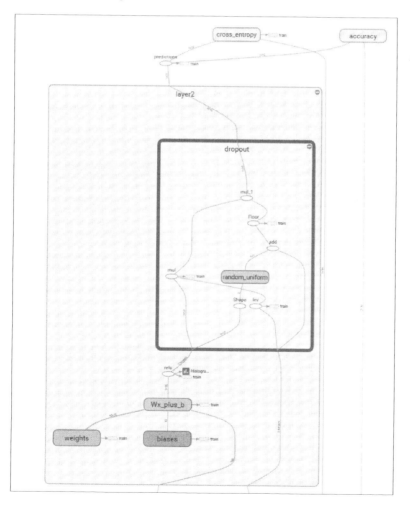

As of late April 2016, the DeepMind team joined the Google Brain team and a broad set of other researchers and developers in using TensorFlow. By making TensorFlow open source and freely available, Google is committing to continue supporting TensorFlow as a powerful tool for model development and refinement.

Knowing when to use these libraries

At one or two points in this chapter, we probably ran into the question of *Okay, so, why didn't you just teach us about this library to begin with?* It's fair to ask why we spent time digging around in Theano functions and other low-level information when this chapter presents perfectly good interfaces that make life easier.

Naturally, I advocate using the best tools available, especially for prototyping tasks where the value of the work is more in understanding the general ballpark you're in, or in identifying specific problem classes. It's worth recognising the three reasons for not presenting content earlier in this book using either of these libraries.

The first reason is that these tools will only get you so far. They can do a lot, agreed, so depending on the domain and the nature of that domain's problems, some data scientists may be able to rely on them for the majority of deep learning needs. Beyond a certain level of performance and problem complexity, of course, you need to understand what is needed to construct a model in Theano, create your own scoring function from scratch or leverage the other techniques described in this book.

Another part of the decision to focus on teaching lower-level implementation is about the developing maturity of the technologies involved. At this point, Lasagne and TensorFlow are definitely worth discussing and recommending to you. Prior to this, when the majority of the book was written, the risk around discussing the libraries in this chapter was greater. There are many projects based on Theano (some of the more prominent frameworks which weren't discussed in this chapter are **Keras**, **Blocks** and **Pylearn2**)

Even now, it's entirely possible that different libraries and tools will be the subject of discussion or the default working environment in a year or two years' time. This field moves extremely fast, largely due to the influence of key companies and research groups who have to keep building new tools as the old ones reach their useful limits... or it just becomes clear how to do things better.

The other reason to dig in at a lower level, honestly, is that this is an involved book. It sets theory alongside code and uses the code to teach the theory. Abstracting away how the algorithms work and simply discussing how to apply them to crack a particular example can be tempting. The tools discussed in this chapter enable practitioners to get very good scores on some problems without ever understanding the functions that are being called. My opinion is that this is not a very good way to train a data scientist.

If you're going to operate on subtle and difficult data problems, you need to be able to modify and define your own algorithm. You need to understand how to choose an appropriate solution. To do these things, you need the details provided in this book and even more very specific information that I haven't provided, due to the limitations of (page) space and time. At that point, you can apply deep learning algorithms flexibly and knowledgeably.

Similarly, it's important to recognise what these tools do well, or less well. At present, Lasagne fits very well within that use-case where a new model is being developed for benchmarking or early passes, where the priority should be on iteration speed and getting results.

TensorFlow, meanwhile, fits later into the development lifespan of a model. When the easy gains disappear and it's necessary to spend a lot of time debugging and improving a model, the relatively quick iterations of TensorFlow are a definite plus, but it's the diagnostic tools provided by TensorBoard that present an overwhelming value-add.

There is, therefore, a place for both libraries in your toolset. Depending on the nature of the problem at hand, these libraries and more will prove to be valuable assets.

Further reading

The Lasagne User Guide is thorough and worth reading. Find it at `http://lasagne.readthedocs.io/en/latest/index.html`.

Similarly, find the TensorFlow tutorials at `https://www.tensorflow.org/versions/r0.9/get_started/index.html`.

Summary

In this final chapter, we moved some distance from our previous discussions of algorithms, configuration and diagnosis to consider tools that improve our experience when implementing deep learning algorithms.

We discovered the advantages to using Lasagne, an interface to Theano designed to accelerate and simplify early prototyping of our models. Meanwhile, we examined TensorFlow, the library developed by Google to aid Deep Learning model adjustment and optimization. TensorFlow offers us a remarkable amount of visibility of model performance, at minimal effort, and makes the task of diagnosing and debugging a complex, deep model structure much less challenging.

Both tools have their own place in our processes, with each being appropriate for a particular set of problems.

Over the course of this book as a whole, we have walked through and reviewed a broad set of advanced machine learning techniques. We went from a position where we understood some fundamental algorithms and concepts, to having confident use of a very current, powerful and sought-after toolset.

Beyond the techniques, though, this book attempts to teach one further concept, one that's much harder to teach and to learn, but which underpins the best performance in machine learning.

The field of machine learning is moving very fast. This pace is visible in new and improved scores that are posted almost every week in academic journals or industry white papers. It's visible in how training examples like MNIST have moved quickly from being seen as meaningful challenges to being *toy problems*, the deep learning version of the Iris dataset. Meanwhile, the field moves on to the next big challenge; CIFAR-10, CIFAR-100.

At the same time, the field moves cyclically. Concepts introduced by academics like Yann LeCun in the 80's are in resurgence as computing architectures and resource growth make their use more viable over real data at scale. To use many of the most current techniques at their best limits, it's necessary to understand concepts that were defined decades ago, themselves defined on the back of other concepts defined still longer ago.

This book tries to balance these concerns. Understanding the cutting edge and the techniques that exist there is critical; understanding the concepts that'll define the new techniques or adjustments made in two or three years' time is equally important.

Most important of all, however, is that this book gives you an appreciation of how malleable these architectures and approaches can be. A concept consistently seen at the top end of data science practice is that the best solution to a specific problem is a problem-specific solution.

This is why top Kaggle contest winners perform extensive feature preparation and tweak their architectures. It's why TensorFlow was written to allow clear vision of granular properties of ones' architectures. Having the knowledge and the skills to tweak implementations or combine algorithms fluently is what it takes to have true mastery of machine learning techniques.

Through the many techniques and examples reviewed within this book, it is my hope that the ways of thinking about data problems and a confidence in manipulating and configuring these algorithms has been passed on to you as a practicing data scientist. The many recommended *Further reading* examples in this book are largely intended to further extend that knowledge and help you develop the skills taught in this book.

Beyond that, I wish you all the best of luck in your model building and configuration. I hope that you learn for yourself just how enjoyable and rewarding this field can be!

Chapter Code Requirements

This book's content leverages openly available data and code, including open source Python libraries and frameworks. While each chapter's example code is accompanied by a README file documenting all the libraries required to run the code provided in that chapter's accompanying scripts, the content of these files is collated here for your convenience.

It is recommended that you already have some libraries that are required for the earlier chapters when working with code from any later chapter. These requirements are identified using keywords. It is particularly important to set up the libraries mentioned in *Chapter 1*, *Unsupervised Machine Learning*, for any content provided later in the book. The requirements for every chapter are given in the following table:

Chapter Number	Requirements
1	• Python 3 (3.4 recommended)
	• sklearn (NumPy, SciPy)
	• matplotlib
2-4	• theano
5	• Semisup-learn
6	• **Natural Language Toolkit (NLTK)**
	• BeautifulSoup
7	• Twitter API account
8	• XGBoost
9	• Lasagne
	• TensorFlow

Index

A

AdaBoost 209
Adjusted Rand Index (ARI) 10
area under the curve (AUC) 146, 179
autoencoders
 about 57, 58
 denoising 60, 61
 topology 58, 59
 training 59, 60
averaging ensembles
 about 203
 bagging algorithms, using 203-205
 random forests, using 205-208

B

backoff taggers 139
backoff tagging 139, 140
bagging 143-146
bagging algorithms
 using 203-205
Batch Normalization 99
BeautifulSoup
 text data, cleaning 131, 132
Best Matching Unit (BMU) 19
Bing Traffic API 176, 185-187
blend-of-blends 215
Blocks 244
boosting methods
 applying 209-211
 Extreme Gradient Boosting (XGBoost),
  using 212-214
Borda count 231
Brill taggers 139

C

carp 138
Champion/Challenger 230
CIFAR-10 dataset 85
clustering 8
completeness score 10
composable layer 81
Contrastive Pessimistic Likelihood
  Estimation (CPLE) 102, 114, 115
convnet topology
 about 79-81
 backward pass 88
 forward pass 88
 implementing 88-92
 pooling layers 85-87
 training 88
convolutional neural networks (CNN)
 about 77, 78, 239
 applying 92-99
 convnet topology 79-81
convolution layers 81-84
correlation 167, 168
covariance 3

D

data
 acquiring, via Twitter 180
deep belief network (DBN)
 about 27, 49
 applying 50-53
 training 50
 validating 54
DeepFace 78

denoising autoencoders (dA)
  about 57, 60, 61
  applying 62-66
DepthConcat element 91
development tools
  about 236
  Lasagne 236
  libraries usage, deciding 244, 245
  TensorFlow 236
Diabolo network 57
dynamic applications
  models, using 221, 222

E

eigenvalue 3
eigenvector 3
elbow method 14, 211
ensembles
  about 202, 203
  applying 218-221
  averaging ensembles 203
  boosting methods, applying 209-211
  stacking ensembles, using 215-218
Extreme Gradient Boosting (XGBoost)
  using 212-214
**extremely randomized trees
  (ExtraTrees) 206**

F

Fast Fourier Transform 88
feature engineering
  about 129, 130, 175, 176
  data, acquiring via RESTful APIs 176, 177
  variables, deriving 187-191
  variables, selecting 187-191
  weather API, creating 191-199
feature engineering, for ML applications
  about 157
  effective derived variables,
    creating 160, 161
  non-numeric features,
    reinterpreting 162-165
  rescaling techniques, using 157-160
feature selection
  correlation 167, 168

genetic models 173, 174
  LASSO 169, 170
  performing 167
  Recursive Feature
    Elimination (RFE) 170-173
  techniques, using 165, 166
feature set
  creating 156
  feature engineering, for
    ML applications 157
  feature selection techniques, using 165, 166
Fisher's discriminant ratio 113
Fully Connected layer 89

G

genetic models 173, 174
Gibbs sampling 35
Gini Impurity (gini) 217
Go 78
GoogLeNet 78, 90
gradient descent algorithms
  URL 157

H

h-dimensional representation 58
heart dataset
  URL 108
hierarchical grouping 67
homogeneity score 10

I

i-dimensional input 58
ImageNet 78
Inception network 90

K

Keras 244
k-means clustering
  about 1, 7
  clustering 8
  clustering analysis 8-13
  configuration, tuning 13-18
K-Nearest Neighbors (KNN) 205

L

Lasagne 236-238
LASSO 169, 170
LeNet 89
libraries
   usage, deciding 244, 245

M

Markov Chain Monte Carlo (MCMC) 36
max-pooling 85
mean-pooling 85
modeling risk factors
   key parameter 229
   longitudinally variant 228
   slow change 229
models
   modeling risk factors, identifying 228, 229
   robustness 222-228
   robustness, managing 230-233
   using, in dynamic applications 221, 222
Motor Vehicle Accident (MVA) 183
multicollinearity 167
Multi-Layer Perceptron (MLP) 29

N

Natural Language Toolkit (NLTK)
   about 137
   used, for tagging 137
n-dimensional input 60
Network In Network (NIN) 91
network topologies 29-32
neural networks
   about 28
   composition 28, 29
   connectivity functions 29
   learning process 28
   neurons 29
n-gram tagger 138

O

OpinRank Review dataset
   about 67
   URL 68
orthogonalization 3

orthonormalization 3
overcomplete 60

P

Permanent Contrastive
   Divergence (PCD) 35
Platt calibration 107
pooling layers 85-87
porter stemmer 141
Pragmatic Chaos model 216
price-earnings (P/E) ratio 161
principal component analysis (PCA)
   about 1, 2
   employing 4-7
   features 2-4
Pylearn2 244

R

random forests
   about 143-146
   using 205-208
random patches 143, 204
random subspaces 203
Rectified Linear Units (ReLU) 91
Recursive Feature
   Elimination (RFE) 167-173
RESTful APIs
   data, acquiring 176, 177
   model performance, testing 177-179
Restricted Boltzmann Machine (RBM)
   about 27, 33, 34
   applications 37-48
   topology 34, 35
   training 35-37
Root Mean Squared Error (RMSE) 173

S

scikit-learn 4
self-organizing maps (SOM)
   about 1, 18, 19, 29
   employing 20-23
self-training
   about 103-105
   Contrastive Pessimistic Likelihood
     Estimation (CPLE) 114, 115

Printed in Great Britain
by Amazon